BELLA!

BELLA!

Ms. Abzug Goes to Washington

BELLA S. ABZUG

Edited by Mel Ziegler

Saturday Review Press

NEW YORK

.

To Martin, whose love made it all possible
To Egee and Liz, our beautiful daughters
To Helene, who carries a double burden
To Mama, who cared first

Acknowledgments

My loyal, patient, hard-working, enduring staff and friends. What would I do without them! And so, to the Washington and New York staffs, to the volunteers who come in at all hours to do all kinds of work, to the devoted group of women who have helped service the community and constituents, to the money-raisers, typists, mimeo operators, writers, researchers, envelope stuffers, message runners, car drivers, doorbell ringers and all the others who help make the wheels go round, to the New Yorkers from all boroughs who worked in the fifty-first state campaign, and to the many friends whose encouragement and support have meant so much to me, my deepest thanks and appreciation.

BELLA!

Introduction

I've been described as a tough and noisy woman, a prizefighter, a man-hater, you name it. They call me Battling Bella, Mother Courage and a Jewish mother with more complaints than Portnoy. There are those who say I'm impatient, impetuous, uppity, rude, profane, brash and overbearing. Whether I'm any of these things, or all of them, you can decide for yourself. But whatever I am—and this ought to be made very clear at the outset—I am a very serious woman.

I am not being facetious when I say that the real enemies in this country are the Pentagon and its pals in big business. It's no joke to me that women in this country are terribly oppressed and are made to suffer economic, legal and social discrimination. I am not evoking a wild fantasy when I claim that I'm going to help organize a new political coalition of the women, the minorities and the young people, along with the poor, the elderly, the workers and the unemployed, which is going to turn this country upside down and inside out. We're going to reclaim our cities, create more jobs, better housing, better health care, more child care centers, more help for drug addicts; we're going to start doing something for the millions of people in this country whose needs, because of the callousness of the men who've been running our government, have taken a low priority to the cost of killing people in Indochina.

(3)

To some people all this may sound a bit grandiose, but let me tell you something: This is the only thing we *can* do and still survive. I didn't devise the program—it's not my master plan. It's what a half million anguished people—Puerto Ricans, Jews, Italians, Chinese, Irish, Poles, Russians, blacks, even WASPs—who live in an area of Manhattan extending from the West Side down and around the Village to the Lower East Side have specifically sent me to Congress to do. These people have had it! They are fed up and dispirited, almost without hope, cynical, oppressed by economic conditions, overwhelmed by the inflexibility of their institutions, demoralized by the war. Either we begin to help them and all the millions of others who are suffering in this country, or we've *all* had it.

All through the campaign and since the election I have had people come up to me and say, time and again, "Bella, you're our only hope . . ." "There's nobody else to turn to, Bella. Only you . . ." "Bella, if you don't, who will?"

I confess—it scares me. To look at these people and the conditions they live in, to talk with them, to feel their desperation, is so frightening to me at times that I become physically ill with the fear that I might fail them.

There are plenty of people, including my husband, Martin, who think I'm nuts. They don't believe I can get anywhere. They worry that I'm taking on too much. They warn that, at best, I'll be misunderstood; at worst, I'll be spurned and cut down. Who knows? Perhaps they're right.

But I don't think so.

These are very special times we live in. The priorities in this country—against the will of the people—are upside down. At this moment, as the 92nd Congress is about to convene, the mood of the country is one place and its government is someplace else. One poll after another shows us that the people are against the war, that the people are opposed to the President, that the people don't trust the Administration. More clearly than ever in recent history, vast numbers of people in this country share a common goal to change their government and its priorities and policies.

Can it be done? Of course. If the women, who are a majority of the population, and the young people, who are just getting the vote, and the minorities, who more than any other group have been made to pay for this rotten war, can be educated into a new political coalition with working people and small businessmen, it can be done. It will take organization. And it will take leadership. The people are ready and willing. They're just desperate for direction. They're waiting for leaders, a new kind of leader.

They can no longer relate to and they have had enough of the old-style wooden, pontificating politicians who really don't give a damn about them. Instead they want leaders who are people like themselves—real people, as human and emotional and agonized as they are. Like me. I'm one of the same kind of people who elected me. I'm someone they can touch, see, feel and smell. It's very interesting that the man I defeated in the Democratic primary, Leonard Farbstein, who had been in Congress for twelve years, had many of the same views on the issues that I did. His only problem was that—unlike me— he was not part of the constituency. You never knew him or felt him. He was not an activist. "He's like a piece of furniture," somebody said to me in the campaign. "It's time he should be moved."

I am an activist. I'm the kind of person who *does things* at the same time that I'm working to create a feeling that *something can be done*. And I don't intend to disappear in Congress as many of my predecessors have. My role, as I see it, is among the people, and I am going to be *outside* organizing them at the same time that I'm *inside* fighting for them. That is the kind of leadership that I believe will build a new major-

(5)

ity in this country, and it was primarily in the hope of being able to exemplify that kind of leadership that I ran for Congress.

I certainly didn't do it for ego. I wasn't looking for a new career. I am a fifty-year-old woman, an established lawyer, a wife, a mother of two daughters and a founder and leader of Women Strike for Peace. Believe me, the last thing I needed at this point in my life was to knock my brains out to get elected to Congress.

But I felt if we are going to get anywhere, Congress has got to begin to reflect in its composition the great diversity of this country. Although women represent 53 percent of the electorate, there are only thirteen of us in Congress (twelve in the House; one in the Senate). The country has 22 million black citizens, and there are only a dozen black Congressmen. There are no artists, intellectuals, scientists, mathematicians, creative writers, architects, Vietnam veterans, musicians, and not even any leaders of the labor movement on Capitol Hill. There are no young people. The average age of a Congressman is 51.9 years, and a Senator, 56. Two-thirds of these people are lawyers, businessmen or bankers. No wonder Congress is such a smug, incestuous, stagnant institution! It reeks of sameness.

Perhaps the best way to change Congress—to make it more representative, to make it more responsive—is to show people exactly what it is. This is the reason I've decided to keep this diary. I want people to share my personal experiences in struggling with the system. Having spent many years as the legislative director of Women Strike for Peace, I'm no innocent to Washington. I've already had a pretty good whiff of what to expect. The inside operation of Congress—the deals, the compromises, the selling out, the co-opting, the unprincipled manipulating, the self-serving career-building—is a story of such monumental decadence that I believe if people find out about it they will demand an end to it.

(6)

I intend, as best I can, to tell it the way I see it. The reason I'm going to be able to do this is that I have no desire to become a privileged member of "the Club," nor do I care to build a career for myself if it's going to be unrelated to the needs of the people who elected me. What that means, frankly, is that I don't give a damn about being reelected unless I'm able to do what I want to do. I want to bring Congress back to the people. If that proves to be impossible to do by working from within, then I'm prepared to go back outside again—to the streets—and do it from there.

—BELLA S. ABZUG
New York, New York

January 15, 1971

January 18, 1971

For the last month or so I've been flying to Washington at least once a week to line up a staff, set up an office, find an apartment and attend some meetings of the Democratic Study Group, a loose organization of the liberal members of Congress. Some of the meetings were briefing sessions for freshmen on Congressional procedures, and others were discussions on how we could push as a group to end the seniority system. The latter discussions were a little sickening, and I attended just enough of them to verify what I suspected all along: There are a lot of old and not-so-old liberals around this place who cuddle up to some pretty reactionary cop-out ideas when the doors are closed.

For instance, one liberal who's been in Congress since 1954, and who personally is not a bad guy, gave us a lecture on seniority and committee selection. "The seniority system has no legal basis," he said. "It is not outlined in the Constitution, it has never been enacted into law. It's outrageous that we permit it to exist, and it should be challenged legally in the courts."

Pretty strong stuff, huh? Well, in the next breath he went on to say, "If I were a freshman and I were assigned to a committee that I didn't like, I'd try to have patience, because, after all, there's always another time."

"For some of us," I told him, "there is no more time. We can't wait."

What he was feeding us is the old song and dance, the old crap, the anesthesia of the liberals: *If you want to get along, you've got to go along.* We should all wait and be patient and everything will get better.

The fact is that we—people like myself who were elected to Congress from volatile districts where the voters are demanding change—are under a mandate not to wait any longer. The old-timers—the guys who automatically get reelected every two years until they die or retire—don't seem to comprehend this, which is why they continue to talk out of two sides of their mouth about the seniority system.

But for those of us from exploding districts, there is no such thing as automatic reelection. The people elect us one after another, hoping someday they'll get somebody with enough guts to do something. When Farbstein represented my district we pushed him and we pushed him and we pushed him and finally we got him to establish a pretty good voting record. But what's a voting record? He wasn't vigorous, he wasn't a leader, he wasn't a catalyst, he wasn't an advocate, and he just couldn't cope any longer with the dynamics of what the district required. So he got tossed out, and the people elected me. They knew and *I* know that I have no intention of getting along by going along. And I don't have any patience either. That's why I'm holding a press conference with some of the other members calling on the Democratic caucus to take the strongest possible stand against the seniority system.

January 19

Liberals! They're not leaders! If they were real leaders they'd understand that their style of politicking and self-aggrandizement is what's destroying the capacity of any of us to get anywhere. How can two guys like Dick Ottinger and Charlie Goodell look at themselves every day, knowing they're responsible for helping a reactionary like James Buckley get elected

(9)

Senator from New York? Liberals! They're always divided, always fighting each other, always selling themselves out for the sake of their little clubs and their little allegiances. They are very little men.

In today's Democratic caucus, my first one, not only did the liberals not have the intelligence and the get-up-and-go to develop some kind of opposition to Carl Albert's bid to become Speaker of the House, but they completely blew it on the Majority Leader position too. Okay, maybe they never had a chance to beat Carl Albert, but couldn't they at least have given a guy like Hale Boggs a rough time? No. Instead, two liberals, Morris Udall from Arizona and James O'Hara from Michigan, ran *against* each other, making Boggs from Louisiana a shoo-in for Majority Leader. It's disgusting. If these phony liberals don't stop screwing each other, we're never going to get anywhere.

The caucus was so full of dealing and double-crossing and nose-counting that it got me sick. Instead of getting together behind *one* candidate so they would have a chance to knock the whole power structure out, many of our wonderful liberals didn't oppose Albert and Boggs because they wanted to be in a better position to beg them for favors.

Examples? Well, there's my neighbor Congressman, Hugh Carey, from Brooklyn, who represents a district, like most in the city, that has an urgent need for health, housing and education programs, a district that is demanding an end to the war. He made a seconding speech for Hale Boggs' nomination. If that wasn't bad enough, he went on to call Boggs a "Great Reformer." I'm sorry, but that was too much to take. The only way you can make Hale Boggs look like a liberal is to compare him with the other men from Louisiana. He's not a segregationist. He's for integration. So, big deal. As a politician, he's old style. And where is he on the major issues of the day? I'll tell you where—he's nowhere.

You know why Carey did it? He was supposed to become

the Majority Whip. But they screwed him. They never made him Whip. So what did supporting Hale Boggs get him? Nothing. He just wasted his vote. He was tricked by a bunch of double-cross artists. He and God knows how many other so-called liberals.

January 20

I'm convinced that the only way to fight the inflexibility of Congress is to turn the system against itself. There must be a way, somehow, to take all these damn rules and regulations and limitations—which the power structure now uses to squelch anything that sounds too liberal—and turn them around to our advantage.

As far as I can tell, there are very few experts on procedure in the House. Those few experts we do have are old-timers, and not liberals. The average liberal thinks up what he wants to do and then runs off to somebody else to ask, "Now what procedural step do I take in order to do this?" Consequently, liberals rarely get anything significant accomplished.

I'm determined to become an expert on procedure, but unfortunately it takes time. Most of the rules and regulations are so cumbersome and so complicated that even when you learn them, which in itself is not easy, it's still a whole other matter to know how to *use* them. Worse than that. The precedents haven't been compiled since 1936. They're all in the head of the parliamentarian, Lew Deschler. He's been ordered to publish them, but nobody knows when that will happen. You've got to be creative, experienced, and know how to use the library to ferret out what you need. What this requires is a good, solid, dependable staff. I spent the last two months interviewing dozens of people for various jobs I had to fill in my Washington office: an administrative assistant, a legislative assistant, a caseworker, a receptionist, a personal secretary and scheduler, people to answer letters. Some of them had communicated with me after the election and expressed a desire to join my staff; others listed themselves with the Democratic Study Group; and there were still others I had heard about who had worked for Congressmen who had been defeated.

I knew exactly what I was looking for: people experienced on the Hill who were also activists and radicals. But as you can imagine, people with that combination of attributes are not readily available, if they exist at all.

In all, I must have talked to more than a hundred people. Most of them, unfortunately, left me pretty cold. They had been working on the Hill just long enough to become unimaginative. Although they wanted terribly to be identified with a radical like me, they didn't seem to have any idea of just what kind of a radical I am. Many had already worked for other Congressmen and they seemed to have taken on the same characterlessness as the men they worked for and the Congress itself. It was very disappointing.

So on the whole I didn't get the kind of experienced staff I wanted. A few people I wanted I didn't get—they went to other Congressmen. It just takes a long time to put a good staff together. For my caseworker I hired a young woman by the name of Sharon Oper who had been working at the Weizmann Institute in Israel. I have some confidence she'll be pretty good. I also think my administrative assistant, Esther Newberg, who has worked for Robert Kennedy and Abe Ribicoff, will turn out well. I have a very good young woman, Ever Terry, who'll be answering the legislative mail and doing a lot of heavy steno and typing. A young man named Jim Crawford is going to be working exclusively on military-related matters.

For my New York office I hired a friend since childhood, Mim Kelber, as my speechwriter and co-thinker. She and I, of course, are very close friends, and she's going to be invaluable to me. Not only is she a professional writer, but we worked together for eight years in Women Strike for Peace. She and I share the same political reflexes. She's crazy to give up her job to work for me, but I wouldn't be able to do without her.

The most difficult job to fill turned out to be the post of legislative assistant. When I couldn't get the type of person I wanted, I ended up hiring—in what will probably be a temporary arrangement—two young women lawyers, each of whom will work part-time, back to back, sharing the job. They don't have as much Hill experience as I would have liked, but I was impressed enough with both of them to try them out. One has done some work in urban and community law and the other had what I thought was a very creative approach when I interviewed her. "I'm a radical," she said, "and the reason I want to work for you is because I don't think you can make it, but I want to watch you while you try."

January 21

After being officially sworn in on the Floor today, I came out to the Capitol steps, where I conducted my own ceremony for about a thousand women, friends and family, most of whom came down from New York for the occasion. Shirley Chisholm, the black Congresswoman from Brooklyn who is a friend of mine, administered an oath to me in which I pledged "to work for new priorities to heal the domestic wounds of war and to use our country's wealth for life, not death." A lot of other Congressmen came out to watch me being sworn in. It's a first, they tell me.

After I recited the pledge I gave a speech and then went back to the Floor where, as my first official act, I dropped a resolution in the hopper calling on the President to withdraw all American armed forces from Indochina no later than July

4 of this year. Twenty-eight other Congressmen and Congress-women co-sponsored the resolution with me.

As far as I'm concerned, ending this dirty, immoral war is the most urgent thing this Congress has to do. President Nixon, with his phony "Vietnamization" schemes, is nothing but a wind-up, wind-down mechanical man who thinks he's fooling the American people. He and his pals in the Pentagon are full of lies and deceptions; they manipulate words as if they were playing parlor games instead of dealing in human suffering. They're making us live through a B-movie rerun of the Johnson script, which promised "no wider war" but brought just that.

Can you imagine telling us to rejoice because *only* forty American kids a week are getting killed over there now? This is going to be a no-hands war, Nixon says, and so what if it goes on? No ground troops, he says. Just hundreds of bombers dropping thousands of bombs on innocent villagers. Very clean, isn't it?

Well, if he thinks he's going to get away with it, he's nuts. Whether he knows it or not, the people are against him. They've had it. And so have I. That's why I've decided to fight for a seat on the House Armed Services Committee. It's not going to be easy, but it's the best way I can figure out to use my position to try to bust up the war from the inside.

January 22

The first time I officially raised the issue that I wanted a seat on the Armed Services Committee was at a dinner for the New York Congressional delegation a few weeks ago. Every-body seemed to approve, except for one guy by the name of John Rooney, from Brooklyn. He's a reactionary. While I was speaking, he was sitting there drinking beer, as he always is, and he got the notion to rib me a little.

I concluded my speech by saying, "I'm looking forward to your unanimous support in my bid for a seat on the committee, and that includes you too, John."

"Agriculture for you," he piped up. "You start at the bottom. You stay at the bottom."

"John," I said. "I can't believe you would be so mean to a still unseated member of this delegation."

"Like I said," he went on. "You start at the bottom, you stay at the bottom—with your seat. And you got a pretty good seat."

Nonetheless, these guys, including John Rooney, know that I'm not up to any funny business in this thing. I've been thinking about a seat on Armed Services ever since the campaign. But you've got to understand a couple of things first, if you want to know what's involved in actually getting it.

First of all, the tradition down here is that new members, like myself, take what they get. They don't make a lot of noise; they don't ask for anything unreasonable; and they humbly go through the proper channels. In other words, we are expected to defer to the seniority system, which dictates that we shut up and listen to the tired old men who run this government.

Secondly, the House Armed Services Committee is not just another committee. I recall its chairman, Mendel Rivers, who died just before the session opened, once saying, "This is the most important committee in Congress. It is the only *official* voice the military has in the House of Representatives." He wasn't kidding. Armed Services is and always has been a special interest committee, loaded with reactionaries who, few questions asked, annually husband through in the neighborhood of $80 billion as a blank check for the military. Its hearings are largely held in secret, because almost everybody who testifies before it is either in the Army or pro-military. I doubt they've ever listened to a hostile witness. Last year, for instance, when the committee heard thirty-four witnesses on the $20 billion weapons procurement and research bill, all but one were from the Pentagon. The last was a Congressman in whose district the F-111 plane was built. Another series of hearings ran to three thousand pages of testimony from three hundred witnesses. Two hundred and ninety-eight of these witnesses worked for the Pentagon or within the military services. The other two represented the National Rifle Association.

The men who serve on the committee often represent areas with large defense establishments. They regard it as their special function to get their districts more and larger defense establishments. More defense contracts, more Army bases, more Naval bases, more war factories—they go on and on aggrandizing themselves and their districts while the American people are faced with the destruction of their economy, while the American people are driven to utter despair over this war. There are already so many defense establishments in places like South Carolina, where Mendel Rivers lived, that they used to say one more would sink the state into the sea.

The guy who's running the committee now, Edward Hébert, from Louisiana, is said to be less of a tyrant than Rivers, but he's made it clear that he intends to maintain the same symbiotic relationship between the committee and the Pentagon. In other words, under Hébert, the committee is going to continue representing the interests of the Pentagon instead of the interests of the American people.

Well, this is appalling! It should be an independently functioning committee of the legislative branch that exists to challenge the military—not to speak for it. Those admirals and generals and munitions-makers should have to answer for themselves, every step of the way. If I get on the committee, I'm going to raise tremendous objections to their requests for appropriations, to their cost overruns, to their never-ending need for this new weapon and that new weapon, and I'm going to get the hearings opened up so people can see what's going on.

(16)

January 23

One of the basic reasons that I'm claiming a right to a seat on the Armed Services Committee is that I'm a woman. A woman hasn't served on it since Margaret Chase Smith, and that was twenty-two years ago. I can't tell you how outrageous that is. Do you realize that there are 42,000 women in the military? Do you realize that about half the civilian employees of the Defense Department are women—290,000 of them at last count? And, as if that isn't enough, there are one and a half million wives of military personnel.

All this was the central point of a letter I sent today to Wilbur Mills, who's the chairman of the Democratic Committee on Committees, which will determine whether I get the seat on Armed Services. Believe it or not, the letter, which urged that I be appointed to the committee, has the unanimous backing of the New York Congressional delegation. Yes, even John Rooney.

The power structure is aware, however, that I have a pretty good argument on this woman thing, and they are not sitting idle. I read a newspaper column in which it was reported that Mendel Rivers, before he died, wanted Louise Day Hicks, the recently elected conservative Congresswoman from Boston, on the committee. "Dahhhling," he is reported to have said to her, "Ah want ya'll on mah committah."

Since I suspected a Tory plot to undercut me, I went to Mills a few weeks ago, before the session, and told him flatly that nobody was going to take the woman thing away from me. "If you guys want Louise," I said, "fine. Then we'll have two women on the committee."

January 27

I represented the Democrats in the "freshman class" at the annual political dinner of the Women's National Press Club, a very fancy affair attended by almost fifteen hundred people, including cabinet members, Senators, Congressmen and, of course, the press. The other speakers included Carl Albert, Hugh Scott, Jack Kemp, from upstate New York representing the freshmen Republicans, and Adlai Stevenson III, from Illinois, Lawton Chiles, from Florida, and James Buckley, representing the new Senators. We were all given instructions to be "funny" for two and a half minutes.

I broke them up with the story about what my older daughter, Egee, said on election night. Egee worked very hard for me during the campaign when my slogan was "This woman's place is in the House—the House of Representatives." After the results came in and we were in the middle of a victory celebration, she got up and told everybody, "Thank God we're getting her out of *our* house and into *their* House."

"After being in Washington for a week," I said, "I'm beginning to get the impression that a lot of fellows are feeling the same way as my daughter, except in reverse. 'God,' they're saying, 'if we could only get her out of *our* House and back into *theirs.*'"

Carl Albert spoke after me and he said, "I notice that we in the House have only half as many people here to speak for us as the Senate does. But, of course, we have Bella Abzug."

Then came Senator Buckley. At which point, even before he said a word, I intentionally stopped smiling, and froze my face to show great displeasure. I find nothing about that guy funny.

He started out his spiel by saying, "When I first received the invitation to speak here at the *Women's* National Press Club, I was shocked that I was to share the same platform with Bella Abzug, particularly as this is a sexist organization."

He went on with some other garbage. I forget exactly what it was, but it was ill-conceived humor, and in poor taste.

Last week an invitation came to my office to attend a White House reception tomorrow for freshmen Congressmen. My staff and my friends have been pressing me about whether I intend to go or not, and up until tonight I couldn't make up my mind. It's not exactly the kind of thing that serves my ego. And who wants to listen to his pious idiocies? On the other hand, I have to admit I'm a little curious. After ten years of protesting on the sidewalk outside the place, you get to wondering what goes on inside.

Martin called tonight from New York to tell me he had his tuxedo cleaned for the occasion. He has said all along that if I was willing to go, he'd go too. But I think he's even more curious than I am, because, after all, he's a writer, and he's interested in experiencing different situations. Martin, incidentally, has published two novels—*The Seventh Avenue Story* in 1947 and *Spearhead* in 1960. He now works as a stockbroker.

So since he's got the tux ready, I told him to fly down and we'll go. I decided my own special reason for going will be to tell Nixon exactly how I feel about some things.

Tonight, as I was getting my hair done in the House Beauty Parlor, I was sitting under a hair dryer next to Louise Day Hicks, and the first thing she said to me was, "What are you going to wear tomorrow? Long or short?"

January 28

I decided to wear a short dress so I could also wear a hat. I didn't want to deprive the President of that great event. I figured I'd let him see me in my whole regalia.

Some kids from my office drove us over, but we had trouble finding the correct entrance to get in by car. Finally Martin and I just got out and walked up to the outside gate to make the approach by foot. I didn't want to be *too* late. You're supposed to arrive before the President does, and I figured it would look too much like a plan to upstage him if I arrived afterwards. I don't need any plans to upstage him. Anyhow, I wasn't planning on being smart-alecky.

So we got out of the car, passed the gate and started up the long walkway. Two or three times guards stopped us to demand, "Who goes there?" and we had to explain who we were. Everybody else was coming up in their limousines, Martin and I noted, while we the peasants arrived on foot. We felt there was something unintentionally symbolic about that.

When we finally got there, it was all red carpet and long gown and dapper people. With all the regalia, it actually looked more British than American to us. We got a big kick out of it. With the Marine band playing in the background, we started up the gold and marble steps and lo and behold . . .

There He Was. His Wife Too. Even though there wasn't a camera in sight, he had his makeup on. We got in the reception line, and then . . .

"Oh," he said. "I've been looking forward to meeting you."

"President Nixon," I said, unsmiling, "I want you to know that my constituents want you to withdraw from Vietnam and they're unhappy that you haven't."

Whereupon his hand stiffened up immensely and locked mine into what Martin described as an Indian hand wrestle.

"We're doing much better than our predecessors," he said.

"Well, your predecessors didn't do very well, but you're doing worse."

He stiffened up further, and his whole body became sort of rigid. "Yes, yes," he said, and pushed me on to Pat.

"Oh, I've been looking forward to meeting you," she chirped. "I've read all about you and your cute little bonnets."

In the course of the evening we met a lot of cabinet members and people on Nixon's staff. Martin cornered the Secretary of

Commerce to chat about the stock market, which is in trouble. "I was lucky," the Secretary, Maurice Stans, told him. "I got this job and got out of it."

Almost everybody I met had seen me at the Women's National Press Club last night and they said they enjoyed me. They were a lot more relaxed than Nixon. Some of them even had a sense of humor. I was having a good time until at a certain point Senator Buckley walked up to me and held out his hand and said, "Hi, Bella."

"I don't shake your hand," I said.

"Why not?"

"Because I didn't like what you said about me last night."

"I was only kidding," he said. "I was trying to compliment you."

"Then you better get yourself another speechwriter."

All done with a smile, but I meant every word.

January 29

Just as I had hoped, my campaign to get a seat on the Armed Services Committee is taking on national proportions. I'm being interviewed all over the place by the press and radio and television, which is giving me the opportunity to drive home a number of points about the nature of the committee. In so doing, I'm stirring up pressure for change, and even if I don't succeed in getting seated on the committee, and I doubt I will, I'll have shaken them up and perhaps even made it possible for another liberal to get on.

Incidentally, those talk shows are something else. When I was on the *David Frost Show*, the producer came out during the commercial and said I was being too rough on Nixon. Would I please let up, he asked.

"What do you want me to talk about?" I said. "Tulips?"

I bumped into Ed Hébert on the Floor. I went up to him, put my hand on his shoulder and said, "Ed, look at how all this looks to the country. Here you are, the most hated committee, the committee that's taken our tax dollars and handed them over year after year to the military and here I am, considered probably the most opposite to you of all the people in Congress. Now, let's face it, you would show that you have great breadth and depth if you put me on your committee. Certainly, if you think you're right, you can take someone on who disagrees with you."

"You know it's not up to me, Bella," he said. "I have no objection to your being on the committee, but it's up to the Committee on Committees to put you there."

January 30

The news came late yesterday from Hugh Carey, our geographical zone leader on the Committee on Committees. He called and said, "Bella, I'm sorry, but you didn't make it. You got some votes, but not enough. A lot of people said there were already two Democrats and two Republicans from New York on the committee, and they didn't feel it was right to put any more New Yorkers on."

"What do you mean? These guys are great at making exceptions when the exceptions suit *them*. Let them make an exception and put me on the committee."

"Bella, you know they're not going to do it. Now what do you want me to do?"

"I don't give a damn what you do," I said furiously. "This is outrageous. You're like the rest of them. I don't care what you do. If I were you, I'd resign. You have no power."

"Look, Bella," he said. "I'm in the committee now and we're deciding. Will you consider any other committees?"

I had never listed any second or third choices, or even

thought about them. I've been figuring that if I don't make Armed Services, I'll just conduct my own hearings on the military.

"Well, Bella, will you consider any other committees?" Carey pressed.

"Interstate and Foreign Commerce, *maybe*," I said, because this is the committee that regulates all the regulatory agencies and the alleged public services agencies that are killing us in this country. You know, Con Ed and the Telephone Company.

"Okay," he said. "Is there anything else you'll consider?"

"Banking and Currency, because it deals with housing, or Government Operations—*maybe*," I said. "So you'd better get back in there and get me on one of them. This geographical excuse for me not getting on Armed Services is baloney."

An hour or so later Carey called back.

"You got Government Operations," he said, "and you ought to be happy. It's the committee that is going to be handling Nixon's reorganization plan, and it's very rare for a freshman to get on it."

"That's a lot of baloney," I said. "You're not fooling me. Tell those guys that I never say die. As far as Armed Services is concerned, I'm not finished yet."

As soon as I hung up I called Carl Albert.

"Now look, Carl," I said. "Let me tell you something. You're the Speaker and you're the only one, really, to whom there is an appeal, and I want to tell you that there are three reasons from *your* point of view to have me on the Armed Services Committee." I then went into the business about the committee having no representation from the women or the cities, and the fact that it was a special interest group.

Then I went on to say, "Now what is this *new look* you're supposed to be representing in the Democratic Party. There's no *new look*! It's the same old sectional politics. Everybody who's in power is either from the South or the Southwest.

Now, if you really want a *new look,* and if you really want to show people that the Democratic Party has the capacity to cope with change, then you'll do what I tell you to do. You'll take the one person who most represents change—the one who has the largest electoral mandate for change—and you'll put her on the Armed Services Committee. You'll overrule the old style! You'll show that you guys are willing to appreciate change, and people will appreciate you."

"Well, Bella," he said, "you're right—there is a desire for change and your arguments are very persuasive. Let me see what I can do."

I'm sure he was just putting me off. He's not going to do anything. My only hope now is to take the fight into the Democratic caucus next week, which has the power to reverse the Committee on Committees.

January 31

Paul Cowan, a reporter for *The Village Voice,* invited me to go with him this afternoon to meet a couple of nuns involved in the Justice Department's wild charges about a plot to kidnap Henry Kissinger and bomb government heating systems. A federal grand jury sitting in Harrisburg has issued a number of indictments naming the Berrigan brothers and others in the Catholic peace/resistance movement as conspirators or co-conspirators.

We went to an old brownstone in the West Nineties which houses the Religious Order of the Sacred Heart of Mary and there in a plainly furnished basement parlor I drank tea and talked with two remarkable women. Incidentally, neither one was dressed like a nun. They're part of the new breed of Catholic that is more concerned with substance than outward form.

Sister Elizabeth McAllister, the younger one, has actually been indicted and is out on bail. "I feel as though I'm trapped in a J. Edgar Hoover nightmare," she said. The other one, Sister Jogues Egan, is a really distinguished scholar and the former president of her order's Marymount College. She's fifty-two, white-haired and chic in a quiet way, and is considered part of the church establishment. She's an unindicted "co-conspirator" and has just spent a couple of days in Pennsylvania jails for refusing to testify before the grand jury. The jury's on a fishing expedition and apparently is now looking for testimony to justify the indictments it issued.

Like a lot of peace people who get thrown into jail for the first time, Sister Jogues was so appalled by the conditions she found there that she wants to go into jail reform. As unbelievable as it may seem, she said, they took away her watch so she lost all sense of time and they also took away her Bible so she couldn't read. Then they had her cleaning toilets!

Unlike the Berrigans, she said, she had never wanted to commit any acts of civil disobedience because she didn't want to go to jail. But when she was called before the grand jury, she decided to refuse to answer their questions, insisting that her conscience bade her "obey a higher court than this one."

She and Sister Elizabeth said they were harassed for weeks before the indictments were handed down. Their phones were tapped and they'd get mysterious calls at all hours. It's really incredible what the FBI gets away with. That's one of the issues I must take on in Congress.

These women have guts—and humor. Just as I was leaving, Sister Elizabeth mentioned that she was especially annoyed at Henry Kissinger's having told the press that the nuns probably decided to kidnap him because they wanted a man. "So why would we pick Kissinger?" she asked.

February 1

I've been on the phone almost constantly the last day or so, trying to line up support for myself in the caucus, but I've been having a difficult time. Why? Because Les Aspin from Wisconsin and Michael Harrington from Massachusetts, both considered liberals and opponents of the Indochina war, have been appointed to the Armed Services Committee. While I consider their assignment a personal victory for myself, neither they nor anybody else in Congress represents the kind of activism and the kind of movement for change that I do. Nobody. I was firmly against this war when many of these "war critics" were enthusiastically presenting Johnson with his Gulf of Tonkin Resolution, and before that too. Ten years ago I was out in the streets protesting nuclear testing, organizing the mothers and other women of this country in a movement for peace and disarmament. It was largely because they were worried about the "mothers' vote" that the Senate ratified the partial nuclear test ban treaty. (Now they're going to have to worry about the "women's vote" too.)

I used to come down to Washington several times a year as a lobbyist for Women Strike for Peace. I would go from one Congressman to another, warning them, "You guys better do something about this war or we're not going to put you back in office." I'm no Joanna-come-lately, believe me. I've been here all along—outside. It's just that now there are enough people who feel the way I do so that they've been able to get me into Congress. I'm not going to betray them.

The more I look at this committee system, the more outrageous I realize it is. Of the grand total of twelve women in the House, five have been assigned to the Education and Labor Committee, which, for some reason or another, the gallant men around here are shaping into a female repository. Maybe they figure if they get us all in one place we'll cause less trouble.

Only one woman will serve on the very powerful Ways and Means Committee, and two on Appropriations. None of us has been assigned to the Rules Committee, the Judiciary Committee or, of course, the Armed Services Committee—as if the jurisdictions of these committees have nothing to do with 53 percent of the voting population in this country, which is female.

Besides women, New Yorkers are severely discriminated against. On the six major House committees, New York City's twenty Congressmen occupy only seven out of two hundred places. Only one Representative from the city is a committee chairman, and under the hideous seniority setup only four are high up enough on the list to have any hope of ever becoming chairmen.

So if you're a woman and a New Yorker too, watch out! Two years ago Shirley Chisholm from Brooklyn, not exactly the most pastoral of regions, was assigned to the Agriculture Committee. When she raised a fuss they shifted her to Veterans' Affairs. I don't know whether it's true or not, and I don't want to know, but this year it was reported in one of the papers that Shirley voted for Hale Boggs in the secret ballot against Morris Udall for Majority Leader. She did it, the article said, because "it was a deal, and the only way she could get on the committees she wanted to be on." She was assigned to the Education and Labor Committee. Believe me, if Shirley has to be driven to something like this, you can understand the degree to which the Tories have this place locked up.

February 2

The caucus is tomorrow. Today the Democratic Study Group voted to endorse my bid to have the Committee on Committees' decision reversed. Am I hopeful? Let me quote the early edition of the *Times* tonight: "Although the study group vote is supposed to be binding on its members, there have been reports that some of the organization's members have voted contrary to the group's stated position once they were in closed caucus."

February 3

Well, I lost—for this session anyway. The caucus didn't overturn the decision by the Committee on Committees. It's really a shame. A lot of people have been trying to make me feel better by telling me that I'm responsible for getting two other liberals on the Armed Services Committee, but that doesn't exactly compensate.

In any case, a number of other liberals fared better than I did. Ron Dellums, the black Congressman from California who supports the Black Panthers, got a seat on the Judiciary Committee. Father Robert Drinan from Massachusetts, also a freshman liberal, not only got a seat on Judiciary but on the ultra-reactionary Internal Security Committee. Herman Badillo, the Puerto Rican who represents portions of the Bronx, Manhattan and Queens, was successful in getting his assignment changed from Agriculture (can you imagine that?) to Education and Labor.

Badillo's been making a big fight, as I have, and I guess now he looks like the winner while I look like the loser. I wonder, however, if people understand what I was fighting for. Education and Labor is already the most liberal committee in the House.

I feel that if you're going to be a pathfinder, you have to fight, as I did, for a seat on a committee that has *no* liberals on it because that's where you're going to have the most impact.

February 4

Hugh Carey has told some people, including a reporter for *The Village Voice* in my district, that "if the Second Coming was

(28)

tomorrow, even He couldn't get Bella Abzug on the Armed Services Committee." I don't know about that, but I do know one thing: Hugh Carey certainly couldn't get Bella Abzug on the Armed Services Committee.

February 6

In the last several weeks a few items suggesting I use profanity have appeared in a few newspapers. I suppose I should deny it, but who would believe me? I'm a very spontaneous and excitable and emotional person, and I do have a way of expressing myself pretty strongly sometimes. Big deal. I don't see where it matters. What matters—all that matters—is that I say what I feel, and I always do *that*. The press is stupid to get all excited because I'm prone to use a few choice words now and then.

Listen to this crap from the Associated Press:

"Did she [meaning me] respond to a suggestion that she take a spot on the Agriculture Committee with an expletive meaning male animal manure?"

Well, the fact is that I don't remember, but if I did, it would have been an appropriate response.

"How about gossip that she suggested House doorkeeper William 'Fishbait' Miller perform an impossible sexual act when he told her she couldn't wear her famous floppy hats—her campaign trademark—on the House floor?"

What the Associated Press doesn't understand, besides the fact that this is absolutely untrue, is that I'm not here to fight about my hats, and if I were, the last guy I'd fight with is Fishbait Miller. He's very friendly. He has been since I met him. I was having a very serious discussion about my committee assignment a few weeks ago with Wilbur Mills. The door opens up and this little man comes in, a stranger, and kisses me.

"Whoever you are," I said, "I think this is an overresponse."

"I'm Fishbait Miller," he said, "and I wanted to greet you."

In a speech to a National Women's Democratic Club luncheon I told a little anecdote about Abigail Adams (wife of John) who was one of the earliest recorded voices for women's rights in this country. When her husband, along with the other founding *fathers*, was in the midst of drawing up the Constitution, she wrote him the following note: "My dear John. In the new code of laws, I desire you would remember the ladies and be more generous and favorable to them than were your ancestors. Do not put such unlimited powers in the hands of husbands. Remember, all men would be tyrants if they could."

To which John replied: "My dear, we men know better than to repeal our masculine systems."

I'll tell you something: the man wasn't kidding. Just to get the right to vote it took women, as one of the suffrage leaders pointed out, "fifty-two years of pauseless campaigns, 56 state referendum campaigns, 480 legislative campaigns to get state amendments submitted, 47 constitutional convention campaigns, 19 campaigns to get suffrage planks in party platforms, 19 campaigns with 19 successive Congresses to get the federal amendment submitted and then the final ratification campaign."

Now, some fifty years after we've won the right to vote, women are finally beginning to realize that we haven't even begun to learn how to use it. Most women, to the extent that they're involved at all in the masculine political power structure, are still kitchen slaves. We ring doorbells, stuff envelopes, distribute leaflets, lobby, parade, demonstrate. We find ourselves relegated to the drudgery, the dirty work, the detail work of politics.

It's outrageous! Just imagine for a moment what life in this country might have been like if women had been properly represented in Congress. Would a Congress where women in all their diversity were represented tolerate the countless laws now on the books that discriminate against women in all phases of their lives? Would a Congress with adequate representation of women have allowed this country to reach the 1970s without a national health care system? Would it have permitted this country to rank fourteenth in infant mortality among the developed nations of the world? Would it have allowed the situation we now have in which thousands of kids grow up without decent care because their working mothers have no place to leave them? Would such a Congress condone the continued butchering of young girls and mothers in amateur abortion mills? Would it allow fraudulent packaging and cheating of consumers in supermarkets, department stores and other retail outlets? Would it consent to the perverted sense of priorities that has dominated our government for decades, where billions have been appropriated for war while our human needs as a people have been neglected? Would it have voted for ABMs instead of schools, MIRVs instead of decent housing and health centers? Does anyone think that a Congress with large numbers of women would ever have allowed the war in Vietnam to go on for so long, slaughtering and maiming our children, and the people of Indochina?

For fifty years women have been trying without success to get through Congress something as basic as an amendment to the Constitution that would guarantee equal rights for women, and we haven't even been able to do that! We still have to listen to men like Emanuel Celler, who last year when the Equal Rights Amendment was being debated on the House Floor said, "Ever since Adam gave his rib to make a woman, throughout the ages we have learned that physical, emotional and psychological differences exist and dare not be disregarded."

Then, in a reference to Michigan Congresswoman Martha Griffiths, who was leading the fight for the amendment, Celler had the nerve to add, "Neither the National Women's Party nor the delightful, delectable and dedicated gentlelady from Michigan can change nature. They cannot do it."

This is exactly the same psychology they used to try and keep the blacks down. The political system denies fair representation to a segment of the population, and then politicians turn around to picture those of us who are underrepresented as having created the situation ourselves because of our own personal inadequacies.

February 9

Some people have suggested to me that I may be coming on too strong down here, that I may be offending some people and alienating them. I don't think it's true though.

Everyone I've talked to has been very cordial; they don't seem to have any complaints about accepting my "presence." In fact, if anything, I intrigue them.

And even if these guys are a little intimidated by me, I can't concern myself. I have to show them that I'm not going to be cowed by the atmosphere. I have to show myself that they aren't going to stop me, or else I'll be dead.

February 10

I've been boiling about Nixon's adventure in Laos for days now, but this morning was the limit. I picked up the *Times* and read more double talk from Laird and Rogers, trying to reassure us that what's going on in Laos is not an "invasion" but an "incursion." There was the usual nonsense that expanding the war will shorten the war. We good clean Americans are only killing people from the air so we can't see the bodies we're mangling. What perverse morality! Lies and distortions, one after another. Sickening. The Gallup poll shows that 73 percent of the people favor total withdrawal, and

Nixon invades Laos! I'm sure that bastard has ground troops in there too, no matter what he says, and in a day or so I'm introducing a resolution to have Congress conduct an on-the-spot investigation.

February 14

I've been feeling very run-down and sick for the last week or so and tonight for the first time in a month I spent a few hours at home in New York with Martin. He was telling me about a guy who called him recently to say, "What kind of life is that you lead? That's no kind of life, alone. Couples should be together." Martin slammed down the phone on him. The guy is divorced.

A lot of people are very curious about Martin—what kind of man he is and what he thinks of my views. Martin's very stable and mature, and a great source of strength to me. For years, however, he's been telling me that I'm too selfless, that I'm crazy to knock myself out the way I do because people don't appreciate it. When it comes to politics, he knows what's going on but he's not as interested in it as I am. He likes to tell people that when I come home and talk about the issues, he goes to sleep. Once he even demonstrated it.

It was during the campaign. *New York* magazine sent somebody over to interview us. The interview progressed and I started to talk about how it's society—not women—that emasculates men, and Martin, who had been up all night writing, started to doze off.

When I finally woke him up, here is some of what he told the interviewer:

"My first reaction to Bella was wonderment. It still is. I'd never met anyone like her. [We met on a bus in Miami on the way to a Yehudi Menuhin concert.] She wanted to practice law. I encouraged her. She was one of the pioneers in the civil rights movement, which entailed a lot of sacrifices on her part. She was involved in a rape case in Mississippi in 1952 when she was pregnant. All this inconveniences married life, but we've managed to make adjustments."

Martin and I had two years of discussions before we were married about how I was going to be a wife, a mother and a lawyer at the same time—and it was with his understanding that I've been able to manage all those roles. It takes a special kind of man to be able to cope with this kind of thing. A lot of men feel threatened by me, but that's obviously only because, unlike a man like Martin, they have feelings of insecurity.

February 15

For a few months now I've had the idea to put together a "Peace and Priorities" barnstorming tour of Senators and Congressmen to canvass the country and arouse the people to organize against the war. Since all the end-the-war resolutions are still in committee—with no sign that they'll get passed without mass pressure—the whole idea of the thing is to show people they still have leaders and to show the leaders that the people are demanding to be led.

Like the people themselves, a lot of Congressmen have grown cynical. They are coming to feel that they are powerless, which, I guess, up until recently has been true. Congress gave its power to the President. But now there are rumblings. They want it back. They feel put down. The President conducts his war without consulting them. Their dignity is offended. They're getting a lot of flak from home. They know they can't cope with domestic problems while the war goes on, and they're very annoyed with the way Nixon is behaving. They feel corroded, impotent.

The younger ones and the newer ones, interestingly enough,

(34)

are no longer that awestruck by the whole rigamarole—the little clubs, people opening doors for them, people bowing and scraping to them, people making them feel important. They don't care so much about their special privileges or special attention, special license plates or special elevators. The country is beginning to fall apart, and they realize it.

So the mood in Congress is slowly changing. The magic numbers are 218 in the House and 51 in the Senate. Those are all the votes we need to set a date for the withdrawal of all American troops from Indochina. Two hundred eighteen and fifty-one! Those numbers are not nearly as unattainable as they once were.

We just have to push and push and push. I'm going to bring it up in every Democratic caucus until we get a majority favoring complete withdrawal by the end of the year. At the same time, the barnstorming—which a private businessmen's organization called the Fund for Priorities is helping to finance —will get underway hopefully next month.

February 17

Another visit to the White House. The occasion this time: a briefing on taxes and revenue sharing. I made a special point of sitting at a table near the door so I could make a quick escape when it got dull, as I expected it would. At my table were a bunch of Representatives from Texas, Indiana and Tennessee.

When the President walked in he went from table to table, shaking every Congressman's hand as they all stood up. I noticed that he kept stealing glances at my table—and at me. He was obviously reluctant to come over, because he knew damn well what was going to happen. It was so evident he was avoiding us that everyone at the table was kidding me.

For a moment or so, while we were laughing, I lost sight of

(35)

the President, and then, suddenly, out of nowhere, I felt this heavy hand on my shoulder from behind me, pressing down so hard I could hardly turn my head.

Then the voice of America: "All you men and this one charming lady."

The men at the table stood up, and I started to also, but by this time Nixon had both his hands on my shoulders, and he said to me, "Don't get up." Not even a "please." He released one hand to shake hands with the others, but I could still hardly move, let alone turn around and say anything to him.

I must say he bested me.

February 20

In addition to Government Operations, they've assigned me to the Public Works Committee. Both will be meeting for the first time in the next week or so. They are supposed to be pretty good assignments for a freshman; some people feel I got them as a concession for losing my fight to get on the Armed Services Committee. I don't know, but maybe that's true.

Government Operations is a committee that could have extensive power, but its chairman, Chet Holifield, is not interested in challenging the system. Its most useful function, as far as I'm concerned, is that it has investigatory powers over parts of the government. Potentially, it could investigate the military, the CIA, the FBI, the Treasury Department, anything it wants, and it could make all those guys pay for the way they've been tyrannizing over the lives of the people in this country. At the moment, I'm angling for a seat on the military operations subcommittee of Government Operations, because that's where I'll be, well, let's say "more useful."

Public Works is also potentially powerful because it's the pork barrel committee of Congress. It's where the authorization to build bridges and dams and highways and things like that originates. It will give me a chance to look out for the economic development of my own district. And since a lot of people from the South and West and Midwest and Southwest want to get on this committee, it's possible if I don't like it that I'll be able to trade it for another assignment in the next session. This is a fairly common practice.

As far as both these committees are concerned, I've decided that if I can function on them and make some kind of contribution, then I'll stick with them. If not, I'm not going to waste my time and energy and the hell with it. I'll just hold my own hearings about things that concern me. I already have one of these scheduled for next week in New York—on child care, which is one of my pet projects. It doesn't matter to me that I'm not on the Education and Labor Committee, which is handling the child care bill. The only thing that matters is that there's a terrific demand in my district for twenty-four-hour child care centers where working women can leave their children.

February 21

Some guy I met today who is not very familiar with politics asked me if the reason I didn't get on the Armed Services Committee was personal. The answer is no. In fact, it's quite the contrary.

These men in the Club down here are very charming to me, very gracious and very complimentary. Of course, they can *afford* to be this way, because they have all the power.

Besides, they like me personally. I'm a very personable woman. When I deal with them, I'm usually—although, I admit, not always—very relaxed and conversational. They respect me because they've seen that I can wage a good battle, and that I'm not thrown by a lack of familiarity with the rules. They admire my persistence and they're full of compliments about my skill and knowledge. Since they're convinced I'll never be able to effect the kind of change I'm talking about, they don't feel threatened. That's right—as long as I'm not a threat to them, they're prepared to see me as interesting and dynamic and, most of all, not boring.

February 22

I'm still feeling washed out. My friends and my staff keep telling me to cut down my activities or I'm going to break down. But I can't. There's just too much to do. As it is, working seven days a week, morning, noon and night, I'm still not able to get *half* of what I want accomplished.

I held a special hearing on child care centers in the auditorium of the Veterans Administration building, where my New York office is located. For hours, Mim Kelber, Georgia MacMurray, who's going to be the head of the city's Agency for Child Development, Shirley Chisholm and I listened to the testimony of women hospital workers, elevator operators, telephone workers, post office employees and others. They desperately told us that they can't work and take care of their kids at the same time. In effect, they said that either we get them child care centers or they're going to be forced to go on welfare. One woman who works at night in the Post Office was so frustrated that she begged us to do something already and stop talking. "Please don't study us anymore," she said. "We have been studied to death."

Legislation to institute a universal child care program in this country is very high on my personal list of priorities. As a matter of fact, I've drawn up a bill and passed it on to Shirley Chisholm, who's now working on it and who will be its cosponsor, in which we ask for at least $10 billion for child care facilities by 1975.

Ten billion is a trifling amount when you consider that since the Second World War this country has spent more than one trillion dollars for military purposes alone. Ten billion is one-eighth of the annual military budget. Can you imagine that? We could have a universal child care program in this country for what it costs to maintain the military for a month and a half.

When it comes to child care, the United States is at a primitive stage compared to countries like Israel, Denmark, Sweden and Russia. We have more than 4 million working women with children of pre-school age. We have countless other women with young children who are on welfare because they have no other choice. And what about all the women who believe that having a husband and kids should not bar them from developing and utilizing their talents and abilities? For all these people we have exactly 640,000 places in the entire country available in licensed day care homes and centers and the Nixon Administration, apart from education programs, has budgeted just a little more than $655 million this year for Head Start, child welfare services, maternal and child health services and the Juvenile Delinquency Act combined.

This, ironically, is about the same amount of money Nixon is asking us to *give* Lockheed Corporation, one of the major defense contractors, to bail it out of financial troubles. These figures—$655 million for the needs of children and $600 million as a giveaway to a corporation that has been digging into our treasury for decades and turning out lousy planes besides—should tell you just how insane the priorities in this country are.

February 23

Like most nights, I worked in my Washington office until 10:30 (sometimes it's even later), signing mail, preparing for my committees, meeting with people and researching some upcoming projects. I grabbed a sandwich on the way home and ate it in the cab. It's my usual practice to either do that or get a quick bite in a local slop joint. I don't have time, as many of my colleagues seem to, for long lunches and dinners in the fine restaurants of this city.

Eating is only one of the things I don't have enough time for anymore. My family, unfortunately, is another. Luckily, it doesn't *require* a lot of time. Both Egee, who is twenty-one, and Liz, eighteen, are away at college and don't get in that often. As for Martin, he and I—even years before my election—were often so busy during the week that we didn't get to spend much time together anyway. We did, however, often have weekends to ourselves. Now we don't even have that. Weekends are the only time I'm in New York, and my schedule in my district is usually merciless.

The family plays a very important role in the lives of working women like me. The tough thing, of course, is trying to adjust the family situation to the realities of your life. You can't put either ahead of the other. There must be a balance, and you've got to strive to keep that balance. The family grows with it. The kids know that the mother is a woman, a wife and, in my case, a lawyer. A total person. It makes them better people.

Let's face it: Some of us have been and are more privileged than others. I, for instance, had a wonderful housekeeper, Alice Williams. To this day (she's now retired) she likes to tell me, "I all but had those kids." My husband, too, played a more domestic role than most do. He helped with the shopping and spent a great deal of time with the kids. I always tried to make it home for dinner every night, but often it was impossible. Once on a visiting day when the kids were very young and away at camp, I had an important trial and couldn't go. I felt so bad that I sent Martin, his mother, my mother and the housekeeper to substitute.

(40)

I don't mean to imply that I'm all guilt-ridden about being a working mother. I'm not. For the most part I rarely missed a school visiting day or school play. I have two great kids and a great husband. On the other hand, there are moments when I think back and say to myself, "I should have been more available." But what can you do?

February 25

My New York office is in the process of putting together what I feel is the broadest package of community services ever offered by a member of Congress. It includes—operating right out of my offices—a legal guidance center, a Social Security guidance center and a consumer information service. This is what I mean when I say I'm an activist. You *do* while you're trying to show people that something can be done.

We run a very big operation in New York, with lots of volunteers. Dora Friedman, a widow with two grown children who's a long-time activist in the peace and civil rights movements, and a Democratic district leader on the West Side, is starting next month as my administrative assistant in New York. She had been working for ten years as an administrator in the Department of Psychiatry at Columbia University. In addition to her and Mim Kelber and Howard Brock, who handles my press relations, I have also hired a caseworker, Sylvia Epstein, and a community organizer, Steve Max. Sylvia, whom I met during the campaign, is doing an excellent job helping hundreds of individual constituents each month with problems concerning welfare, Social Security, food stamps, the draft, housing, immigration, drugs, abortions—and whatever comes up. As an example of the unusual kinds of things she does, she helped one man who has a pizza parlor in my district get a $1500 refund from Con Edison, which had been double-billing him for electricity. Steve works primarily with groups and organizations in the district on economic development, housing, crime, health and similar problems.

We see to it that whoever calls or writes us gets whatever service we can provide. Sometimes people don't understand I have a staff to take care of things for me and they do everything they can to get through to me personally. Like tonight when my phone rang at home. It was a drunken cab driver. He wanted to know if there were going to be more cab medallions issued, or something like that. I was too exhausted to go into it with him so I told him Mrs. Abzug was not at home.

"Whaddya mean?" he said. "You sound like Bella to me."

"No," I said, "I'm her daughter."

That didn't seem to faze him though, and he spent ten minutes telling me about his problem. Actually, I could have shut him up, but I didn't really want to. Why frustrate him further? In the meantime, I listened and convinced him to call my office in the morning. I'll prepare my staff for his call, and they'll do what they can. After all, he's entitled to help.

I get a lot of support from cab drivers. They like me because I'm outgoing and tough and rough and ready. Cab drivers, truck drivers, they all like me. And I like them. It's fun when they holler out in the street as they drive by, "Hi, Bella, give 'em hell!"

February 26

After watching our great liberals in action down here for a month now, it takes an awful lot to shock me. Believe me, with these guys I expect just about anything, but yesterday at the first meeting of my Government Operations Committee, they proved themselves even worse than I could have imagined.

Government Operations is the committee that a few years ago drafted the Freedom of Information Act, a law that requires that the executive branch furnish on demand information requested by the press and the public. It's a great breakthrough law, and the guy who's responsible for it, John Moss from California, is still on the committee. Okay. Got that?

No sooner did I walk into the committee room than I found myself in the midst of a vote *to exclude the press from the meeting.* Chet Holifield, the chairman, had decided that we were going to have what he called "an executive reorganizing session" and the press had no reason to be there. The vote went 19-18 to order the press to leave, with only John Culver, from Iowa, me and the Republicans, who were going through a ritual protest, voting against. The guys who voted with Holifield included Mr. Freedom of Information himself, John Moss, as well as such liberals as John Conyers, the black Congressman from Detroit, Ben Rosenthal from Queens and Henry Reuss from Wisconsin.

The doors shut tight, Holifield then started his "executive reorganizing" by proposing to play hanky-panky with the rules approved by the Democratic caucus, which apply to all committees.

The first rule he decided to get around is a new one which decrees that nobody can be chairman of more than one legislative subcommittee. It so happens that five of the men who chair Government Operations subcommittees are also chairmen of subcommittees elsewhere. Rather than compel them to resign, Holifield simply announced that he was turning most of the legislative subcommittees into "investigative" committees. Just like that. So anybody could go on being chairman of as many subcommittees as he wanted. Well, this was a complete violation of the rule—the one-chairmanship regulation applies to all the subcommittees of a parent committee with legislative jurisdiction, such as Government Operations. Think about it: A chairman like Holifield can do whatever he likes to the rules, and there's not even a whimper from the liberals.

As if all this wasn't enough, Holifield—remember now, press barred—then went on to *combine* two major subcommittees that have nothing in common: government reorganization and military operations. As far as I'm concerned, this is the most appalling thing he did. It was an outrageous trick! To top it all off, he made himself chairman of this new super-subcommittee which will now have to deal with Nixon's grandiose plan to reorganize the government into fewer departments. This means that it's not going to have any time to look into matters of "military operation." What Holifield did, in effect, was kill the military operations subcommittee.

The most insane thing is that the guy thinks he's going to kill Nixon by denying him government reorganization. My God, doesn't he realize that he could do it a lot more swiftly by investigating the rotten military which is depriving us of an opportunity to live like decent human beings in this country?

And where were the liberals when all this was going on? Guess. Holifield's plan to combine the two subcommittees passed with a tie vote. Conyers, Moss, Reuss and Rosenthal all voted *for* it. Why? I think because they feel a need to survive in the Club. Unfortunately, They think they have to kowtow to the chairman, because they think that's the way to get power. What they don't understand is that by kowtowing they are *giving up* their power. Think about it: Had any one of those four guys I mentioned voted against Holifield, we could have had the press inside the committee room to report about what he was doing.

February 27

I'm going through an ordeal. The past week or so I've been on television three times, I've been interviewed by the press on my peace views at least a half a dozen times, and I've been to so many meetings I can't remember them all. I'm wondering whether I'm pressing the peace issue in the right way. Maybe I should be out there barnstorming the country—by myself, if necessary—to help move the people into a new political coalition which will bring change. I don't know. It's so difficult to figure out whether you're getting anywhere.

Well, there has been at least one indication that I am, and it was sort of amusing. Emanuel Celler, not one of our superliberal Congressmen by any means, usually asks me to sit next to him at meetings of our New York Congressional delegation. As a result he always hears me at close range *hocking a cheinik* about the war. Well, the other day he followed me on the TV program where I called for the withdrawal of all troops by the end of the year. To my utter surprise, he came on and did me one better: "The war should have ended yesterday," he said.

February 28

For the first time in a few weeks I managed to steal a few moments to visit my eighty-two-year-old mother. Not long ago she fell at a bar mitzvah and broke her hip. Since her release from the hospital, she's been recuperating in a nursing home, and I feel very guilty about not being able to see her enough. My poor sister Helene has had to take on the whole burden of looking after her.

She's a remarkable woman, my mother. She was the source of many interesting anecdotes during the campaign. On primary night she told me, "Well, Bella, congratulations. Let's hope next time it will be for President." The way she said it, she could have been saying, "Let's hope next time it will be a boy." At the victory party after the general election she got up before the crowd and said, "I always knew Bella would make it. She always did her homework and practiced without being told to."

That same night, incidentally, Martin said, "I hope you constituents deserve her." That was very sweet of him and characteristic. He doesn't think anybody deserves me.

Liz, I'm sure, had some wise remarks prepared too, but a friend of hers had just been hospitalized and she couldn't come. Like the older one, Liz is very tough on the outside. But neither is really tough, you know, they both pretend. They were both proud of my election, even though I think it was a little hard for them. They don't want to be known only as my daughters, naturally. They want to be known on their own. Egee is a talented sculptress and Liz has a beautiful voice. I'd like Liz to become a professional singer, but lately she's been talking about becoming a lawyer. Egee is planning on becoming a clinical psychologist.

March 1

This has been one of my best days so far—the kind of day when I feel like I'm making a mark. This morning I testified before the House Armed Services Committee for repeal of the draft.

Here is some of my prepared testimony, which I thought was very good:

"I am unalterably opposed to military conscription and believe it should be dismantled. . . . Conscription, no matter how worthy the avowed purpose, no matter in what sophisticated packaging it is wrapped, is involuntary servitude. To keep using the word 'service' to describe actual slavery is a mockery.

"Therefore I do not advocate any type of draft reform. I view attempts to make the draft allegedly more equitable as both romantic and pernicious—romantic because the achievement of equity within a conscription system is impossible, and pernicious since by instituting minor changes and holding out false hopes these attempts tend to make the draft more palatable to the public."

(46)

I said I'd agree to a volunteer army only as a transition.

"Transition to what?" they asked.

"I would hope, gentlemen," I said, "that we would understand that the survival of civilization in this nuclear age rests upon our looking toward the possiblity of having general and complete disarmament under an international and universal public authority, and that we would begin to realize at some point that the hopes of this world rest upon settling our international disputes by peaceful means, for which we simply won't need the kind of military we now have."

I must say I really got a kick out of my testimony. It was an opportunity for me to tell these guys philosophically a lot of things they never get a chance to hear. I wasn't loud and angry, either, but in a very quiet and instructive voice I lectured them on how my concept of foreign policy is quite different from theirs.

When I finished, Ed Hébert, who's really a very pleasant man, came over to me and said, "Bella, you can appreciate how lucky you are not to have gotten on the committee. Had you been a member you would have been limited to only five minutes. This way you got forty-five."

March 2

My experience so far with the Public Works Committee has been a lot more pleasant than it has been with Government Operations, I'll tell you. The chairman, John Blatnik, says he's anxious for me to utilize my brain for the benefit of the committee, and so he's been swamping me with subcommittee assignments. It's as if he's in cahoots with the establishment to keep me so busy handing out dams and bridges that I can't stop the war.

In any case, part of my district, the Lower East Side, has been declared a "special impact area" under the Public Works and Economic Development Act, and I'd like to be in a position where I can help the people there get all the assistance they need. I accepted seats on the rivers and harbors subcommittee because of the Hudson River situation, and on the subcommittee on investigation and oversight because I'm very interested in pushing mass transit at the expense of cars, and this committee might be investigating scandals in the administration of the highway program. As if this weren't enough, Blatnik also assigned me public buildings and grounds. It's nice of him, and everything, but he's not going to get as much time out of me as he thinks he is, because I just don't have *that much* time.

March 3

I was invited, for the third time, to the White House the other day. The occasion was a prayer breakfast. I didn't go. It's not my style.

March 5

I dropped by a party for Bill Ryan tonight. Ryan, who is one of the originators of the reform movement in New York, has been in Congress for ten years. He was the first guy in the House to speak out against the war. He represents a portion of Manhattan, and there's a chance that in the redistricting based on the 1970 census, they'll eliminate one of the four districts in Manhattan, and this means, theoretically, that one of us—Ryan, Ed Koch or me—could be forced to run against the other in 1972. I'm sorry to say but this seemed to have some people at the party a little bit uptight.

I left early, just after receiving a telephone call from United Press International. It seems that Spiro Agnew was speaking tonight at a fund-raising dinner in Maryland, where he said,

"Republicans should work for adoption of environmental programs, welfare and revenue-sharing and *most importantly, we have to keep Bella Abzug from showing up in Congress in hot pants.*"

The UPI reporter asked me to comment.

"I have no intention of wearing hot pants in Congress," I said, "because they are not my style—any more than Mr. Agnew is. Besides, before long—and at least by 1972—I expect hot pants will disappear from the national scene, along with Mr. Agnew and Mr. Nixon."

March 6

Everybody's kidding me about Agnew's remark, which I guess is funny in a stupid way. I really can't get angry. Some guys would like to dismiss me with silly comments about my hats or my four-letter words or my figure. Maybe they think that by dwelling on aspects of my flamboyant character (Norman Mailer has said my voice "could have boiled the fat off a taxicab driver's neck. It was as full of the vibrations of power as those machines which rout out grooves in wood."), they can divert attention from the things I really dwell on such as child care, repeal of the draft and an end to the war. All I say is that anybody who thinks he can take me lightly because I'm fresh and colorful had better watch out.

March 8

This afternoon I was trying to reach a fellow by the name of Tony Podesta who works with Common Cause to help me organize the barnstorming. My secretary placed the call, and as is protocol, once he was on the line, I picked up and started to talk.

"Tony, look," I said, "we're organizing this barnstorming

tour against Nixon so we can show the country that Congress-men can really mobilize . . ."

"Wait a minute," he said. "What do you mean *against* Nixon. Mrs. Abzug, I *work* for Nixon."

"Huh?"

"Do you know who I am?"

"Yeah—Tony Podesta. Right?"

"No," he laughed. "Bob Podesta. I'm not even any relation to Tony Podesta. I'm the Assistant Secretary of Commerce in charge of economic development."

I roared. "Well, as a matter of fact, I've got something to say to *you*, too—about economic development on the Lower East Side. You must know I'm a multifaceted human being."

I worked late in the office and an old friend, Curtis Gans, who was the national coordinator of the McCarthy campaign, dropped in to see me. He has this idea to set up a new super-structure composed of people like John Gardner, Clark Clifford, Kingman Brewster, Leonard Woodcock and others in that middle group who've finally come to realize they've got to do something about the war. With them at the core he wants to form an umbrella group out of which all kinds of organized opposition to the war would flow.

I think he's wrong and that's what I told him. We're well past the stage where we need these kinds of middle groupings that organize people for one march a year and then fade away into oblivion. What we need instead is a political organization that will mobilize the people for broad-based change and that will go beyond the simple protest phase. We need to organize existing power so that it's more visible; we need a coalition that will not only work to end the war, but will stay in form *after* the war to make sure the priorities are turned around. And, furthermore, I don't like the idea of super-umbrella structures because I know damn well that they probably wouldn't be inclined to use radical tactics, and I'm not going to put up with that.

Curtis and I talked until about 11:30, when I started coughing uncontrollably. I was really feeling miserable. I also had some pains in my chest, which I made the mistake of mentioning to him, because he started to insist that I go to the hospital. Finally, I was able to persuade him that I had no time to go to the hospital, that it was a ridiculous idea, and he drove me home.

March 9

I woke up feeling awful, but went to the office anyway. My body seemed to be failing me.

Early in the afternoon Ed Michaels, the husband of Charita, a very close friend of mine, dropped by the office to see me. He was in Washington for some scientific conference. No sooner did he walk in than I had to go to a press conference. I asked him to come along.

The press conference had been called by the U.S. Servicemen's Fund, a group that is sponsoring a "message" variety show for troops staged by such antiwar entertainers as Jane Fonda, Elliot Gould, Donald Sutherland, Dick Gregory, Peter Boyle and Barbara Dane. They are having a problem with a show scheduled for next week at Fort Bragg, North Carolina. The Commanding General there refuses to permit them on the base because, he claims, their show would "disrupt the discipline and morale of the troops."

A captain and a sergeant came up from Fort Bragg and presented a petition with eighteen hundred signatures from the base asking that the show be allowed to go on. I made some remarks about how the Army has no right to abridge freedom of choice, opinion and speech, and that it was shocking that the generals were trying to censor this thing. Actually, to be truthful, I felt a little put upon. A number of other Congress-men supported the petition, but I was the only one who showed up for the press conference. The entertainers weren't even there! I don't know—I guess it's just my cross to bear.

Because of my bad throat and because I believe in a change of pace once in a while, I gave a kind of soft-sell presentation. Some people may not realize it, but being able to switch from an impassioned speech into a soft sell is all part of the diversity of personality that I possess. I don't want the press to think that I operate on only one note. I don't think they do, actually, but I worry about it, because I'm conscientious. I'm always concerned that I'm going to be boring, even though as some-body once said, "Whatever else you are, Bella, boring you're not."

Whether I'm doing a soft sell or one of my impassioned speeches, it always takes self-control. In either case, I not only have to be aware of my emotions, but I have to watch the timing and get the phraseology just right. Some people think this comes naturally, but actually it's very thoroughly thought out. Even if it's not studied, it's thought out.

After the press conference I went to a meeting of the Demo-cratic Study Group, inviting Ed to come along for the drinks and crackers they always serve before the session. I must have looked really awful, because he kept telling me how important it was for me to save myself and not get sucked into every kind of activity.

During the meeting I learned that there was some confusion about a request I had made to bring up a discussion of the war in the upcoming Democratic caucus. It's very complicated, but what it boils down to is this: Under the rules of the caucus you have to give nine days' notice to the chairman and the members if you want to put any matter on the agenda. I notified Olin Teague, who's the chairman of the caucus, and all members that I wanted to put before the caucus the question of Vietnam. Unknown to me, however, a group of guys notified Teague, *but not the members*, that they wanted to specifically raise for a vote the Vietnam Disengagement Act. (This is the House version of the McGovern-Hatfield Amendment, which calls for our troops to be out of there by the end of the year.)

Therefore, they had not complied with the rules of the caucus, as I had; yet I had not requested a vote on a specific resolution, as they had. The upshot, we were informed, is that they wouldn't be on the agenda at all, and although I would, I wouldn't be able to call for a vote on the Vietnam Disengagement Act.

Outrageous, isn't it? But you see what the problem is? Simply, that the Democratic leadership does not want the specific resolution brought up in the caucus. So they're playing games with us.

The members of the DSG listened sympathetically to the problem, but I'm pretty disgusted with them too. They haven't done much of anything. They don't take binding votes. All they do is discuss and discuss and discuss until it comes out of my ears. Oh sure, they do provide a certain amount of guidance in bulletins they put out weekly on what's coming up on the Floor, and they do try to arrange a unified approach to liberal causes—but in the end each of these guys falls out to do whatever he wants. As far as I'm concerned, a group like this should *never stop* until it figures out a way to utilize its talent and energy to bring up the issue of militarism and the war on the Floor every single day until they force Congress to do something.

After the meeting I came back to my office, hoping to work at my desk for a couple of hours instead of running around, since I was feeling progressively worse. What I discovered, however,

(53)

was that I was scheduled to speak before some dinner of another women's press club. This angered me no end. My secretary is the easiest target in town for all these appointments.

By the time I got there I was feeling so sick I thought I might collapse on the spot. I started to worry about what kind of speech I'd make. I have this little envelope I carry around with me with various speeches for various occasions, but I don't often use them since I'm more effective when I'm being spontaneous. Tonight, however, as never before, I needed a prepared speech. So wouldn't you know it? There was no lectern for me to place the paper on. I nearly died. I turned to the woman sitting next to me on the dais and asked her if it would be all right if I just answered questions instead of giving a speech. "Let's just see what happens," she said, smiling.

Well, she introduced me and, of course, I started a very impassioned speech, giving it to them hard on Nixon and how terrible the war was and all that stuff. I felt myself growing more and more tired, more and more down, fading and fading. Somehow, and I don't know how, I kept it moving until when I was finished three-quarters of the audience rose in a tremendous standing ovation. After this, I answered some questions, and there were more ovations. Everybody was pretty fired up over what I had said about how the political power structure was going to have to reflect the diversity of America itself, how the institutions were going to have to change and how women were going to be seen and heard. By the time I sat down I was in a cold sweat. Curtis Gans was there. He put me in his car and drove me to Bethesda Naval Hospital.

March 10

It's all been very strange. In the car last night I kept telling Curtis I was tired, that I wanted to go home and go to sleep, and the next thing I knew I was here in the hospital where

(54)

they were giving me a cardiogram and taking chest X rays, and the doctor was insisting that I at least stay the night so he could get the results of the tests. I argued with him, but finally I consented.

This morning, Dr. Rufus Pearson, the Capitol physician, came to see me. He seemed a little put out that I had not gotten in touch with him first.

"I wasn't able to reach you," I explained.

"I don't know why," he said. "I was home watching television."

"Well, I guess my secretary didn't have the correct number."

"Well, no matter," he said. "You're on the wrong floor here. I've made arrangements for you to be moved to Tower 16, which is where Congressmen go."

"This is fine here," I said.

"No, no, no," he said. "We won't have it."

A little later a nurse came in and told me to get my things together. I said to myself, if these people are going to make such a fuss about me going to this so-called Tower 16, the least they could do is get my things together for me. But they didn't.

Tower 16 was filled with male patients and male staff. Not a woman in sight. Most of the nurses were young corpsmen from the Navy who all seemed to be in a twitter when they saw me because there has never been a woman on this floor before.

The dozen or so beds up here are occupied by mostly captains and admirals. There are two doctors who look after us, in addition to a number of specialists who are always coming in and out.

I've been just lying here, exhausted. The medical corpsmen, it turns out, know who I am, and they're very curious about me. One of the things they seem to ask a lot about is women's lib. Tonight I was trying to explain to a group of them that women should have the right to control their bodies, and a right to equally participate in the economic, political and social issues of our time. I went into women's consciousness and the deeply ingrained roots of male chauvinism.

Our dialogue was interrupted every few minutes by a senile patient on the floor, who couldn't hear what was going on but who kept yelling, "Baby, baby, let's go to bed, baby. I'm ready anytime, baby. You ready?"

March 11

The tests are just about completed and I seem to be in working order, suffering only from exhaustion and a bad throat. They've told me to rest another day or so, and they'll release me.

The corpsmen won't leave me alone. All day they've continued to press me about women's lib, the war, why I ran for office, you name it. I guess I love it. I ended up lecturing them for hours. I'm a proselytizer, you see. Wherever I go, something like this happens. It's because I'm only human, and when I get a chance like this I like to explode a lot of myths that have sprung up around me and about me. It's important that I do this because I want people to understand that I'm motivated by feeling.

The corpsmen are all very open, which, in a military institution like this, surprises me. I really enjoy them. Not only are they honest, liberal, relaxed and intelligent, but they're also very sympathetic to my views. Not only the corpsmen, but the doctors too. From what I can tell, very few of them are interested in saber rattling.

One doctor—a throat specialist who says he makes $33,000 a year—came in to see me and complained that it was wrong for a vast hospital like this to be part of the military. "We service a half million people, including civilians," he said, "and we'd have a much more efficient operation if the military wasn't doing the administrating."

A few of the guys—corpsmen and doctors—asked me to help them get raises in pay.

"Not me," I joked. "You should know I'm against this military stuff."

March 12

Released at last. The doctors wanted me to stay over the weekend, but I insisted I be let out. Martin met me at the airport and we drove to Connecticut to spend a few days relaxing with Charita and Ed Michaels. They have a great place on the water in East Norwalk.

March 13

I'm still feeling very tired and sick, but maybe it's the result of some cold pills the doctor gave me, which are the same ones the astronauts use for *their* colds. "They better work," I told him, "or I'm going to cut the space program."

The people we're visiting are old friends. Charita is very chic, very pretty and a fashion stylist. We often used to go shopping together, looking for bargains at Loehmann's and Alexander's.

These days not only do I hardly have time for bargain shopping, but I'd like to do something as simple as get my hair done and I can't. Never a free minute anymore. I want to switch my hair style to something they call the American Afro, the little girl look with curls. As it is, my hair's always a problem. As we all know, from newspapers, I can't wear my hat on the Floor of the House, so I have to take it off and leave it in the vestibule. This usually leaves my hair messy, but to comb it I have to walk what seems like a half a mile to the only women's room. A hair style like the American Afro I wouldn't have to comb.

Under the influence of the astronaut pills, I slept most of the day, but tonight, unfortunately, we were invited to the home of a friend of the Michaels' for dinner. Of course, since I wasn't in the mood, we got into a big political argument about Ralph Nader.

I was feeling cantankerous and annoyed at being questioned when I was so tired, too tired to be able to even argue effectively. Afterwards, we all went to see a Dustin Hoffman movie which bored me, and I went to bed angry.

March 14

This morning I got up and read the *Times* and found out that the antiwar show did debut last night at Fort Bragg. It took place in an off-base coffeehouse, and the paper said five hundred soldiers attended. This made me feel good and forget about last night.

Toward late afternoon we drove home to New York and went out to dinner with our two daughters who were in for the weekend. When we got to a place called Victor's, a Cuban restaurant in the West Seventies in my district, it was jammed, and we started to walk away. But then Victor saw us through the window and came out and offered us a table.

My daughters, of course, were very embarrassed, because they thought I had pulled my rank, which I didn't. I usually don't ask for special favors. Victor just saw us and he was insistent.

(58)

You know what that Holifield decided to do to me? He assigned me to the conservation subcommittee! On top of that, he had the gall to come up to me and say, "Bella, I hope you like your subcommittee."

"I don't like my subcommittee," I said to him sharply.

"Why not? You requested it, didn't you?"

"Yeah—as my last choice. And if you think that's the way you handle people, you've got another guess coming. You listen to me: *If* you want to beat Nixon, you beat him on the grounds that he's destroying this country by the continuation of the war. I don't like what you did to the military operations subcommittee. You should have left it alone to function by itself and you should have put me on it."

"I couldn't have put you there anyway," he said, "because you don't have the seniority."

"Look," I said, "don't think that because we just came to Congress that we're children. Don't treat us like children, you understand? The fact is I'm not interested in your rotten seniority system, and I have a strong electoral mandate to be on any number of committees other than the one you assigned me to. I have a long background in understanding the military and the way it operates. I could have made a very significant contribution on military operations, if you hadn't disemboweled it."

"Now, Bella . . ."

"And it seems to me that you would be better off if you would understand that seniority is not the only basis upon which committees should function. Had you had the guts to put newer members, like myself, on committees which have something to do with our mandates—because most of us are from areas demanding vigorous change—you might have helped the whole rotten Congress, if not the country. You, mister, have made a terrible error."

(59)

The members of the committee, who were all witnessing this exchange, were astonished.

"Well, I'm sorry you feel that way," Holifield said.

"I'm sorry too, and you better know you are making a big mistake."

At this point, Henry Reuss, the chairman of the conservation subcommittee who over the years has done a lot of wonderful things in the field, walked over to me and said, "Bella, I want you to know that nevertheless you're very welcome on our committee, and I hope you'll do a good job." It was a very warm gesture.

Then I walked out.

The only heartening thing that happened at the meeting was that Holifield was forced to abandon his devious plan to turn the legislative subcommittees into "investigative" subcommittees, which would have made it possible for him to be chairman of as many as he wanted. Also, I would like to point out that a few of the liberals who had gone along with him on this thing the last time got their comeuppance. They had been chairmen of special subcommittees which Holifield now says he's eliminating altogether. So, see, it did them no good to compromise, and I hope it teaches them a lesson.

Added to the tremendous deception and the illegal activities on the part of the Nixon Administration's conduct of the war, a whole new factor seems to be emerging: oil.

Thanks to a number of recent articles in the press, we are now being alerted to the implications of the bidding by U.S. oil companies about to take place in Saigon for oil tracts off the Vietnamese coast. Two recent exploratory expeditions seem to indicate that there is a fortune in oil out there, and, as far as I'm concerned, this raises a lot of questions about the role of the U.S. government.

(60)

It's inconceivable that with a financial investment which David Rockefeller has estimated at $8 billion at stake, the government hasn't made a few assurances to somebody. Let's face it: Would the oil companies risk their money in a war-ravaged country unless somebody in high office told them they could expect American troops, fleets, planes and soldiers to be around there for a long time to come?

I have a pretty strong hunch that some funny business is going on. So I had my staff work up a resolution calling on the Government Operations Committee to investigate the whole matter. You've got to keep your eyes open all the time around here.

I overdid it today, and I'm exhausted. People have been asking, "Bella, are you going to cut down now that you've been in the hospital?" I'd like to, but I just don't know how I can.

It's very tough, this job is. It's hard work and yet much of it is not very productive. Introducing bills, co-sponsoring bills, making speeches on the Floor, putting things in the *Congressional Record*, making speeches to different groups, being interviewed, running around the country and at the same time working hard in my district, meeting with constituents and discussing their problems, trying to relate to them, to give them hope, trying to move things along—God, it's tough.

And yet there's no other way. It all has to be done. You know what it requires? Seven days a week, eighteen hours a day, that's what. Too much. Much too much. The question is, can I keep this pace up? The issue is, will I accomplish enough if I don't put in that much time? I don't know anymore.

March 16

This morning George Meany, the president of the AFL-CIO, testified before my Public Works economic development sub-committee. He's a guy I disagree with on a number of things, and so I gave it to him hard about the disproportionate rate of unemployment for women and about how blacks have not been able to get anywhere in the construction trades. He sat there listening to me, hemming and hawing. The more I pressed, the more he squirmed.

After it was all over, he started to walk over to the chairman but instead came right up to me and said, "You keep sockin' it to us, ya hear?" And he walked away. I was floored.

My conservation subcommittee met later on. I thought about not going, but I did, primarily because of Henry Reuss. He's a very sweet guy and one of the most able men in Congress. As the first order of business, he said he had read my "Dear Colleague" letter about the Vietnam oil lease investigation, and since one of the committee's jurisdictions is the Department of the Interior, which concerns itself with oil, he said he was going to send an inquiry over to them.

I had a chat with Senator McGovern at a reception tonight, mostly about barnstorming, which he said he wanted to participate in. "Good," I said, "because a presidential candidate isn't worth anything unless he's an activist who goes out and organizes the people around their concerns." Just to be sure he didn't read *too* much into my compliment, I added that *"generally speaking,* and *so far"* he's spoken out more strongly than any other candidate.

Otherwise, I really wasn't too sociable at this reception, because just before I left to go there I received a call from the Whip's office. The message was that there would be no vote at the caucus tomorrow on the Vietnam Disengagement Act. Some real skullduggery has taken place, and I'm furious.

As I've been able to piece it together, the leadership called the guys who were going to bring up the resolution and told them that (a) because tomorrow is St. Patrick's Day not many people were planning to come and (b) that "Doc" Morgan, who's the head of the House Foreign Affairs Committee, has asked for time to prepare his opposition. Prepare his opposition! Can you imagine that? The opposition has been in the driver's seat on this war for ten years!

The audacity! Boggs, Albert, Morgan—they all know we have the votes to win this thing and this is the only way they can stop us. It's a bluff! If you convince enough people that there's not going to be any vote, then you don't get a quorum. And without a quorum they can keep a vote from taking place. So you know what our great liberals did? They agreed to postpone the vote until next month. Just like that. Without thinking. They were taken! And they didn't even ask for anything in return!

March 17

I got to the caucus at 8:15 A.M., all set with my hot little speech in my little hands, and a press release waiting upstairs. "Doc" Morgan was there when I arrived and he said, chomping on his cigar, "You're here so early."

"That's right."

"Well, I want you to know that I came just to hear you speak."

"Good," I said.

By 8:30 only a few people had arrived, and I began to get the feeling that the jig was up. It was apparent that the leadership, with its ploy of spreading the word that the vote was off, had gotten just what it wanted. Most people decided not to come. In the next few minutes a few more people trickled in, but we were still obviously far short of a quorum. Then— even before we got to any of the items on the agenda, including my speech—somebody asked for a quorum call. We only had 80 of the 127 heads we needed there, so Olin Teague, the caucus chairman, promptly declared the meeting adjourned.

We got screwed.

I headed right for Carl Albert and let him have it: "Now you listen to me, Carl," I said. "I'm sick and tired, because it's about time this caucus went on record against the war. The people want the war to end! And here you are, the Democratic leadership in the House, stifling a vote like this. What's the matter with you? I know why you're doing it, too, Carl. Because if you hadn't prevented this vote we would have won it, that's why, and that's what you're scared of."

"What do you mean by these charges?" he said angrily. "What you're saying is ridiculous. Anyway, how do you know how *the* people feel about this war?"

"Because I know how my constituents feel and how the people across this country feel. I go out there and I talk to them, and they tell me they want this war over. I also know how you feel about it too."

"You don't know how I feel."

"I sure do. You agree with Nixon. You support the war."

"How do you know that?"

"How do I know that? For one thing, when Nixon invaded Laos, you said it was a 'prudent' move. Well, if anything was ever a 'prudent' move, *that* sure wasn't, and neither was what you said."

By this time he was furious with me, really furious. "I don't like the way you're talking," he said, "and if you weren't a lady . . ."

"Being a lady has nothing to do with it, understand? I'm a Congresswoman with an electoral mandate, and I'm going to fulfill it."

"Well, I don't know why you're so angry with us. We've been very nice to you."

"What are you talking about? You've done *nothing* for me in this House. Nothing! You didn't give me a decent com-

(64)

mittee. You stopped this vote. If you had any damn political sense you'd know the only way to defeat Nixon is to have a vote which opposes his Vietnam policies."

"Well, lady, that's your opinion."

"Yes, that's *my* opinion," I said and walked away, disgusted.

This is my week for telling off the political power structure, I guess. About twenty people saw me shouting at Carl. I couldn't help noticing that a lot of them had secret smiles on their faces.

I started to storm out of the room, but instead I circled around for a moment. Albert's a real shrewdy. Something he said hit me. He said he'd been nice to me, and in a way I knew he was right. He was in New York when I was campaigning and made a point of being friendly and helpful. Even though when it really matters on political issues he's nowhere, I felt bad for what I had said to him, at least for the tone I had used.

He was watching me pacing around, and he came over to put his arm around me. He's a little fellow, so it was kind of funny. "Come on, Bella, let's go get a cup of coffee," he said.

"Look, Carl," I said in a much gentler tone of voice. "You know I'm trying to do my best. I've got a lot of things to offer this House, and if you'll only give me a chance, such as getting me on the Armed Forces Committee . . ."

"Well," he said, "I don't know if that's possible, but I've been thinking there may be a vacancy on the Joint Economics Committee—nothing definite—but if there's room, would you like to come on it?"

"Yeah," I said. And then I walked off again, turning back to say, "We've got to have a vote on this Vietnam issue, and don't you forget it, Carl."

The House convened at noon to debate the SST. My contribution: "There are a lot of arguments against the SST . . .

but there is only one real argument for it: profits for a very few people. While we debate such false issues as the SST's effect on the balance of payments or the dangers of Russia or England or France producing the first 'White Elephants,' children in this country suffer from not having enough food to eat. . . . How long must the working people of this country watch their taxes spent, not for anything that might benefit them or their fellow human beings, but for useless pieces of metal that make some rich people richer?"

At lunch I went out for a bite with Ella Grasso, who's a new Congresswoman from Connecticut. Ella's a great gal who had served as Connecticut Secretary of State for twelve years before she was elected to Congress last year. We're both about the same age, and she has two kids too. Where we differ is that she, unlike me, is a real party regular. As a result, she has a very good relationship with the House leadership. Unlike some of the others in this situation, I like her because she stands where she stands, she's very straightforward and makes no pretense. If she votes with the leadership she's honest about it. She says she does it to preserve her good relationship with them. No phony moralizing. I often find I have a lot more in common with her than with people who *theoretically* agree with me on the issues, because she empathizes with me in a real human way. All through lunch she scolded me because I'm trying to do too much and because I'm not taking care of myself. Before the session convened, we considered living together down here, and in a way I'm sorry we didn't. We both lead lonely during-the-week lives, having to come back to our rooms alone after long, hard days. I mean, you should see my telephone bills from late night calls alone.

Ella was telling me an interesting story about a meeting she attended the other day with a representative from a huge airplane company in her state. A number of other Connecticut Congressmen were there with her, including a freshman moderate named Bill Cotter. When the guy from the corporation told Ella, "We hear you're friendly with Bella Abzug. We don't like that. She's against everything we need," Bill Cotter objected strongly.

"I know Mrs. Abzug too," he said, "and she's a very fine, sincere and charming woman. You have no right to say that about her."

March 18

I was in the office until past midnight last night, reading, writing, being interviewed and waiting desperately for my legislative assistant to bring me testimony she was preparing for my appearance today before the general labor subcommittee of the House Education and Labor Committee. Finally, at eleven o'clock she brought it in, and while two secretaries typed it up, somebody went out for some soul food. I didn't eat any because I'm trying to diet.

I woke up with a terrible sore throat. I testified at 9:30, suffering. My main point was that since women and minorities are still castoffs in the American economy, we should strengthen the enforcement authority of the Equal Employment Opportunity Commission, which can now only sweet-talk employers into obeying the Civil Rights Act of 1964. A press release and a transcript of my prepared remarks were available to the press, but I had to leave without answering questions since I had a subcommittee meeting of my own to go to.

I got to the Floor around 2:30 and the place was jammed. The SST debate was raging. I was disappointed that I had already made my remarks yesterday to an almost empty House, but I sat through the debate anyway, finding a chuckle here and there, such as when Gerry Ford got up clutching a photograph of the Russian SST. "If you vote against an American SST," he said, "you are ensuring that the Soviet Union, the

British and the French will dominate the market in advanced aircraft over the next two decades." He was so funny, I booed out loud. After me, several other people booed too.

Several times I was called off the Floor by labor lobbyists. It was really pathetic to see unions fighting for the SST because jobs were involved. People's livelihoods should not be tied to war and pollution when there are so many things we really need in this country, such as hospitals and housing and schools. Finally, the vote got underway, and as it started to shape up, it looked like we might win. Hale Boggs walked by at this point and I heard him say, "We're losing by ten votes."

"What do you mean *we're* losing by ten votes?" I said. "*You're* losing, not *us*. And this is only the beginning, only the first defeat. From now on, it's going to be one after another. Next we're going to beat you on the war. We're going to beat you because we're where the people are, and you and your guys might as well face it."

I was ecstatic.

When the vote was officially announced, we won 216-204 and we were so happy that we violated the rules of decorum and applauded. A great event.

I didn't have much time to celebrate, unfortunately, because of my usual last-minute weekly rush to get my clothes and files together and catch the plane back to New York. I call this my clicking-off moment. Clicking off the problems of Washington and clicking on the problems of New York. It happens every Thursday. Anyway, I barely made the third section of the shuttle, arrived in New York at five o'clock, went home, made some calls, met Martin for dinner, spoke at the Village Independent Democratic Club, spoke at the Phoenix Democratic Club, went home, made some more phone calls, the last one to Ronnie Eldridge, my good friend who works as a special assistant to Mayor Lindsay. We talked about personal things, mixed in with some politics, and then

I went to sleep, exhausted. I can't go on this way every day. I'm going to collapse.

March 19

After an impossible schedule all day, there was no time left, as usual, for dinner and all I was able to have was some cottage cheese in the car on the way to Lincoln Square Synagogue, where I was scheduled to speak at, so I thought, 8:30. It turned out when I got there that I really wasn't scheduled to speak until 9:30, and since I was hungry and rushed, I was very angry. I wondered why the hell my office couldn't figure out that I have to be places later rather than earlier. Then, after thinking about it, I realized it probably wasn't their fault at all. People treat politicians like children. They swear up and down that an event is an hour earlier than it really is so they'll be sure we arrive on time. Well, I think this is rotten. After all, time is all I've got. It reminds me of when I was a lawyer. People'd call me for long, chatty conversations, and then they'd be startled when they got my bill.

In any case, I tried not to show my annoyance because this was a very important event to me. During the campaign, this synagogue and its rabbi had been very hostile toward me because they had swallowed some vicious political garbage my opponent, Barry Farber, had been spreading. He had picked up on a speech I had given in which I had noted—and that's the proper word for it too, *noted*—that selling jets to Israel was not a total solution to the Middle East crisis. Well, the way people reacted you'd think I had suggested giving the country back to the Arabs or something. It was unbelievable! Fueled by the Jewish Defense League and Barry Farber, a tremendous smear campaign was launched against me. Up and down the Jewish neighborhoods I was held responsible for, among other things, killing Jews in World War II. Boy,

(69)

did they make me suffer for those words. Those lunatics from the JDL even went so far as to say that since I was a peacenik, I was anti-Israel. People got hysterical, really hysterical. No matter how much I tried to set things straight, the malice and viciousness spread until a lot of people were convinced that Bella Abzug was not only not a good pro-Israel Jew, but possibly anti-Semitic. It was terrible, and quite honestly, it hurt me so much at times that I broke down and cried.

Lost in all this hysteria were the facts: Ever since my youth I've been a Zionist, and I worked hard for the cause of a Jewish homeland too. I've visited Israel and I raised my kids with a very strong background in Jewish culture. Besides that, I spent a couple of years of my life as a Hebrew teacher! To try to make me out as anti-Israel was nothing but rotten and vicious. And the awful thing was that Farber had them all so worked up that even Rabbi Steven Riskin from this Lincoln Square Synagogue, who's usually a very sensible man, denounced me from the pulpit.

You can understand, then, that it was with more than a little trepidation that I went back there tonight. The place was packed for the occasion. I felt as if everybody had come to see the monster, the self-hating Jew, or whatever they call me. But when I started to chat with a few people, they weren't bad at all; they were even sort of warm and cordial. Then, suddenly and out of nowhere, a guy walked up to me and pulled a letter out of his pocket which I had sent to him as a prompt reply to something or other and which I had signed with the word *shalom*. Well, to see the word *shalom* on official Congressional stationery was such a very big thing to this guy that it broke the ice for me, and I began to feel a lot better. Not only that, but he and the others couldn't get over that I could speak Hebrew and that I knew the rituals of the service. That, of course, wrapped it up for me. If there was any hostility, it dissolved immediately. They knew I was true.

By the time I finished my prepared speech on the problems of Jews in the Soviet Union and the survival of Israel, into

(70)

which I mixed some of my preoccupations about America, they all realized finally that I feel as related to Israel as anyone, and that I'm also very concerned about my own country. Once they understood this, they felt a lot better, I felt a lot better, and they proceeded to be very laudatory.

March 20

I worked late again at a number of projects and then rushed uptown to have my hair done for a dinner given by the Inner Circle press club in New York, an annual affair where they spoof local officials. I was late for my appointment at the beauty parlor and they made me wait, which got me furious. Afterwards, I rushed downtown, got dressed, and, of course, arrived at the dinner in plenty of time. In retrospect, I don't know why I was so hectic about it, because I wasn't particularly excited about going. Ronnie Eldridge had heard that I was going to be lampooned and Saul Rudes, a lawyer who's a very good and generous friend of mine and who worked day and night for me during the campaign, insisted that it was only proper for me to attend. Little did I know.

Martin and I were Saul's guests at a special table he had reserved. The place was packed at $100-a-plate with thirteen hundred people, including every newspaperman I ever knew and every politician right up to the Governor. I wasn't too happy being there when I saw the setup. The Inner Circle has a long tradition of being a sexist organization and there were only a few women like myself who were allowed to sit on the main floor. From what I understand, this was the *first* time they allowed women on the floor at all. The wives and most of the other women were still forced to sit by themselves in a balcony section.

I really hate to go into the details of what happened once the skits began, because I was subjected to a great deal of humiliation by a group of men engaging in megalomania or male-omania, if there is such a word. What they did and said was vicious and repulsive and disgusting and vulgar, a product of their *Playboy* mentalities.

To begin with, some reporter from the *Daily News*, his shoulders and rear end padded substantially, a floppy hat on his head, came out on stage in a satin blouse and a skirt with a flower pattern. He was supposed to be me. He and another guy, who played Mayor Lindsay, then had this exchange:

Lindsay: "I stole two elections, but how the hell did you win?"

Me: "I have broad-based support and something else."

At this point they broke into a song, the lyrics* of which went something like this:

> I guess I've never been the high-fashioned kind,
> Mother Nature gave me a big behind.
> Wherever I go, I know I won't fall flat.
> When I just wear my hat . . .
> Oh, I'm filled with jubilation
> For women's liberation
> We rang our liberty bell
> We'll burn a bra and girdle
> But dammit there's one hurdle
> When we take them off
> We all look like hell . . .

After the song somebody came out in a white apron with frills and he was depicted as "Mrs." Martin Abzug, which was probably the most vicious thing they did all night.

Whereas I'm perfectly willing to receive *political* criticism, satire, jousting, spoofing, lampooning and whatever, and I

* *I didn't remember this garbage. It comes to you courtesy of the* New York Post.

(72)

get it all the time, what these guys did was very crude and in poor taste. To make an attack on a woman's figure or physical appearance is to make an attack on all women. You see, it's just a reflection of a male approach to women that dictates that if you're not gorgeous, svelte and sexy, you're somebody to make fun of. And if you are gorgeous, then that's all they see. None of the men were lampooned for the way *they* look. Everybody else was satirized in terms of what they stand for and what they believe in. But I as a woman was considered fair game to be ridiculed for what I *look* like. It was not only vulgar, but discriminatory at the same time.

I thought about walking out as a matter of protest. By so doing I would communicate to the other women there that these sexist idiots were taking apart in denigrating fashion the one woman in their midst who was a major political figure. But I made the mistake of hesitating, and before I knew it a half dozen people were on top of me, trying to console me. All *kinds* of people, and the interesting thing was they didn't know I was upset. They just sensed I should be, and that's why they started to migrate toward me from all parts of the floor. The first was John Marchi, the ultra-conservative state senator who ran for Mayor in 1969, who was full of compassion, even though I greeted him, "Hello, you reactionary." He was very sweet. Then came Howard Samuels, Ed Koch, Ronnie, Saul, Doug Ireland, Dick Aurelio, Bess Myerson, Carter Burden, Jerry Wilson of CBS—there must have been twenty of them, all telling me how repugnant they found it, all urging me not to leave for fear I'd be making more of a fuss over it than it deserved.

So I didn't leave. I tried to cool down. I realized I can take it. I learned over the years that to dish it out, you have to be able to take it, and I certainly have dished it out a lot, though never in such a sexist, degrading way as they did to me. But I was still, and am still, angry. I'm a very frank and open person and I don't stand on great ceremony, but I felt it was undignified. And insulting. And who knows? Maybe I was really sore because I *do* have a big behind. It's only recently that I got fat, and I *am* very defensive about it. It's one of the mysteries of my metabolism that during the campaign when I worked harder than I ever did in my life, I gained forty pounds.

March 21

I was at the opening of a consumer center on the Lower East Side when Bess Myerson, the city's Commissioner for Consumer Affairs, appeared, looking very pretty in her gorgeous six feet of gaucho pants, black boots and suede cape.

"So you'll answer them, Bella," she said. "You'll answer them at your own affair next Monday." (She was referring to a fund-raiser I'm having March 29 at Katz's Delicatessen.)

"Well, I'm thinking about it," I said, lying. The truth is that last night I came home and forgot about it. That's the way I am. I never have enough sustaining anger in me to hate.

In a way, it's too bad, because I've always felt that if I could hate more, I'd be more effective. Instead, it's my nature to just say, "That son of a bitch, I'll never talk to him again," and then turn around and talk to him. You know what I mean?

Tonight I ventured into semi-hostile territory again, this time for a dinner of the Chinese Democratic Club, an organization that supported Farbstein in the primary, and then me, half-heartedly, in the general election. They're old-line regulars, not reform types by any means. Martin, in one of his rare appearances, came along for moral support. He was in a very gay mood.

When Peter Wu, the club's president and a very wealthy shrimp importer, introduced me, Martin interrupted him to start a round of applause. And then, to my utter surprise—because he *never* does it—Martin insisted on speaking before I did. Peter consented and added, "This is the practice in our country, anyway. The man comes first."

Which led me to pipe up, "Well, things are going to change around here."

Martin got up and told a story about Madame Ky. "A few years ago," he said, "she went to have her eyes broadened, to be Westernized." Well, I don't need to tell you, I nearly died! Here he was talking to Chinese people! "But Madame Ky," he continued, "obviously didn't know the fashion. Now, Bella, on the other hand, who reads *Harper's Bazaar, does* know the fashion, and if you'll notice she had her eyes Easternized."

Then he sat down. That's all he said. I'm not sure they thought it was so funny either, because there were only mixed laughs. He's something, my husband, he's so unpredictable. Even though he appears very stable and placid to some people, Martin's every bit as much of an individualist as I am. When he opens his mouth, you never know what he's going to say. As a matter of fact, when he's approached by a reporter to be interviewed, my friends warn me, "Don't let him! He's going to say *something!*" And inevitably, he *does* say something. He's very uninhibited. But I don't mind. In fact, I kind of like it.

How can I complain about what he told the *Washington Post*, for instance? "She's got a lot of guts, that woman," he said, "more guts than the whole Army. Bella comes on strong, but she's not domineering. She's very generous and very sensitive. The best I can describe her is she's hard on the outside and soft on the inside."

Martin is one of the few unneurotic people left in society. He's very mature and very stable; he's not self-conscious in the least; he's not vain; and he's not aggressive. What he *is* is natural. One of the few naturals left. Once when one of our daughters was having a little difficulty we had to see a

(75)

psychiatrist. Martin had the attitude that he couldn't be bothered. So I went alone with my daughter three times, until finally the fourth time he came along. Well, the psychiatrist looked at both of us quietly, without saying a word, as psychiatrists will often do when you are under treatment. He remained silent for so long that I began to feel uncomfortable, and turning to Martin, I said out loud, "Dr. So and So would like us to say something."

Martin gave me the most incredulous look, cleared his throat and said icily to the doctor, "Well, we're very happily married." As if to say, "Now look, fellow, if you think the problem with our daughter is because of us, forget it!" The doctor nearly fell off his chair. That's Martin.

After dinner we went to the Fillmore East for a benefit to help Al Lowenstein pay off his campaign debts. I made a few remarks in between some variety acts. Al, of course, was defeated in the last election, largely because of redistricting. He's now into this Dump Nixon thing, but unlike with the Dump Johnson movement, where I worked with him, I think he's making a serious mistake. I mean, you can't have Democrats trying to operate inside the Republican Party, it's ridiculous. To run Pete McCloskey in a primary against Nixon, as they're talking about doing, is a good antiwar, anti-Nixon tactic. But you just can't have a dump anybody movement unless there's an insurgency inside his party such as there was in 1968 inside the Democratic Party.

So my preoccupation is still with the barnstorming tour I'm putting together, which is the kind of thing we need to organize a real grass-roots coalition to trounce the power structure. Once this coalition becomes a political force—with the women, the young people, the poor and the minorities all recognizing their common interests—we'll be able to demand that candidates speak to our needs. Or we'll be able to de-

(76)

mand a candidate of our own. That's why I'm not supporting McGovern or McCloskey or anybody right now.

March 22

I visited my mother for a little while before I flew back to Washington. I've managed to do that every week at least. She's still recuperating in a nursing home, slowly getting better. However, my sister and I don't feel that she's going to be able to maintain herself alone in her apartment once she's released, and this has put us in kind of a desperate situation. She obviously can't live with us, because I'm never there. My sister works all day too as a teacher. At the moment what we're trying to do is to get her into a residence for the elderly so she won't be alone. She does better when there are other people around, so she's ready to give up her apartment. But, as usual, there have been various delays in getting her admitted —there are incredibly long waiting lists—and I'm getting a little impatient. I don't want to intervene directly, but I did call a friend who works for the city to ask her to try to speed things up.

It's one thing after another these days. My two legislative assistants are giving me all kinds of headaches. In the beginning they both insisted on the part-time arrangement, even though I wasn't that hot for it, and now they're complaining that working part-time for me is like working full-time for anybody else. They don't believe it's possible to stick to twenty hours a week and still meet my demands. Maybe they're right. I could actually use a dozen L.A.s. I don't know. I just don't understand young people today, quite frankly. During the campaign the staff had to work in two or three shifts to keep up with me, even though many were only half my age. It's a hard life they have, but a different struggle from my generation. Our struggle was political, ideological and economic, and we felt we couldn't make something of ourselves unless we bettered society. We saw the two together. The individual young person today is first and foremost concerned about making something of himself or herself—internally. And then, and only then, relating to something external.

This week in the Public Works Committee we're marking up three major bills which we'll report out to the Floor: the Accelerated Public Works Act, the Economic Development Act and the Appalachian Regional Development Act. Under the Civil Rights Act there can be no discrimination due to race, color or national origin in any federally assisted program. But there's no ban on sex discrimination. So I have insisted that an anti-sex discrimination clause be included in these bills. The men—after making their little remarks about how they're all in favor of sex—have unanimously supported my amendments. Now if they pass on the Floor, I will have made legislative history. For the first time sex discrimination will be specifically prohibited in federally assisted programs.

March 24

All day I was very uptight about getting to testify on the Equal Rights Amendment to the Constitution. Although I was scheduled to appear before the House Judiciary Committee, things didn't turn out the way I would have liked.

Martha Griffiths, the Congresswoman who was responsible for last year's discharge petition to get the amendment off the shelves and onto the Floor after forty-seven years, was the first to testify, and she was followed by Senator Sam Ervin from North Carolina, after whose testimony we recessed to go to the Floor. When the committee reconvened at 2:00 P.M., I was supposed to be the first to testify, but I came in late and they had let some young woman from Bill Ryan's office go before me. As I was waiting for my turn, Andy Jacobs from Indiana, the House Wit, got her into a discussion on women pages in Congress, as if that were the key issue of women's lib, and the two of them seemed to drone on forever. Meanwhile, I was growing very impatient, sitting on tenterhooks waiting to testify, with my testimony all prepared and a press release waiting upstairs. By the time they got to me, a quorum bell sounded, meaning we all had to go to the Floor. So they asked me to please *summarize* my testimony. That was the limit!

"Look," I said. "This is a serious matter to me. I'm one of the few women who came to Congress on the equal rights issue, and either I testify entirely or I simply submit my testimony, but there's not going to be any summary. Understand?"

They understood. I began testifying and then they convened again later in the afternoon to hear the rest of what I had to say about the Equal Rights Amendment, which I'm co-sponsoring. I consider it a legislative landmark in the struggle for human equality and recognition of the reality of women's political power. The Equal Rights Amendment—which passed the House 350-15 last year but never came up for a vote in the Senate—legally establishes, as I see it, that women as a group are physically, mentally and culturally suited for every kind of activity for which men are suited.

It will have two major effects. First, laws that confer benefits of one kind or another will be extended to both sexes. This means, for instance, that in any and every case both men and women will qualify equally for things like Social Security payments and alimony awards. It also means that child custody cases will be determined strictly in accordance with the welfare of the child, not by favoring women because of the traditional role of the sex.

Second, laws that restrict opportunities would be declared unconstitutional. By this I mean "restrictive" work laws (such as weight and hour limitations), special restrictions on property rights and all other provisions that now penalize women—or men—because of sex. The amendment would wipe the whole slate clean by eliminating all existing legal distinctions based on sex. The fact that it would abolish state protective labor laws is the main reason some guys are against it.

But, you see, that's a phony issue. The test for whether or not you can hold a job should not be the arrangement of your chromosomes. It should be, simply, whether or not you're qualified, whether you have the necessary training, whether you need the job and whether your skills will permit you to perform it effectively. Women may want jobs involving heavy labor and overtime because they need the extra money to survive. There's no reason why, if they want, women can't be crane operators, or bus drivers or construction workers. If there are going to be protective labor laws, then there should be standards that make sense. The test for a weight-lifting job should not be whether you're a man or a woman, but how much weight you can lift! After all, a 120-pound man is more likely to get a hernia from lifting a heavy weight than a 160-pound woman.

The amendment is essential to women, because although we make up more than 38 percent of the work force, we only earn a median wage that is a little more than half of what men earn. Many of the 31 million working women are actually paid less than men for doing exactly the same work. It's revolting! A few years ago, while 17 percent of the men earned less than $5000, only one out of two women was making *as much as* $5000. To make matters worse, about two-thirds of the women in the labor force are married, most have children, and the only reason they're working at all is to survive.

March 25

Late yesterday afternoon I had sixty minutes on the Floor to myself to harangue all I wanted about the war in Indochina.

(80)

Technically, I had requested what they call a "special order," which entitles you to a block of time at the end of a day's session to say whatever you want on any issue. It's a poor substitute for debate, but what are you going to do? They don't allow you to debate the war around here.

The reason I asked for the special order is because there's been no discussion of the way Nixon keeps escalating the air war and I want to get some licks in before next week's caucus. Actually nobody stays around to listen to these things, except for a few people in the gallery, so in effect I was standing there and talking to my friends. Herman Badillo, Ron Dellums, John Dow and Bill Anderson of Tennessee joined in. But the stuff does get into the *Congressional Record*, where most of these guys will read it. I figure you've got to get it across any way you can.

Two interviews today. One with the Cleveland *Plain Dealer*; the other with United Press International. Both uneventful. They always ask me the same questions, like "What do you think you can accomplish?" It's very boring. I don't like being asked those kinds of questions because here I am, day in and day out, working like a damn machine. What do I think I can accomplish? It's a stupid question. I must say, however, that they never seem bored with my answers.

March 26

I'm dying to get some new clothes and I promised myself that I'd do some shopping today. I started out and bought a few pairs of shoes and some more hats, of which I already have a couple of dozen, but I didn't have time to look for dresses, which I need the most. I also missed another beauty parlor appointment.

I had to rush to get out to Great Neck, Long Island, where I was scheduled to speak at the Great Neck Forum. I wasn't up to it at all. But I had promised Amy Swerdlow, one of my closest friends and a co-worker in WSP, that Martin and I would have dinner at her house first.

I told the forum about how we won on the SST, and then gave them a few anecdotes, including the Melvin Laird story. Which goes:

I was going up in the elevator in the Capitol when the door opened at one floor and Laird and his staff walked in. We were introduced, and he said, "Yes, I know who you are. Why don't you come over to see us someday?"

"I was already there," I said, referring to the Women Strike for Peace march on the Pentagon in 1967. "But they wouldn't let me in."

Even though she and Elliot Gould have been advertised as the co-sponsors, Jane Fonda had to back out of the $30-a-plate fund-raising affair set up for Monday at Katz's Delicatessen on Houston Street. When my staff told me this, I called to see if I could straighten things out.

"You know, it's very embarrassing to me, Jane," I said. "I'm sort of out of the planning for this stuff—I'm so busy with Congress and my constituents—that when an event like this comes up, I can't get involved in it. But when the other people who are running it told me you were planning to come, I was very pleased, because I think you, more than anybody else in the theatrical field, represent much of what I stand for. We have a lot in common in that sense."

"Bella, I'm really sorry," she said. "But I'm *booked* to speak at Stanford Monday night, and nobody told me about your affair until yesterday. There's nothing I can do."

"Nothing?"

"No, really, I've got to be at Stanford."

(82)

"Well, gee, then, I'm sorry about the mix-up," I said. "I would have loved to have seen you. I'm very embarrassed for you and me. As we say, it's just too upsetting."

March 27

We did a trial run of the barnstorming in the New York area, and it went so well that I was all over the tube tonight. The theme of my remarks was, "It is long past the time when we doves in Congress can sit in Washington and wait for the people who come there to demonstrate and lobby against the war. We must go out into the nation ourselves and organize grass-roots pressure to be brought on recalcitrant members of the House and the Senate who are frustrating the American people's will by preventing legislative action to end the war. We in Congress and in this country are not suffering a lack of power, but a failure of leadership. If we can't get this war over, which is what the people want, we might as well all resign and stop pretending to be representatives of the people."

While Ben Rosenthal, the Congressman from Queens, Herman Badillo and a few others were trooping through Queens, I was up in the Bronx and Westchester with Bob Abrams, the Bronx Borough President. Ogden Reid, the Republican Congressman from Westchester, showed up to meet us in Scarsdale. He had told me previously he wasn't coming, so I can only assume our efforts have had some effect. This, of course, is what the barnstorming is all about.

I wound up the day at a cocktail party in Scarsdale, which was attended mostly by rich peaceniks, and though I'm not their usual style, they seemed to react and care about what I had to say. The high point of the day for me was in the Bronx. It was very strange to be back there now—under these circumstances.

There I was, standing in the neighborhood—on the very street corners—where I grew up, appealing with all my passion for peace. My parents would have loved it.

My father—his name was Emanuel Savitzky—fled to the United States from czarist Russia when the Russo-Japanese War broke out in 1905. He was the kind of man who hated war, all war, and he hated it with such an intensity that his spirit affected everybody around him—family, friends, neighbors, even strangers. In the days following World War I he managed a butcher shop on Ninth Avenue. You know what he named it? The Live and Let Live Meat Market.

He and my mother, another Russian immigrant whose maiden name was Esther Tanklefsky, were among those Jews fortunate enough to set up housekeeping in the East Bronx instead of on the Lower East Side. To those who could afford it, the East Bronx was paradise. Now it's declined into one of the worst slums in the country—crumbling buildings, garbage-ridden streets, backed-up sewers, dope addicts lingering on corners and in the hallways of abandoned tenements.

I was born ("yelling," my family used to say, prophetically) in 1920, just after the war. I was the second daughter. My sister Helene was already a few years old.

Because my father was not very successful at business, we never had much money, although there was usually enough. When the Live and Let Live Meat Market failed, he worked as a bookkeeper and sold insurance. He was a very good and generous man and because of him we had a warm and close family life. He loved music. He was always singing folk songs in Yiddish and Russian, and when he wasn't, his favorite Caruso record was on the Victrola. Helene played the piano and sang. I learned to play the violin. Later on I taught myself to play the mandolin—it's easier. On Friday night after the traditional lighting of the candles, our apartment—where my maternal grandfather and one of my mother's bachelor brothers also lived—turned into a virtual concert hall.

We were a religious family. My grandfather went to the synagogue twice a day, and whenever I wasn't in school, he took me along. I learned to recite the solemn Hebrew prayers like such a wizard that he always made it a point to show me off to his friends. Incidentally, it was during these visits to the synagogue that I think I had my first thoughts as a feminist rebel. I didn't like the fact that women were consigned to the back rows of the balcony.

Where there wasn't such institutional oppression—such as in the streets—I fared well with the boys. As well, in fact, if not better than they, I played Red Rover, leapfrogged over ashcans, skated, played stickball and Immies, a game that left my pockets sagging with marbles I won.

When I was twelve I joined a pioneer Zionist youth group known as Hashomir Hatzair, and from then on all I could think about was working on a kibbutz and going to Palestine to build a Jewish homeland. Wearing our brown uniforms and ties, my friends in Hashomir Hatzair and I spent hours and hours casing the subways and street corners to collect pennies for the Jewish National Fund. In fact, it was in the subways between stops that I made my first speech.

My father died in the midst of the Depression at a time when I was entering Walton High School, an all-girls school in the West Bronx, where we were then living. My mother supported us on the insurance money and by working as a cashier and saleswoman in department stores. My mother sent Helene to college while I, enthusiastically athletic, earned money in the summers as a camp counselor. During the school year I attended a special Hebrew High School after school, and later enrolled at the Jewish Theological Seminary in Manhattan. On weekends I taught Hebrew and Jewish history and culture to young kids. Can you see why I was so burned up during the campaign when they tried to make it look like I was against Israel?

Meanwhile, I was elected class president in my high school

(85)

and later student body president at Hunter College. As student activists of that time, we demonstrated and marched to protest the spread of Nazism and the American, British and French trade embargoes against the legal Spanish Republican government during the civil war in Spain.

By the end of World War II I was a practicing lawyer with a degree from Columbia, where I had been editor of the *Law Review*. I joined a firm that specialized in labor law. By this time I had met Martin.

We were married in 1944. Our first daughter, Egee (Eve Gail), was born in 1949, and Liz (Isobel Jo) came three years later. In between I became involved in my first civil rights case. The man I defended—Willie McGee—was accused of raping a white woman, even though he and the woman had had a long-standing sexual relationship. That fact, of course, only made the crime all the more heinous to the Mississippi jury, and McGee was sentenced to death. Challenging the traditional practice of excluding blacks from the jury and arguing that Southern judges and juries reserved the death penalty for "rape" as a cruel and inhuman punishment for blacks only, I managed to get the Supreme Court to stay the execution twice. But, in the end, Willie McGee was executed.

In the early fifties I concentrated on labor law and spent a lot of time fighting McCarthyism. By 1960 (strange how my life has been divided into decades) I became a peacenik. It all started when the Soviet Union and the United States resumed nuclear testing. Almost overnight, women across the country, I among them, began to protest. We founded Women Strike for Peace in Washington, New York and other cities. Calling for a ban on the bomb, we warned of the danger of radioactive contamination in our children's milk resulting from nuclear test fallout. We fought the arms race, and in the process became the most unlikely experts on all the horrible weapons and missiles being devised. We held one demonstration after another at the UN and at the White House, and we lobbied in Congress. I served as both political action director and legislative director for WSP.

In 1963 the limited nuclear test ban treaty gave us a limited victory. Testing of hydrogen bombs in the atmosphere was outlawed. But underground testing continued, as it does today, and the arms race just continued to mount and mount. Meanwhile, the American intervention in Vietnam was just becoming alarming, and we immediately began to stage protests. The rest is history.

While military costs for this atrocious war slowly ate up the country's wealth, I watched my own city—with its housing shortages, its mass transit needs, its inadequate health facilities for the poor, its welfare mess, its too few hospitals, its polluted air and water, its drug epidemic—fall to pieces.

In 1967 I organized peace action committees in the city to get into politics, and in 1968 I led in efforts to build a coalition among the peace movement, liberal Democrats and Republicans, women's groups, poor people, blacks and other minorities, and young people. All that ended abruptly in Chicago in August—for the meantime.

I'm still working on building that coalition. By temperament and conviction I'm an activist and I deeply believe that people, given the truth and the freedom to organize, will act in their own best interests. It takes hard work, hip leaders and a breaking of the old political molds.

March 28

More barnstorming—this time in Queens for a mass rally of six thousand people. It was one of those rare times when I was upstaged. The actress Julie Newmar came along, glamorously done up in a skin-clinging dress. When she was speaking to the crowd, Ben Rosenthal, who was on the platform with us, kept dropping pieces of paper on the floor to, I presume, get a clearer look at Julie's legs. "Sit up, Ben," I finally said to him. "Your wife's looking at you."

The rally itself was terrific. The pressure from the peace groups was so great that even the old-line politicians turned up, and the Queens organizers were delighted. Don Riegle, a Republican from Michigan who's become a dear friend of mine and is an important peace voice, flew in from Washington to speak.

More guys are changing their minds about this war every day, and so far we've lined up at least a hundred votes for the caucus Wednesday when we're going to call again for the withdrawal of all troops by the end of the year. If the leadership doesn't pull any tricks, there's a good chance that this time we'll make it.

A group of state legislators from around the country came to Washington this morning to present a petition to Carl Albert calling for total withdrawal from Vietnam. I attended a press conference with them, and later on, on my way to the Floor, I bumped into Carl.

"Carl," I said, "I'm getting old." I was feeling really run-down.

"Old?" he said. "You're not getting old. You've got more energy than most of these guys who came down here today, and most of them are younger than you."

Afterwards, he took his seat in the House and then sent word to me that he had something to say. I walked up to the chair.

"Look," he said, the petition in his hand, "I know how you feel about this war. You've been against it from the beginning. But these other guys are just a bunch of phonies jumping on the bandwagon."

"So?" I said. "You jump too."

(88)

Later in the afternoon I flew back to New York for the "Ball for Bella" fund-raiser at Katz's, which I approached with a great deal of reluctance. I feel very self-conscious appearing at a function where money is being raised for me. I find it a terrible chore. We still have that campaign deficit.

To make matters worse, I had nothing to wear. I ended up with a dress that was too dressy for the occasion, and that started me off feeling very uptight. Also, I had asked that the press not be invited in their official capacity, but as guests. Unfortunately, they brought their cameras with them, and all that clicking and flashing when I walked in made me even more nervous.

I did begin to feel better after a little while, though, because the spirit in the place was just great. But I still can't get over the strange mixture of people who were there. Some who should have been, like Jane Fonda, weren't, but others whom I would have least expected did come. Elliot Gould, whom I don't know very well, for instance. He said that while he wasn't very political, he wanted to do something to help me because he believed in me. He looked strange, I thought, very scruffy, but I guess that's the acting field. I don't make judgments on it. It's just hard to relate to sometimes. Some other actors and actresses were there too. Leonard Nimoy (from *Mission: Impossible*) flew in from the Coast, Elaine May, Kim Hunter, their husbands, and Bob Evans. Oh yes, Julie Newmar too. In hot pants. Strange people of one kind or another, such as one guy in an Afro costume who wore a bird cage with a live bird in it for a hat. And lots of old friends: Mayor Lindsay, Saul Rudes, Doug Ireland, the brilliant young man who managed my campaign, Jerry Rowe, Jean Wolcott, Joan Dierckx, Mary Halloran and other veterans of the campaign. But more than that, as Mary Perot Nichols of *The Village Voice* commented, a slice of the community was there—Puerto Ricans, Jews, Chinese, Italians—even kids off the street, who wandered in and sampled the hot dogs.

The setting was also a little bizarre. Izzy Tarowsky, who

owns Katz's Delicatessen, closed the place to the public for the first time in eighty-three years, he said, so the party could be held. A sign he had made during World War II hung in glaring irony from the ceiling: "Send a Salami to Your Boys in the Army." Everybody was stuffing themselves with hot dogs, sauerkraut, pickles, french fries and corned beef.

After I got rid of the press and questions like why wasn't I wearing my hat, Howie Samuels, the head of the new Offtrack Betting, asked me to dance. I also danced with my husband, which, for some reason, surprised a lot of people. It surprised me that they were surprised. We're both excellent dancers. We've been doing the fox trot, the hora, the marengue and a lot of other dances all our lives.

One of the people I had a rather long conversation with was Gertrude Samuels. She had done this whole write-up on me for *The New York Times Magazine,* but they never printed it. It was during the election, and they thought it was too much of a rave. "I'm so upset about it, Bella," Gertrude said. "I don't think I ever felt so badly about anything."

"Don't be upset," I said. "It's not your fault. It's your editor's fault."

The reporter who wrote the story about Martin in the *Washington Post* was also there. She amused me.

"Your husband is so vital and dynamic, so vigorous," she said.

"So?" I said. "What did you expect?"

March 30

We raised $10,000 last night, which is a nice sum. I still have campaign debts totaling between $20,000 and $30,000 though.

Back in Washington, this was the first day of debate on the bill to extend the draft, and I got up to give a speech unlike any speech I've given on the Floor yet. "I'm tired of listening

to a bunch of old men who are long beyond the draft age standing here and talking about sending our young men over to be
killed in an illegal and immoral war," I said. "It's all very well
and good for you men to be talking this way, because nobody's
sending you over to be killed. . . ." I was really very harsh and
emotional, and when I finished, the gallery, filled with a lot
of young people, burst into applause. That was a very exhila-
rating moment for me. But applause from the gallery is for-
bidden by House rules, so Ed Boland of Massachusetts, who
was presiding, rebuked the kids. Of course.

The debate will continue tomorrow when the amendments
are slated to be brought up for a vote. Thursday we'll vote on
the entire bill. This gives us three days of debate, which, in a
way, is unbelievable. Mendel Rivers would have never permitted it. Ed Hébert's a lot smoother. He's clever enough to
give us a lot of rope to hang ourselves. And why not? He's still
got the power. And he knows it.

He's perfectly willing to be a gentleman. Besides, he and his
cohorts like to be entertained a bit. I don't mean in a ha-ha
funny way, but in an interesting way. I am different from most
people in the House, because I say things more frankly, and
they find this interesting. But you can be sure that if I had
power, interesting or not, they wouldn't let me talk.

Later in the day I went to this miserable reception of the
Democratic Study Group where Hubert Humphrey came,
allegedly to convince everybody to vote for the December 31
withdrawal resolution in the caucus tomorrow. He chose instead, however, to give us a campaign speech, which I found
so boring I folded my arms and closed my eyes. Afterwards
some guys approached me and said they had made a private
bet with one another. One bet I was angry. Another bet I was
bored. Another bet I was sleeping. I told them to divide the
money up three ways.

What a day this was! We were mowed down in the caucus. The whole thing was a fraud from beginning to end.

I had gone there, of course, expecting a vote on the Vietnam Disengagement Act, which calls for withdrawing all the troops by the end of the year. As of yesterday I figured we had at least one hundred votes, and it seemed to me that with everybody so mad about Nixon's invasion of Laos, there was a good chance we'd get enough extra votes to win.

Little did I know—we never even had a chance. A deal had been made. Deals, deals, deals, deals! These guys have got compromise in their blood and guts!

In order to understand what happened, you've first got to understand a big con game that takes place all the time around here. It works like this: When the reactionary power structure is pushing for some measure that it wants very much to pass, it fishes out a liberal and makes him its spokesman. Conversely, when the liberals are pushing for something that they want passed, they go and find a moderate and make him their spokesman. Old games. Everybody thinks they're conning somebody, but in the end nobody's conning anybody, believe me. The people outside are way ahead of all of them. They don't give a damn if a moderate pushes for a liberal resolution or if a liberal pushes for a reactionary resolution. All they care about is the resolution. If it's right, it's right; if it's wrong, it's wrong.

So what happened before we even went into the caucus is the liberals got some moderates to push for and bring the Vietnam Disengagement Act up for a vote. Naturally, these guys—having fairly recently decided they're against the war—are not really inclined to go out there and fight. You can't rely on them to stand firm. The theory that if you get them pushing on your side you'll arouse broader support is ridiculous. They are too ready to compromise.

Which, it appears to me, is exactly what they did. We never even got a chance to vote on the Vietnam Disengagement Act. No sooner did we walk into the caucus room than we found ourselves voting on whether to accept a substitute amendment, presumably one that was vague and watered down, on the theory that the original resolution itself couldn't get enough votes to pass. By one lousy vote, 101-100, the caucus agreed to accept a substitute. Can you imagine that? One goddamn vote!

At this point the leadership recognized Richard Bolling from Missouri who offered a substitute resolution providing for setting a withdrawal date—*without specifying when it would be*—and calling on Democrats to work with Republicans to end the war, or something like that. You know, the old bipartisan baloney that has ruined this country.

Then up gets Carl Albert to tell us he supports Bolling's resolution because he wants to see us work together with the Republicans to end the war. I was appalled! Here was the Speaker of the House—a man in that kind of position—giving us more old-fashioned, desperate, moldy garbage from the past. Since World War II the Democrats and the Republicans have been "joining hands" to fight international communism, and where has it gotten us? We've created a nuclear monster and a vast, uncontrollable military machine. We've inspired guys like Joe McCarthy and Spiro Agnew to level all the opposition. The military and the industrialists and the munitions-makers have moved in to take over our power structure, influencing it, manipulating it and dominating it. All for the sake of good old bipartisanism; all for the sake of good old anticommunism.

It's the kind of thinking that has knifed democracy and the people of this country all along. We've been so tricked by this crap about bipartisanism and anticommunism and national security and Americanism that we're now faced with runaway government. An autocracy. The President can act without the consent of Congress and without the consent of the people.

To add to Carl's nonsense, John Dent from Pennsylvania

(93)

proposed an amendment to strengthen the Bolling resolution by specifying that the House work "to end the United States military involvement in Indochina" sometime before the end of the 92nd Congress. In other words, by 1973.

What the Dent Amendment did was to make Bolling's resolution more palatable, more acceptable, more likely to be approved. Anybody with any brains who wanted the war over as soon as possible should have voted against it, because that way we could have probably beaten down Bolling. Unfortunately for all of us, the liberals don't think this way, and so with their help the Dent Amendment passed. A few minutes later, by a vote of 138-62 (with fifty-four members not voting), the caucus accepted the Bolling-Dent resolution.

We lost. Number one, because the liberals who voted for the Dent Amendment gave the moderates something they could chew a bit more easily, and in so doing killed their own chances to get the troops-out-by-the-end-of-the-year resolution passed. So they're stupid in addition to not being really committed. Number two—and this is what really burns me—a few guys who should have been there to vote were absent. If just two of them had been present we would have won the original vote not to accept any substitutes and the caucus very likely would have gone on record as favoring a withdrawal by the end of the year.

Now what makes this all so bad and pretty inexcusable as far as I'm concerned is that this afternoon on the Floor *we also lost* on an amendment offered by Chuck Whalen, a Republican, to extend the draft for only one year (instead of the two years Nixon was asking for) by *only two votes*. As part of a strategy I had worked out with Chuck and Mike Harrington, we gave the House three separate chances to protest the draft: first, my amendment for repeal; then Mike's amendment to end it as of June 30; and finally, the one-year extension. And Eddie Hébert yielded to us in that order.

I couldn't even get enough people to stand up *and vote for* having a recorded teller vote on my amendment to abolish the Selective Service System and the President's power to induct men. Why? Because the liberals who *were* in town were out to lunch when the amendment came on the Floor. They figured an amendment offering an extreme position didn't have a chance of passing, and they didn't want to exert themselves until it was time to compromise. It was very sad.

The draft vote was disastrous. I get the feeling that a lot more of these guys would have voted against the draft except they're all hung up about the volunteer army concept, which is the alternative. They're afraid that a volunteer army will mean a professional army, and they're afraid that with a professional army there's too much of a risk that the military will run the country. I'd like to know who they think is running the country now. Anyway, they don't understand that manpower means warpower, and that if we didn't give the military the men, it wouldn't be in business so much.

I must admit I was so angry that I made a very shocking speech before the vote, part of which went like this: "You people may not be listening to what's going on, but I want you to know that the women in this country are examining their economic, political and social status and they aren't going to forgive anybody here. And their sons who are between the ages of eighteen and twenty-one are about to get the vote too, and they are not going to forgive you either, for trying to send them to an illegal war. This combination of mothers and their sons, along with all the other people who've been made to carry the burdens of this war—I want you to know before you cast your vote—are going to vote against everybody who votes here today to prolong the war and a draft which makes it possible."

That's a very tough way to talk to members of Congress. It's like you're not one of them. It's like saying, "I'm here to tell you that you are going to lose your seat." I said it though, because it was essential to say, and frankly, I was looking to scare up a few votes, which I believe I did. There were a lot of guys who were upset though. I could tell by their reaction. They didn't like what I said because it was too truthful for them.

So the Democrats gave Nixon exactly what he wanted today: two more years of the draft and an invitation to end the war by election time.

And yet somebody like Phil Burton, who's head of the Democratic Study Group, is calling the caucus vote a "victory." He's so proud because this is the first time we've had an opportunity to vote on the war—or even discuss withdrawal as an issue. I realize he and others have been fighting against the war for a long time. But from the point of view of the people, it was an utter, rotten defeat. The liberals should begin to think about radicalizing their tactics because the people are way ahead of them.

April 1

One of the guys from Alabama—I forget his name—came up to me and said, "Bella, you take it easy, hear? When you made that speech on the draft, your face got red as a beet, and there was a stiffness around your lips. I worry about you. You're all over the place. You're into everything. We know how deeply you feel, but you got to take it more easy."

Interesting, huh? The guy totally disagrees with me, but he's not unsympathetic. Some people thought these reactionaries would run around hating me, but they don't. Not that there aren't guys who hate me. I think there are, but I'm not sure. It's just a feeling I get, and since I can't be sure I'm not going to name any names. One thing I'll tell you though. It's not the people you'd expect, not the Boggses and the Alberts and Héberts—the guys I usually holler at and scream at and carry on about.

After the final vote on the draft bill, I rushed to New York for a peace rally at Hunter College. When I was introduced, a heckler started hollering about how I'm a hypocrite since I'm for the sale of jets to Israel, and so on and so forth. I get it from both sides on Israel. He kept it up and kept it up until finally I stopped and said, "Well, okay, you speak. I'll wait."

As I expected, that did it. It always does. He had nothing more to say.

"Okay," I said. "I've listened long enough to you. Now I'll talk and when I'm good and ready I'll answer you." Then I pointed out how he was here shouting and hollering while the House just passed the draft bill because people like him failed to come to Washington to lobby and pressure Congress. Then I went into my speech, and when I finished, I turned again to the heckler and said, "As for you, my opinion is that every country has a right to survive. Every nation that is threatened with extinction by other nations has the right to be given the means which will help it survive. Furthermore, I feel Israel should have the arms it needs, but the long-range solution for peace is in direct negotiations with the Arabs. Period."

April 2

I'm out in Los Angeles for a convention of the California Democratic Council, which is a liberal grouping inside the Democratic Party. I was asked to be the keynote speaker by the CDC Women's Caucus.

It was a long flight and I got here around 3 P.M. local time, checked into my room and found, as usual, that my dresses were all creased. I wanted desperately to have them pressed, but the hotel didn't have an iron, and the valet shop was closed. After I got over being a little annoyed, I steamed them out myself in the bathroom. Then I went down to have my hair done.

Afterwards I rested for a while, and called my sister-in-law and brother-in-law who live out here, and told them to come over. They didn't want to come because they thought they'd be in the way. This is my husband's brother—shy people. "Don't be silly," I said. "You know I don't know anybody out here."

While I was waiting for them I made a few more phone calls, one to Barbra Streisand, whom I haven't seen since my election. I met her in a restaurant during the campaign when she came up to me and said she had a young son and wanted to do something for peace. She gave a fund-raising event for me in her new house in Manhattan, did a show and radio spots for me, and even came out on the streets and campaigned with me. "Ya betta win," she used to say. She was great, and I really feel indebted to her.

"How was the ball at Katz's?" she asked when I got her on the phone. "Sorry I couldn't make it."

"It was fine," I said, "but to tell you the truth, I felt a little funny about having Elliot [Gould, her husband; they're separated] as one of the hosts."

"Why?" she asked. "He's the father of my child."

"Well, I thought you'd kind of resent it."

"No, not at all. How was he?"

"Fine."

It's interesting: Elliot had also said he wanted to do something for the cause of peace and, like Barbra, said he couldn't think of a better way to do it than to help me.

Early in the evening I attended a short CDC reception, then visited in my room with my in-laws, and it wasn't until 10 P.M.

(98)

(1 A.M. *my* time) that they called me down to give my speech. I was pooped. I had worn a black low-cut dress to the reception, but because I wanted to wear a hat (how could I deprive them!) I changed into another less dressy outfit. After I listened to a few speeches, I was introduced, and in the course of the introduction, they staged a huge demonstration for women's rights up and down the aisles—replete with some original suffragettes. I can't imagine where they dug them up. Then I went into my song and dance and moved them to a five-minute standing ovation—very spirited crowd, this one. I must say though, it happens everywhere I speak across the country.

April 3

By the time I got back to my room last night it was 2 A.M. New York time, and I was exhausted. Then Al Lowenstein, who had also been one of the speakers, along with California Congressman Jerry Waldie, appeared and insisted on talking to me. You should have seen him! He got this wild gleam in his eye, this urgent excitement in his voice, as he started to talk about how in this presidential election we're going to inherit the political power structure. He was unbelievable. He is a very bright, very *brilliant*, and very, very, motivated guy with a touch of madness. It's a fascinating thing, but he thinks he's a messiah. He's a believer, largely in himself, which is the key to being a believer in others. His defeat for reelection to Congress was a tremendous personal setback for him, even though his district was stolen from under him by gerrymandering. I think he misses Congress a great deal.

Al and I have a lot of differences, but the most striking I guess is that he is more of a liberal than I am. He worries about the radical left. I don't. He's afraid that the radicals will gain too much influence. I'm not. Why worry about it, I keep telling him. The fact is the radical left doesn't have any influence, and if it did, it wouldn't be such a terrible thing. The trouble with this country is that it doesn't have and never has had a cohesive radical movement. If we did, we'd have a lot more change. Besides—and I tell this to Al—there is only a very fine line between worrying about the radical left and red-baiting.

Al kept pressing me and pressing me to join his Dump Nixon movement. "Look, Bella," he said. "You know what you can do to audiences. I saw what you did tonight, I don't have to tell you. We need you. You've got to be with us on this thing."

He knows I disagree with him about the whole thing, but he also knows I'd like to keep my finger on any movement to dump Nixon. At the moment, I'm not sure what I'm going to do though. It's a tough one, I'll tell you. Not only am I worried that a large effort *inside the Republican Party* to dump Nixon is a waste of time, but what happens if we succeed? Do we open the path for a Republican like Rockefeller, who would be more difficult to beat than Nixon? The Dump Nixon movement can't be anything like the Dump Johnson movement, because there's no real insurgency inside the Republican Party. If we organize a Dump Nixon movement and bill it as a pro-McCloskey movement we run the risk of pushing the kids into registering as Republicans—therefore losing vital votes for a stronger liberal Democratic candidate. On the other hand, if we define the Dump Nixon movement strictly as a peace movement, in which Democratic and Republican presidential candidates are encouraged to participate, then it can serve as a massive and focused youth registration drive. In that case, my role can be to talk the hard stuff—about changing the power structure with a coalition of women, youth and minorities.

This morning I addressed the Women's Caucus meeting, and despite a preface in which I said I'd try not to get too psychological, I spent a lot of time discussing my belief that our society operates on a masculine mystique. Our culture demands that men be strong and virile, all-capable, all-doing and all-knowing. Ironically, all this emphasis on proving one's masculinity only ends up emasculating men and the society itself. Because they are constantly on the line to prove themselves in some super-duper way—which breeds racism, Pentagon chauvinism and Nixon's need to have a military victory in Vietnam—men in society have developed all kinds of problems that women don't have. We don't have any Freudian obsession with missiles. Society doesn't require us to prove our superiority or to accomplish in some super-human manner. We have very, very little to prove. That's why, in terms of political power, I feel we'd end up being a lot more sensible. And more peaceful.

Then I got political. I talked about how we wouldn't even have effective political parties without women, how they keep all the clubs going, and the committees, and how they do all the work in the campaigns, filing, typing, mailing, telephoning and fund-raising. Let's face it: There are no campaigns where women are not the mainstay. Women are also always at the forefront of demonstrating, lobbying, picketing, organizing. We control everything in politics but the power. So, I said, in light of this we ought to demand to get out of the back rooms and into the front rooms—into the forefront as both public officials and elected representatives. And if we organize, we can do this.

Afterwards, a lot of people came up to tell me how glad they were to hear me. Some suggested I run for President. I'm always touched when this happens, but I have to laugh it off. It really doesn't make sense. All it proves is that the country is hungry for leadership, and that people are pretty united on what they don't want: Nixon, the war, inflation, unemployment. They want a society that builds and that doesn't de-

(101)

stroy. All they want, really, is a little love and humanity in leadership, which they sense in me.

But I'm a pragmatic and very realistic person. I realize that no convention is ready to nominate a woman for President next year. Before we start thinking about the White House, we have to organize our political power and put pressure in the places where we can get *real*—not symbolic—results. I and a number of other women are in the process of organizing a National Women's Political Caucus as a cohesive power group in every state. That's the first step. Once we are united in such an organization, then we'll worry about the candidates, although I can see some women deciding to run in a couple of presidential primaries to make the point that women are entitled to political power. This, of course, could be useful. But all I can say is that at the moment I'm not happy with any of the existing candidates.

April 4

I arrived back in New York at one o'clock in the morning, and there was nobody there to pick me up! They didn't think it was right to have somebody come out to the airport at that hour in the morning. It makes no sense. A staff is there to work for a Congresswoman, isn't it? Well, sometimes people have a misplaced sense of relationships.

Early in the morning I got up to be driven to Easton, Pennsylvania, where I addressed some students at Lafayette College. Martin came along. By the time the day was over, he managed to make himself the guest of honor, and I loved it!

He was very funny and entertaining and clever, talking about the economy, literature, whatever. He's an awful lot of fun to listen to when he's in one of these moods. I love when he decides to come along with me, because a lot of times he doesn't want to. We don't get to spend much time together anymore. Outside of Martin and the kids, I don't feel very related to most people at this point. Since I'm totally absorbed in thinking of where it has all got to go and what I've got to do to get it there, there just isn't time to function in ordinary social situations. Since my schedule is always packed on weekends anyway, it would be artificial to sandwich in a social life, and I just don't want to do it.

Funny enough, most people who know me would not think this to be true, because on the surface I appear to be very involved in a lot of social relationships. But that's just not the case, because inside I'm not relating to anybody. I find it all a strain and an interference. I feel detached in social situations. I'm always thinking about other things, about Congress, about the issues, about the political coalition I'm trying to organize. It never leaves me. I even have trouble relating to some of my closest friends, though God knows I still love them, even if they don't know it.

All my life I've been a private citizen. Now suddenly I'm in the papers all the time and on television, and I'm instantly a public personality. I enjoy it, but it's tough, because I'm not used to it. I'm recognized everywhere—in the streets, in airports, at the movies, in restaurants. The people who come up to me are always very demonstrative, always full of warm feeling. It's very rewarding. The only time it upsets me is when they say, "We're countin' on ya, Bella." Too many strangers say that to me. It makes me feel as though I've created a monster, and that I'm not going to be able to live up to their expectations. It makes me feel a tremendous burden, one I obviously can't handle all alone. I'm only one person.

Before I started my speech, I invited the local John Birch Society that had picketed me and was now standing in the back to come in and sit down. Instead they left. I spoke to the students and asked them why I had heard nothing about radical activity at Lafayette College. "The student body is mobile," they said. "Students are responders, not leaders," they said.

(103)

"We've had our Cambodia, and now we're into ourselves," they said. I guess that's the way it is. Egee says now it's "in the head." First, they are going to make the revolution in their heads. "They're into themselves," she says. Frankly, it's something I never understood.

I'll tell you something else that troubles me: the utter cynicism among students. They have the attitude that they tried it once, it didn't work, and so why bother. You know, they want the instant approach to change.

This is precisely why there have never been any matured movements in this country. Demonstrations, insurgencies, eruptions—yes. *Movements*—no. If what the students had begun as antiwar activity a few years ago had gone on, we might have built something. Was Kennedy its leader? I don't know. Obviously McCarthy turned out not to be its leader because he refused to give it leadership. I don't think Bobby Kennedy was, though toward the end he was beginning to feel people's real needs. But these men were really part of the establishment, which has got to be changed. Unlike others, it's true, they were prepared to attack the military, but were they really ready to make fundamental changes? Of course not. The best we could have done had we gotten Kennedy into the presidency would have been to establish a people's victory that might have enabled us to build a broader, deeper political movement. But we were routed, as usual, and we fell apart. Now the question again is, who's going to put the movement together? We have little leadership.

I think I'm one of the leaders, but I have a problem, a conflict. I can be a good Congresswoman and take care of my district, and I can be a national leader, but it's tough to be both at the same time.

You have no idea of the kind of national recognition I have. I have a special group called National Constituents for Bella Abzug functioning in Washington just to service all the response I get from across the country. Barbara Bick, an old friend from Women Strike for Peace, helped put it together, and Eleanor Garst, who's a terrific writer, is doing a newsletter. The trouble is we don't have any money. I have to find a money angel, and I'm not good at that. Nor is anybody in my entourage. That's one of my big problems. I still owe a lot from my last campaign—and I'm going to be looking for more campaign money next year.

From Easton we drove to Scranton for a Jewish Federation dinner to honor my first cousin, Al Geffen, who's been the head of the Jewish Family Agency there for some twenty years. He's one of the most industrious and decent guys I know, and I didn't want to miss the event, except with three hours' sleep in me from the past three nights, I hated to face another speech.

When we got to Al's house there was all this excitement about Al's cousin, the Congresswoman, you know. Then there was the usual problem for me of what dress to wear. At the dinner I was tired as hell. The guy I was sitting next to, the master of ceremonies, was a pants manufacturer and one of the do-gooders of Scranton. He told me they were building a synagogue there for a million dollars!

Then when he introduced me for my speech, I got up and called him an unliberated pants manufacturer, because he only makes pants for men. That got a big yak, and I was off and going.

April 5

Back in New York, I was so exhausted when I woke up this morning, I could barely pull myself together. When I'm this tired, I'm miserable. I've been hollering and screaming at everybody all day. I was so tired, as a matter of fact, that I attended a rally downtown and for the first time ever I *read*—yes, *read*, right off a piece of paper—my prepared statement on Rocke-feller's soak-the-poor budget.

It was an interesting experience: there was absolutely no response from the audience. I couldn't stand it. So I put the paper down, and in all my rage, really lambasted Rockefeller and Nixon and the whole crew. Well, that got me a little response anyway.

After dinner Martin drove me up to see our friend Ronnie Eldridge and we talked about my staff problems and Lowen-stein and Lindsay. She was kind of sad. She's a terrific gal, but her husband died six months ago, and she's got all kinds of problems—kids, no money and an uncertain future. And being a special assistant to the Mayor, no matter how good it sounds, is like being a glorified social worker.

Originally, I wanted Ronnie to be my administrative assist-ant, but she thought I was crazy. She didn't want to move to Washington, she wouldn't be getting enough money, she's on the staff of a man who may run for President—and I just couldn't persuade her. I guess she just didn't see the potential. If she did, she was afraid of it. Some people feel she feared the competition. I don't think so, though, because she never wanted to run for office. She's been associated with the Ken-nedys, with Lindsay—you know, that kind. I guess that's big-ger than Abzug. Bigger maybe, but not better.

How do you like that about Hale Boggs charging that the FBI has been tapping his phone? That's really something, isn't it? I mean, I have no doubt that they've been tapping my phone all along, but to hear that they're doing it to a fellow like Boggs, that just shows you how outrageous they really are. Anyway, I'm thankful for Hale's timing. For weeks now, my staff has been preparing a resolution calling for an investigation of the FBI, and now that Hale's thrown the discussion wide open, I'm going to introduce it in a day or so.

April 6

All these guys have been eating up their one-minute speeches before the session to relieve themselves of what they have to say on Hoover, the FBI and Calley. You should hear how they're carrying on, lauding the FBI, commending and defending Hoover. I mean it's really disgusting. You'd think the man was a great American hero. You could puke from it. Well, I'm going to knock them all for a loop tomorrow.

As if Hoover weren't enough, Lt. Calley seems also to be the hero of the day. Believe it or not, I even heard one guy compare him to Jesus Christ. When word reached the Floor that the President was going to intervene in the case, they actually burst into applause. Next thing we know they'll be giving the guy the Congressional Medal of Honor.

A lot of people say that Calley is some kind of sacrificial goat offered up by the Pentagon to deflect attention from its own sins. I believe that. But I still feel he's guilty and he deserves to be convicted. Let's face it: If we're going to talk about the rights of the individual, we've also got to talk about the responsibility of the individual. This man is the convicted killer of twenty-two people. There were other soldiers at Mylai who made a moral decision not to shoot down babies. They turned away and wouldn't do it. Calley did. To exonerate Calley now—or to give him privileged treatment as Nixon has done—is to say that it's all right to follow orders blindly, even if the orders entail the slaughter of civilians, as they did at Mylai.

I can understand that the country's going through a moral convulsion. I can understand how everybody's now recoiling in horror and trying to say, "Look, how can we sentence him when it's really *our* fault?" It's the old American sense of fair play.

Still the solution is not to let Calley off, but to find the other Calleys, to unearth the full and unsparing details of American war crimes in Indochina. We already know that the underlying concept of the war is racist, that the military strategy is one of exterminating civilians and destroying the land that sustains them, so we shouldn't stop until we get every last detail of what we've done there. Three other Congressmen—Ron Dellums, Parren Mitchell and John Conyers—and I have decided that since we've been unable to persuade the House leadership to conduct an official inquiry, we're going to hold our own ad hoc hearings. This afternoon we held a press conference to announce that they'll be starting later this month.

Still, it's inexcusable that we can't get a full-scale Congressional investigation. It's just that these guys are scared to death to take a good look at what's really been going on in Indochina for the last ten years. In a way they remind me of the stockholders at Dow Chemical, a group I once saw on television. Some antiwar demonstrators had stormed one of their meetings, rushed to the front of the hall and held up giant blowups of photographs depicting Vietnamese babies mutilated by Dow's napalm. It was a horrifying sight. But what was even more horrifying was the way the Dow stockholders behaved. They simply turned their heads away and refused to look until the demonstrators were booted out. Then the meeting resumed and they all applauded news of higher earnings and dividends.

April 7

Great day, this one, the last before the Easter recess. In a way I was like all those other conventional Congressmen making a big show for the constituents before going home. But, unlike most of them, I didn't plan it that way. It just happened. I was pushed by events.

Okay, first things first. In the morning I attended a press conference called to protest Nixon's order to allow abortions for dependents of military personnel only in accordance with state and local laws. An outrageous action on his part, an arbitrary exercise of personal prejudice to mandate a public policy that violates the rights of women. He calls abortion "an unacceptable form of population control," and bases his ruling on his "personal belief in the sanctity of human life." Isn't that a joke! That can be filed away with his own description of himself as a "deeply committed pacifist." Damn it, can't the man understand that abortion is a matter to be left up entirely to the woman concerned, not the President of the United States?

The afternoon was hectic because I had two things going on at the same time. First, the FBI investigation. In the statement I made by way of introducing the resolution I cited how charges against the Berrigan brothers, leaders of the Catholic antiwar movement, were cooked up by J. Edgar Hoover when he appeared before a Congressional committee to ask for a bigger appropriation, and were only attempted to be justified by an indictment two months later; how an agent who criticized the FBI administration in an academic program was dismissed; how Congressmen and Senators have disclosed they've been subjected to FBI wiretaps; how stolen FBI files have shown that the agency routinely maintains large and inaccurate dossiers on special groups and individuals whose politics Hoover finds personally offensive. Oh, it was great, I'll tell you. The FBI has been making life miserable for a lot of people for about twenty years now, and having represented in my career many people who've been harassed, it was good to have the opportunity now to harass back.

Since the Deputy Attorney General, Richard Kleindienst,

had said earlier in the day (by way of accusing Hale Boggs of either being "sick or not in possession of his faculties") that he welcomed an investigation of the FBI, once I made my speech, all hell broke loose. Everybody from the press wanted to interview me at once. But since I was supporting an amendment to a supplemental appropriations bill (which would give another $75 million to school districts for pupils who live in public housing) that was coming up for a vote, I didn't want to leave the Floor. The press thought I was crazy. Congressmen love publicity. Finally, after they nudged and nudged, I ran out and did a few TV and radio recordings and came back to sit through the appropriations bill debate.

There is a theory around here—and this seems like a good opportunity to tell you about it—that to attend a debate on the Floor is a waste of time. Since everybody has his mind made up in advance, the theory goes, what's the point in going to a debate? Insert what you have to say into the *Record*, which doesn't even require you to be on the Floor, and distribute it to your constituents. If you're seen hanging around the Floor listening to others, you're considered overearnest. You should be up in your office answering your mail. To stay on the Floor is to be unsuave and unsophisticated.

Well, that's the theory, and I, obviously, don't buy it. I hardly ever leave the Floor when the House is in session, because what I was sent here to do is sit and watch and participate. Besides, I don't think debate is a waste of time. I have seen my own arguments sway votes. Like in the draft debate, and today too. I pointed out that the $75 million for aid to education would not go only to New York City, but to certain rural and suburban areas too, and *you should have seen these guys perk up*. They hadn't known this. They were *listening* to me. I saw it on their faces.

So those who tell you that debate is worthless are just cynical. The system has mowed them down. Well, I'm only a neophyte who comes from a movement of social change, and even though I have a fundamental cynicism about the system myself, I still believe we have to push and push to make the process work. Playing handball, paddle tennis, taking massages or going swimming in the pool—which is what a few of these guys do in the course of a day's debate, in case you didn't know—is getting us absolutely nowhere. We can't do anything in Congress unless Congressmen attend the sessions. Of course, it's going to be even harder as the committees get to work, and we all have to choose between attending committee sessions and being on the Floor. Which brings me back to that education amendment. It was part of a package amendment that lost 187-191. Why? Well, a lot of our great liberals have already left town and started on their vacations. Which is precisely why the power structure put the bill up for a vote on a day like this. They knew the liberals would already be gone. One fellow from the South said to me with a big smile, "Bella, where are all your friends?"

April 8

Martin said that on the NBC-TV program they used a sketch of me in the background when they reported my resolution for an investigation of the FBI. He wanted to know how come I wasn't on live because the sketch was horrible.

This afternoon I was working on some aspect of the housing problem, and in the course of it had to make a few telephone calls to some people in the Lindsay Administration. Finally, I got hold of one of the commissioners—I'd better not mention his name—and my temper ran short and I started to scream and yell at him. A few minutes later my friend Ronnie called back to tell me that this fellow had run down the hall to her claiming I called him a four-letter word. Now isn't that ridiculous? A-s-s is only three letters. The man's crying like a baby. Oh, I don't know, I guess it's my cross to bear, these things. I mean, how am I to do anything if I don't scream and carry on? How else do you get action out of these people?

Tonight Martin and I were having dinner with some friends at the Homestead Restaurant near Fourteenth Street when a guy came over to me and said, "Listen, Bella, I'm with you, but I'm standing at the bar with a very reactionary guy from the American Legion and he bet me you wouldn't even come over to say hello to him."

Five minutes and two drinks later, I won another supporter.

April 9

We flew to Freeport in the Bahamas where a friend is lending me an apartment for a few days to relax. Our daughters are with us, which is nice, because I never get to see them anymore. Now I'll have a chance to get caught up on their school activities and friends.

I'm really exhausted. This is the first time in months I've been away from it all, and so I'm sitting here by the pool thinking about a lot of things. I'll tell you one thing I'm beginning to realize, which might shock you: It's not the reactionaries in Congress who feel threatened by me. It's the liberals. Isn't that regrettable?

See, I'm more freewheeling and I'm less bound to tradition than most of these liberals are. I say what's on my mind. And this means, usually, that both the people and the media listen. So some liberals have gotten the mistaken idea that I'm getting undue attention.

What they just don't understand is that I do it as I see it. True, I get tremendous coverage, but I'm not out pushing for it.

The press looks for me because of the things I say and do and the way I do it. I introduce resolutions, bills, call for action—this is where I get my press. I don't call press conferences, except very rarely.

I have a feeling that some of the guys are pretty furious with me for something I did toward the end of the week: I inserted into the *Record* the actual roll call vote from the Democratic caucus on the set-the-date resolution. You see, the press is banned from the caucus, but this time somebody had leaked the vote to the Baltimore *Sun*, so I just took it out of the paper and put it into the *Record* for anybody who wanted to see it. And why not? As far as I'm concerned, these votes should be a matter of public record anyway.

The way people vote in the caucus goes a long way toward determining the policy in the House (even though the votes aren't exactly binding). If the Democrats are ashamed of how they vote behind closed doors, then all I can say is "too bad." They're elected and sent here by the people and their constituents should know what they are doing. Anyhow, I'm sick and tired of a lot of them feeling they don't have to come to the caucus because there's not going to be a recorded vote. So that's that. They'll have to think twice now about how they intend to vote, and about whether or not they come.

April 11

Al Lowenstein has managed to ruin my vacation. He told me last week he's kicking off his Dump Nixon campaign with a rally in Providence, Rhode Island, next weekend, and he's insisting that I go. It's going to be a kind of registration-in for young voters, and it's being held in Rhode Island because the state has one of the earliest primaries.

The problem is this: The same day as Lowenstein's rally I'm due to speak at some lecture series in Seattle. Since they're going to pay me quite a bit of money, it's not an easy thing to get out of. Not that I care about money—it's never what motivates me—but I do need a few thousand extra dollars for my newsletter to constituents and for extra staff, and this will be a good opportunity to make it. I guess if I wanted I could make an awful lot of money—guarantees, minimums, stuff like that—on the lecture circuit, but I don't do it because I don't want to be tied down. Because when I am, something like this always happens.

Something tells me that I have to be in Rhode Island, no matter what. I have to see what Al's up to. Besides, he's a very persistent fellow. I have all kinds of reservations about this thing, but Al doesn't feel my concern about the kids' registering as Republicans is warranted. The main thing, he says, is just to get them registered, because whether Nixon is dumped or not, they'll be a huge progressive vote in the general election. Yet I say we need these kids in the Democratic Party to help us get a progressive candidate in the first place.

So I'm not sure where he's headed with this project and I haven't decided whether to go to Rhode Island or not. One thing I do know, though, is that I don't want to lose any opportunity to help organize this political coalition I've been talking about all along. Incidentally—although it's not generally recognized by history—I played a very big role in bringing a large part of the unorganized Democratic vote into the Dump Johnson movement, particularly the people from the peace movement. So I'm somewhat familiar with these goings on.

April 14

Flew back today, a little rested. Then I took one look at my schedule for the next few days, and couldn't believe what my staff has done to me again.

April 15

I was in Massachusetts to speak at Clark University and it was a very strange experience. They invited me to this special dinner and they all sat around and talked to themselves as if I weren't there. Then, when it came time for me to speak, a bunch of dogs were running around in the auditorium, so I got up and said, "I've been greeted by all kinds before, but never by dogs." Not one of them laughed. Do you think they took it personally? Oh well, they tell me they have a big psychology department at Clark, so maybe they were all just into their psyches. I finally worked them up to some applause, but I must say, it was hard work.

My daughter and some of her friends had driven up from Boston, and they took me back to the airport. The entire trip Liz only wanted to go over some suggestions for a theme she had to write for political science. I figured it's the only reason she came to see me. But I loved seeing her—and helping her. She agreed it was a tough audience I had faced, but she felt I was able to get more out of them than anyone usually does.

I've decided, like a fool, to cancel the lecture in Seattle and follow my curiosity and my sense of obligation instead to Providence this weekend. I'm very concerned that the kids might be misled into thinking that Pete McCloskey is anybody who anyone other than Republicans should actually be supporting, because if we lose our votes to the Republican Party we're not going to get anywhere.

April 16

Back to New York at one o'clock in the morning and out again at nine. This time to Nashville. My staff, you know, has wild dreams that I can be everywhere doing everything at all times. If they don't let up, I swear they're going to put me back in the hospital.

Before I gave a speech at Vanderbilt, which is known as "the Harvard of the South," some students showed me some comments that had been made about me in a student magazine. Stuff like how I used four-letter words, etc. So I bawled them out for writing that kind of crap. "When you get an ally like me in the adult population," I said, "you don't put her down. Understand?" On the other hand, I'm told this was the first time they had ever invited a woman to address this symposium. *That* I was glad about.

April 17

Back to New York at midnight, out again at nine. This time to an Ann Arbor meeting of the Michigan Democratic Coalition. My staff is killing me. Just because Congress is in recess, this whole week was booked without even consulting me. They can't understand that I have other things to do than talk. They just figure I want to "spread the word." And they're right, of course.

Anyway, at one point during the day I ended up at a press conference where some reporters started pressing me about which candidate I was supporting for President.

"None . . . yet," I said. "Because I believe that the candidate I support has to be an activist and I haven't seen any yet."

"What about Senator Henry Jackson," one reporter asked.

"He's one candidate I'm certainly not supporting."

Whereupon I turned around and there was Senator Jackson. I hadn't noticed him. It seems he was in Detroit addressing some other group which was meeting in the same building on the same floor as the one I was addressing.

"I see you're raising hell again," he said.

"No more, no less than usual."

Later I spoke to a University of Michigan woman's group called PROBE. They've been conducting a terrific battle out here on discrimination against women in the faculty and in other university matters. "It may sound incredible to you," I told them, "but the Constitution guarantees women only one right—the right to vote. Protection of women under the Fourteenth and Fifteenth Amendments is still uncertain—and at the discretion of male judges."

April 18

I flew back from Detroit this morning and Martin met me at the airport with Bruce Mertes of my staff and Sandy McLeod, a volunteer, and we drove up to Providence for that big Lowenstein hoopla. About 15,000 people, mostly young kids, showed up. Ed Muskie was there, Birch Bayh, Pete McCloskey too. All low note, low key stuff. You don't do that to a crowd of kids who are dying to hear something inspiring. Lowenstein, too, instead of speaking like a leader of youth, came off like an elder statesman. McCloskey urged the kids to register Republican. I admire what he is trying to do, but that I didn't like. I wanted to get out of there.

I was the last one to speak, and I seriously considered telling the kids that the only way they're going to beat Nixon was not from within the Republican Party, but from outside with a smashing activist candidate. But then I realized that if I told them to register in the Democratic Party, they'd be just as turned off me as they were McCloskey. So instead I gave them one of my rip-roaring speeches about the need to build a new political coalition, and roused them up.

What's wrong with this McCloskey thing is its premise. It assumes that there's an insurgency in the Republican Party. There isn't. The Republicans are very happy with Nixon. As far as McCloskey is concerned, the Republicans have a long tradition of "curing" their liberals. You take Goodell—they destroyed him. Rockefeller, who at one time was a liberal, had to unliberalize himself in order to survive. Javits, who'd like to think of himself as the perennial liberal, is very inconsistent. Okay, so they have a few liberals in Congress, but so what. They can't get any power inside their party, and since they don't know how to organize at the bottom—where they should be organizing to take over the party—they start this grand Dump Nixon movement.

What they haven't considered is that if they succeed in getting rid of Nixon, they're not going to get McCloskey, that's for sure. His following is almost entirely outside the party— among Democrats, independents and liberals. He's an outsider! No party is going to nominate an outsider for President.

April 19

Back in Washington. It's going to be a very exciting week. The Vietnam Veterans Against the War are in town. I gave them a tough speech from the Capitol steps, and they loved it. "Right on, Bella," they called. "Bella for President." Their enthusiasm was unbelievable.

I've been meeting them personally all day, and they're wonderful youngsters, very sincere, very troubled and very angry. And they don't look anything like the soldiers you see on the recruiting posters.

Richard Fulton and another Tennessee Congressman both came up to me this afternoon and said their families and constituents heard me the other day at Vanderbilt and agreed with me. So I said, "Why don't you?"

April 20

I went to a cocktail party for the Vietnam veterans at the home of Senator Philip Hart, and on the way over stopped at the veterans' campsite to say hello. They were all very excited to see me. You should have seen them. They raised their clenched fists and shouted, "Bella! Bella!" So I was feeling pretty good by the time I got to Hart's.

Even though these kinds of parties are not my style (I don't drink that much, and when I do I get sleepy), I had a pretty good time. When I first got there I spotted Senator Fulbright, and I said to somebody who was with me, "I don't know if he remembers me—we met once—and I ought to go over and say hello." But, at that point, Fulbright came over to me. "I wanted to say hello," he said. "There isn't a day I don't read about you in the papers. You're doing a great job." It was good to hear him say that. I've always admired him.

Earlier in the day at a meeting of the Democratic Study Group which was called to discuss strategy for tomorrow's Democratic caucus, I announced that I was once again going to raise the issue of ending the war this year rather than in 1973. They all tried to tell me that doing such a thing would be very foolhardy and one guy even said, "You're going to wear out your welcome."

"It looks like I might not only wear out my welcome in the caucus," I said, "but here too. But I'm going to raise this issue until I get something done, no matter what you guys try to tell me."

These are the great liberals I have to live and work with. Little men. I'm absolutely fed up with them.

April 21

Half the night I was on the phone making sure we'd get a quorum for the caucus this morning. The other sponsors of the original resolution and I divided up the calls.

Well, I got to the caucus room, got the Floor and began to make my motion that we vote on the Vietnam Disengagement Act when suddenly they began to cut me down and hang me up with all kinds of stupid technicalities. They tried to tell me that I was on the agenda first for a *discussion* and later for a *vote*, or something like that.

"You know what the trouble with you guys is?" I said. "You're always trying to figure out ways to block me instead of helping me. After all, I'm trying to raise an important issue, and you're just talking about technicalities."

They went ahead and called a quorum on me. We were nine votes short. You'll have to excuse me if it's beginning to sound like the same old song, but once again many of our wonderful liberals *were not there*. This time the leadership was responsible for keeping people away. They were busy calling everybody this morning to tell them that because there would be no quorum there would be no vote in the caucus—and therefore they should all attend their committee meetings as usual. Herman Badillo said he got such a call just fifteen minutes before the caucus was scheduled to begin. I wasn't the only one who was furious. Andy Jacobs from Indiana—who's been trying to get an item concerning the District of Columbia on the agenda all year—was mad as hell. When we came to the Floor of the House later and we were debating the Public Works bill, he kept making one quorum call after another as a retaliation. This meant that all these fellows had to keep coming out of their plush offices on false alarms. Some guys came over to me and said, "Bella, please, you ought to stop him. You have influence on him."

"Me?" I said. "I don't even know him."

Oh, I loved every minute of it.

Tonight, after the Supreme Court ordered the veterans not to camp on the Mall, several Congressmen, including me, opened our offices for them to sleep in. There were about fifteen who came to my place. One, to show his appreciation, brought a small bunch of azaleas.

He attached the following note:

"Dear Bella,

"I would like to thank you with these ripped-off flowers from the Capitol lawn for coming out to the lawn when they tried to move us. You are really dynamite."

April 22

"There's only one thing I want to know," said Sam Stratton, a rigid hawk from Albany, who saw a TV report on the veterans sleeping in my office. "Did you spend the night there with them?"

That remark is the first time anybody in Congress has said anything untoward to me since I've been here.

"It's not my style, Sam," I said, and that was it.

April 23

Flew to Rochester to address a convention of home economists. They were mostly teachers, dieticians, nutritionists, all very conservative, as was their group, which was afraid of lobbying for its own interests in Congress because it didn't want to risk losing its tax exemption. Nonetheless, I socked it to them pretty hard about women's rights and the war, and ended up getting a pretty good ovation. Oh, I don't know, I guess they filed the speech away under "Permissible Oddities of a Congresswoman." There were a few people who sat on their hands. It must have been quite a trauma for them.

If they weren't comfortable, neither was I—but for different reasons. I didn't feel properly dressed. I never have time to change my clothes anymore. I just get on a plane, get off and get on a plane. It's impossible. I guess I'm more vain than a lot of people realize, because I don't like the idea of not being able to be dressed just right.

One problem is that I have no time to buy clothes. Another is the weight thing. Because I don't have a chance to eat anything but junk and sandwiches, I've put on forty pounds since the campaign. I have an underactive metabolism and what I should be doing is eating regular high-protein meals. But there's no time! Oh, I'm always starting diets, but I can't stick to them. Something happens, like I get agitated on the House Floor, so I go into the cloakroom at the back of the Floor and stuff myself with things I shouldn't be eating. One of these days, though, I'm going to get on a serious diet. Ha, it would really be too much for these fellows if I was svelte. They'd bust a gut. There was a time—just last year—when I was in good shape. I wasn't always like this.

So the whole physical thing has been a very touchy matter with me lately. But I do the best I can. I get to the House beauty parlor at the crack of dawn when I can't get to my usual place in New York. Before I make a public appearance I always get to the ladies room to freshen my eyeliner, tighten my belt a notch (it's like girding your loins to be ready for what's out there) and put some lipstick on with the plastic top from my pen.

Some people ask me why I wear makeup at all, because makeup is fashioned by Madison Avenue, which enslaves women. Well, all I can say is that I've been liberated so long that it will take more than Madison Avenue to enslave me.

April 24

As I told the crowd, everybody was in Washington today except President Nixon. He was in retreat. At Camp David.

There were close to a half million people in town for the largest antiwar rally we've ever had. Fighters for Peace, a lot of new faces and young vets too. Martin and our daughters, Helene and her kids were there. When I got up to address the rally, two old friends, who were coordinating the event, came up to me and said, "Remember now, Bella—one minute."

"You listen to me," I said jokingly. "I'm a Congresswoman now and you can't talk to me that way."

I should say I wasn't entirely joking. After working with these guys for ten years in the peace movement, I see they're still trying to keep women down. Al Lowenstein overheard the exchange. So he put his two cents in: "Do you think they were ever able to tell you what to do when you weren't a Congresswoman?"

It was a magnificent rally. Coretta King spoke, and I thought of that great March on Washington in 1963 when her husband gave his "I Have a Dream" speech.

At 5:30 I caught the plane back to New York and had dinner with Ronnie Eldridge and Marvin and Arlene Gersten. When I walked into the Italian restaurant where I met them, people started to applaud, probably because they had seen me on the *Six O'Clock News*. As for the dinner, I managed to get Ronnie and the others mad at me because I refused to be gracious enough to say the food was great, even though it wasn't.

Afterwards we all went to a benefit for the John Lindsay Association in Brooklyn. When John and Mary first spotted me, Mary said, "You were great. I just saw you on TV. John was sleeping, though, and I didn't want to wake him."

"You should have," I said.

April 25

I went to Albany to speak at the Women's Political Conference of the New York State Democratic Committee. To tell you the truth, I couldn't stand being there because Sam Stratton was one of the speakers. He's hardly my type, but we managed to keep up a polite banter. I don't know why he was invited in the first place, since he's a conservative. He must have some sort of appeal to these upstate women who still have their own form of backwardness, which I hope will change as the movement for women's rights begins to evolve.

The featured speaker was Birch Bayh, who's a nice fellow. At the beginning of his speech he turned directly to Shirley Chisholm and me and said, "When we're in the White House in 1972 . . ."

"Does he mean him or us?" I said to Shirley, out loud.

April 26

The *New York Post* reported that Bayh said to me and Shirley, "After we have taken over the White House in 1972, well, you're going to decide which one of you is to be Vice President."

That's not the way I heard it.

We had the first session of the war crimes hearings this morning, but I'm not at all that happy. We haven't been able to agree among ourselves whether individual guilt should be assigned or the guilt should be all-encompassing. I agree that we should point the finger at political leaders and generals, but I also feel that we have to hold some individual soldiers responsible.

April 27

The hearings picked up today. Much better. Although a lot of soldiers were reluctant to name names, dates and places, they did give some pretty horrifying eyewitness accounts of things that have been going on over there. I asked one guy what he felt like and what he did after tying up a prisoner's genitals with telephone wires.

"We went out and got drunk," he said.

April 28

The entire day was screwed up because I overslept by two and a half hours. The first time I've done it since I've been in Congress. It made for a mean day for me, let me tell you. First of all, I was supposed to go shopping for clothes this morning —before the war crimes hearings—and I had to forget about *that*. Then when I got to the hearings I couldn't stay very long (which made me feel very guilty) because I had to go to a New York delegation luncheon. The delegation has finally decided to meet twice a month to discuss common problems, and I don't like to miss it. Sometimes Manny Celler, who heads the delegation, will come up with some concrete things he wants us all to do, and they're often pretty good. A lot of Congressmen use the delegation luncheon as an opportunity to collect signatures for various letters they may be writing to the Mayor or the Governor or cabinet members. You can bust a gut until they make a law in Congress, so these guys like to write letters of protest and inquiry as a means to get something done quickly.

An amusing sidelight to the way the delegation operates is the big fuss that's made about dispensing various jobs and posts. For instance, everybody was upset with John Rooney because he has been in charge of Democratic patronage in New York City for ten years and hasn't been slicing up the cake fairly. He never even told anybody what patronage exists. So there was a big fight to get the facts, and it turned out that the whole patronage deal for New York is something like one page, one-half of an elevator operator and one-third of a clerk. A big to-do over nothing, really. Then somebody was given the job to be on the statewide steering committee, which meets on occasion with Rockefeller, and somebody else was given the job of being on the House steering committee, which meets on occasion with Carl Albert. Stuff like that, little jobs, big jobs, little power, big power, prestige . . . bunk. It's all job-oriented—who's going to *get* what, not who's going to *do* what, and so, as you can imagine, they're all busy making their little deals with Manny Celler in the same way they make little deals with the House leadership. And this—as by now you should know—is not for me. If I want something, I very plainly say so. I don't operate on a sub rosa level.

I can't concern myself with these guys. They haven't gone out of their way to give me any special work for the delegation, or any help either. Besides, they're a little backward on the women's thing. I think it's clear that I'm doing more and accomplishing more down here *without* the bootstrap assistance of the New York delegation, the House leadership or anybody. And whether they like it or not, a lot of these guys are being forced to accept my leadership. If I may speculate, in a short time they'll be doing things for me too.

When I get out there to fight for the kids, these guys are forced to come out too. When I pick my fights to defend people's rights, again, these guys are forced to come out with me. When I said I was going to barnstorm the country, it may have taken them a couple of months, but now they're ready to come out and barnstorm with me. So ultimately I'm giving them plenty of leadership, and whether they acknowledge it or not doesn't interest me. What interests me are facts, like Hugh Carey, the number two man in the delegation, coming out, as he did recently, in favor of the Vietnam Disengagement Act.

So let them have their old ways. Maybe they feel threatened by me. Threatened both as politicians and *men*. Regrettable, because I'm not in competition with them.

I flew back to the city tonight for the annual dinner of the Village Independent Club. They're a group that worked very hard for me during the campaign. They chose Birch Bayh as their guest of honor. Because he was a presidential candidate, they said. So since I didn't have to speak, I just relaxed. Martin came along, and we danced. They couldn't believe I knew how to dance. It happens all the time to me. A community newspaper once said that I "stunned" the crowds with one of the "coolest bugaloos around." These people don't understand that a person like myself can be many different things. They don't see that Bella Abzug is more than meets the eye. That's what gets me. Maybe they just don't fully dig me.

April 29

Today was the final session of the war crimes hearings. What has emerged from these hearings—and they've been very moving and very revealing—is the sense that it's U.S. policy in Indochina to kill civilians. It's the policy of this country to order saturation bombings, to designate huge areas as free-fire zones in which anything that moves is shot down, machine-gunned or napalmed. It is U.S. policy to burn down entire villages and use chemicals to destroy all vegetation so that people can no longer live off the land. All *policy*!

We have made barbarians out of our soldiers. You should have heard some of the things these veterans testified that they did without questioning. They've told horror stories about how they or others threw prisoners out of helicopters, about how prisoners were tortured to extract "confessions," about how helicopter pilots would zoom down with their crafts just to knock women off bicycles. One ex-sergeant told us about how he personally took part in a 1969 massacre of thirty men, women and children near Mylai. "I didn't even tell my wife about it until last night," he said. You see, most of these guys were so brutalized by the Army that it's taken them two years to realize what they've done.

I can't begin to describe what a horrifying experience it's been sitting and listening to all this. One thing that really disturbs me is how many of these guys tried to defend Calley. Obviously, since many of them are guilty of war crimes themselves, they don't want to see specific guilt assigned. So they're very confused. I mean, here are guys who probably never had a political thought in their lives but who now, in looking back, have come to understand what they were forced to do. They're willing to tell everything because they now realize that the whole mess over there is a matter of politics and racism, and out of guilt, they want to do something, anything, to stop this madness. It's only too bad that they are unwilling to accept individual responsibility.

Let's face it: We need people at all levels to accept individual responsibility for what they've done if we're ever going to get a political movement together that is strong enough to change the present policies of our government, policies that have made the Vietnam war so racist and the entire intervention such a monumental atrocity. What we've done over there, after all, is nothing but an extension of the dehumanization that is taking place in our own society. We've simply exported it to Indochina. We don't go out and shoot women, children and old men in this country yet, but we completely ignore their basic human needs to a point where it's almost as brutal.

The hearings, combined with the veterans' demonstrations last week, have had a tremendous impact down here. They've had the effect of waking up a few more Congressmen and they've scared the hell out of the generals. It's been astonishing to everybody to hear these soldiers testifying directly about their own acts of atrocity.

I dropped in for a few minutes at an Israeli-American Public Affairs luncheon to honor Israel's twenty-third anniversary. I didn't intend to make a big thing out of it, but no sooner did I get there and sit down to eat than the young people began pummeling me with questions. The usual ones, designed to test how committed to Israel I am, how committed to Soviet Jews I am, etc. They're zealots, these people, and I'm a zealot too, and they just want to make sure that my zealousness goes in their directions. They pummeled and pressured and pressured and pummeled me so much I couldn't even get a bite of food swallowed. It was as if I held the power of life or death over the fate of Israel and Soviet Jews. Interesting, isn't it? Actually, I love their intense burning feelings because it's exactly the kind of stuff I'm made of.

Later in the day, back on the Floor, the debate on appropriations for the House Internal Security Committee, the reactionary witch-hunters, was going on. About a month ago I testified before the House Administration Committee about the perniciousness and wastefulness of this dangerous committee. I pointed out, ironically, that it's true that the internal security of this country is threatened as never before—not, however, by those exercising their right to free speech, but by those who would silence all speech. In other words, by those elements befriended by the House Internal Security Committee.

The committee, as far as I'm concerned, plays no role other than to invade people's privacy. It is deeply involved in investigating members of the peace movement, in collecting unproven allegations into unauthorized files which it distributes indiscriminately, in publishing malicious material full of false charges and innuendoes identifying people as Communists, and so on. For these, and its other ridiculous adventures, we pay an appropriation of $850,000 a year, the sixth largest budget of any standing committee, and $300,000 more than we give the Judiciary Committee, which is the legitimate guardian of our security. As far as legislation is concerned, the committee is absolutely useless. Last year, thanks to the good sense of the House, of the twenty-nine bills referred to Internal Security, none became law.

Every year Don Edwards, my good liberal friend from California, leads the fight against the committee on the Floor. This year, he and a few other liberals worked out a strategy to get $200,000 lopped off the appropriations. Going into the debate, we figured there was an excellent chance we'd win. We even had the backing of the Ways and Means Committee and the Administration Committee.

Then Richard Ichord, who's the chairman of Internal Security, got up and started weeping about how $200,000 was too much to take away from him, the usual crap, and before we knew it, some of the liberals had sold us out again. They undercut their own agreement, compromised and decided $100,000 would be enough to cut. So, there we were, routed again as usual. The appropriation was cut by $100,000 instead of $200,000 and some liberals were running around glowing with contentment, congratulating themselves on their "victory." How in 1971 can we be satisfied with an inch? It's disgusting. Compromise has become their way of life.

Back to New York tonight for a dinner dance of the Park River Independent Democratic Club, a reform club in my district. They were honoring Charlie Rangel, Herman Badillo and Bella Abzug. Just to be safe, a black, a Puerto Rican and a woman.

I used the opportunity to make a speech about the need for unity. The reform Democrats in the area are squaring off for another fight—with each other—and I was hoping it could be headed off.

April 30

I had lunch at the *Daily News* with the political reporters, who, believe it or not, are pretty hip people. And except for its backward editorial policy, which they have nothing to do with, they put out a pretty good newspaper too. I may be wrong, but I feel—in spite of what they say about me on the editorial page—the *News* gives me better coverage than any other paper. I can't be sure, though, since I don't follow it that closely, just as I don't look at myself on TV or listen to myself on radio. How can I? I'm on all the time. It's all part of a day's work.

This evening I opened up an office on the Lower East Side in the Educational Alliance Building. It was a great event in many ways. The office will serve one of the most blighted communities in the nation. Joe Cadden, an old friend who's retired from some of his business activities, has volunteered to be in charge. So far my other offices have processed nearly a thousand cases of constituents who have come to us for help. Now we're going to be able to help the people of the Lower East Side with their special problems concerning food stamps, Medicaid, Medicare, Social Security, welfare, the draft, unemployment, veteran's benefits, housing conditions, drug addiction rehabilitation, poverty, you name it. Of course, as I told them, there's not much we can do in some of these areas because of a recurring problem that besets us all—money. Everything requires money. Just to make the point graphic, afterwards in a speech at the New Era Club I told them what the $150 billion we have spent so far to fight the war in Vietnam could have bought us all had we spent it more sanely:

We could have built 15 million new homes.

We could have given virtually free medical care to all Americans.

We could have given annual scholarships of $2400 to each of the 8.8 million college age children of American workers.

For $1 billion alone—1/150th of what we've spent in Vietnam—we could have built 333 hospitals with 125 beds each or 70,000 new low cost housing units.

Incidentally, it was before this same audience that during the campaign I debated Barry Farber. At the time, because of Farber's lies about my position on Israel, there was a lot of hostility toward me. It was a real bloodbath down there, that debate, I'll tell you. He whipped them up to a point where they would hardly listen to me.

Well, back in the old gladiator arena tonight they listened and they listened good. The chairman of the event made the statement that in his thirty-seven years of running these forums he had never heard such a thorough report from a public official. One woman got up and said, "When you were fighting for this seat, you said that if you won, we would win. Well you won, and we are winning." People came up to me and kissed my hand. An orthodox Jew with a beard and a yarmulke came up to the stage and shook my hand, an act that violates the tradition of Orthodox Jewry that a woman is not to be touched because she's considered unclean. That's an indication of how strongly they felt. What a triumph! I turned a hostile audience into some of my greatest supporters.

May 1

I was determined to buy something today, so I went shopping with my friend Charita from Connecticut. We went to Alexander's in the Bronx, where I finally found a dress I liked, and also a hat and a couple of other things. I was so exhausted from standing on my feet that long, I thought I'd die, and with people coming up to me "Bella, Bella, Bella-ing" me every minute. One woman: "Hello, Bella . . . from a conservative." But since I finally bought a couple of things, it made me feel better.

This evening I went to a cocktail party at the McManus Democratic Club—they're regulars, not reformers—in my district. It seemed every judge in New York was there, as well as a lot of old-school politicians to whom I am the very antithesis— and yet a curiosity. Most of them were very nice, but I did encounter a few toughies, two women in particular, one a Republican district leader and the other a regular Democrat. I ended up going out with them afterwards to have a few drinks. I'm not a drinker, but in that atmosphere one of the ways you get accepted is to show that you can drink. I mean, it's not a big deal to be able to drink, but I don't normally do it because I don't need the calories. In politics, though, votes come before calories, and so after a few hail-sister-well-met drinks with these two women, we all felt a lot better.

When I came home to have dinner with Martin, Charita and Ed, I said, "Well, I beat them at their own game."

"What's that?" they asked.

"Drinking," I said, and collapsed on the couch.

May 2

A speech at Boston University, where Liz goes to school. Martin came along. Liz looked gorgeous. The speech was well received, and I'm sure she got a kick out of it, as she always does, especially since I referred to her being in the audience. *That* always gives her a certain delight.

May 3

Where to begin? History will judge this as the day they really did the Constitution in. The papers say there are 50,000 Mayday demonstrators down here (although it's more like twice that number) who vowed to shut down the city today with massive civil disobedience. The event began grandly yesterday with the Administration, in a Gestapo maneuver, dispersing the demonstrators in a dawn raid at their encampment on the banks of the Potomac. Nixon and Mitchell seemed determined to turn what the leaders of the demonstration have termed will be a nonviolent protest into a potentially violent situation.

Having dispersed the demonstrators, the Administration then announced that seventy-three hundred police and Guardsmen would be on hand at six o'clock this morning. When I crossed the bridge from the airport all I could see was soldier after soldier after soldier, as if all the criminals in America were about to strike at its capital city. It was unbelievable. As my cab wound through the streets I saw more cops and more soldiers than I had ever seen in my life, all of them standing there with their guns, guarding against . . . heaven knows what!

Before I go any further, I should say right here that the announced intention of the demonstrators to stop traffic in order to shut down government offices is not my thing. The veterans, the April 24 rally and the war crimes hearings have put a lot of pressure on Congress, and I feel we should play it for what it's worth while it lasts. This kind of activity is very difficult for people to understand, and if things turned violent, it would be a very serious thing. But my major objection—besides the fact that I'm not well acquainted with the people who are leading the demonstrations—is that I don't believe we should start talking about closing down a city when we *can't*, plain and simple. It gives the impression that the people are powerless. They say they are going to do something, and then they can't do it, so they end up just demonstrating their own powerlessness, when, in fact, they aren't powerless at all!

Now, I realize that the demonstrations are intended to be *symbolic*, but people don't have the capacity to conceptualize these great big symbols. If you say you're going to do something, and then you can't do it, then you've failed—as far as most people are concerned. Understand?

Finally, civil disobedience is not my thing. It's no good unless it's truly massive, and that's next to impossible right now.

I've been involved in a lot of debates about civil disobedience in my time. A few years ago I was leading a Women Strike for Peace group demonstration at the White House. The police confined the majority of us behind some barricades across the street, while allowing only a hundred or so to march up and down in front of the White House. So some of the women got fired up, threw down the barricades and sat-in in the middle of Pennsylvania Avenue. They remained there for an hour while I negotiated with the police not to arrest them, and then they left. Afterwards, there was a big polemic in some circles in which I was attacked for not letting them get arrested.

I told them and I say it again: to get arrested is not a sign of any great action. As a matter of fact, it's only a way of confining yourself and having yourself tied up in knots so that you can't act. And that has never been my tactic. Someday it might be—maybe—but only when it's massive. You shouldn't construe any of this to mean that I don't respect people who do commit acts of civil disobedience. I do. I think they show a great commitment of individual conscience. I admire them. In many instances they demonstrate the highest form of patriotism.

Now, for what *happened* today, which is not a story of civil disobedience at all, but of governmental disobedience. The government, not the people, broke all the laws.

I went to my office, and as the morning progressed, word came that the cops were arresting everybody in sight, en masse, without any identification, without any charges, without any anything, and herding them off to a fenced-in football practice field near RFK Stadium, where they were being held without food, water and sanitation facilities. It was like the whole thing was finally coming apart.

I immediately decided I had to go to the stadium. Esther Newberg told me about a friend of hers by the name of Captain Dan who does traffic reports from a helicopter for a Washington radio station.

"Want to go there by air?" she asked.

"Yeah," I said, and a few phone calls later, I was taking off in Captain Dan's flying machine.

(136)

I don't know what's the matter with me. I didn't think. As he started the helicopter going up, I suddenly got this very insecure feeling that I was about to fall out the door. I was terrified.

"I think I'd like to go down," I told Captain Dan. "I'm not going to lose my life over this thing."

"If you just relax," he said, "you'll enjoy it."

"I know, I know," I said. "I once took flying lessons, so I know all about enjoying it, but take me down. Now. Please."

So he started to take me down. He must have thought I was crazy, but I was feeling like one woman risking her life going up in a helicopter to save the world when the world's obviously not going to be saved by one woman. Not even the country. Not even the state. Then, as he was about to land the thing, I suddenly thought to myself, "Gee, what if this is the only way we can see what is happening?"

"Okay, Captain Dan," I said, dwelling on that thought, "I'll tell you what: Let's try it again?"

And we did. And I adjusted. (Look, I'm only human, for godsakes. I'm not made of iron. I have my fears and doubts just like everybody else. Sometimes I have to give in to my frailties too.)

From the air, when I allowed myself to look, I saw quite a shocking scene. All these thousands of people in one large field on this raw and nasty day, wire and cops and soldiers all around them, and off in the distance, machinery and artillery. You wouldn't believe it.

When we landed near the stadium my two L.A.s, Judy Wolf and Nancy Stanley, met me and we walked together toward the gate past an ominous line of cops and soldiers with bayonets. It was gruesome. When we got to the gate, I boomed, "Step aside, I'm Congresswoman Abzug, and I'm going to go inside." And, like the Red Sea parting, they stepped aside.

The moment I walked in I was mobbed—literally. You know, "There's Bella . . . Bella baby . . . hey, Bella . . ." Somebody said, "Everybody sit down," and with amazing discipline, they all did.

I explained I wasn't there to make a speech, and I didn't. I said I had come to talk with them to see what had been going on and whether they had proper facilities and what help I could give. As it turned out, of course, they didn't have any facilities or shelter or food. They had put a few tents and tarpaulins up themselves, but they were shivering. They had had no food or water for hours. They said there were only four makeshift cardboard bins as sanitation facilities for seventeen hundred people. It was utterly shocking. Many of them had been arrested as early as seven in the morning, and this was now four in the afternoon, and there was no sign of the Red Cross. You'd be shocked to know how many little kids— thirteen and fourteen years old—I found there. At a certain point, the soldiers pushed open the gate and tear-gassed the crowd.

Perhaps the most shocking thing of all is the number of people I spoke to who were doing nothing at all to warrant getting arrested. It's clear to me that anybody in the dragnet area who was not wearing a business suit was hauled in. People who just went out to move their cars. Students on their way to classes. Photographers. People walking their dogs. One young man and young woman I spoke to were on their way to get married. People who had merely brought food and thrown it over the fence for those inside were herded inside themselves. I saw old friends, Dr. Spock, Barbara Deming, Grace Paley, members of my campaign staff—all of them arrested for no reason at all. It's very sad—like the Constitution has been suspended, and this stadium is a detention center, a concentration camp.

In my day I've represented many people in the courts, prostitutes, thieves, the worst criminals, and they were given better treatment than these kids. In all my fifty years I have never seen anything like it, believe me.

When I left the stadium I went back to my office and started calling any and everybody I could think of: the Red Cross, the Attorney General's office, Mayor Walter Washington's office, other Congressmen. By this time more than seven thousand people had been arrested, a one-day record for the city—in fact, for the entire country—and I explained to the Red Cross that these people were being treated like cattle.

"Why isn't your organization there helping them?" I asked. "You're supposed to apply humane treatment to everybody."

They had the audacity to answer that the command post had told them the detainees were to be moved momentarily. No matter that they had already been there eleven hours, suffering.

To everybody else I called I said that what was going on was inhuman and outrageous, certainly no way to treat people who have no charges against them. I mean, even if there were charges, they're still human beings, aren't they? There had been no due process. The Constitution was simply suspended. I'll tell you, I was furious. I still am. You know what Mayor Washington's office told me? "We're working on it," they said.

The liberals I spoke to—I can draw their replies into one composite: "Bella, cool down, at least it's not Chicago. At least they're not breaking one head after another."

"You make me sick," I told each and every one of them. "So this is why you're not doing anything to help these kids, is that right? Because it's not Chicago? Because they're not being physically attacked? What's being committed here is a fundamental violence to our Constitution and to our democracy."

"Well, I understand why you're upset," they said, "but it seems to me that they're being treated pretty well."

You know what upset them the most? There were a few reports that the demonstrators had thrown some paint around and had put some nails in the road, that's what upset them. Okay, I don't agree with those kinds of tactics either, but only a

(139)

few people were doing it and it was no justification for what followed.

Finally, later in the night, things started to change. The detainees were moved from the open stadium to the D.C. Coliseum, a sports arena. Church groups, the Medical Committee for Human Rights and the D.C. Statehood Party people started to furnish food, medicine, blankets. Procedures were finally set up to formally "arrest" people after more than fifteen hours of illegal detention. They were being processed out—if they gave the police the information for their arrest forms, paid $10 collateral and entered a plea of guilty.

They had never been properly arrested. No charges had ever been filed. They were not informed of their legal rights. They were denied access to lawyers. They were not promptly arraigned—and as a last insult they were asked to forfeit collateral, thus eliminating their right to trial, in order to be released. Is there anybody who's going to tell me that the Constitution meant a damn thing to the government today?

I went over to the Coliseum with Congressman Parren Mitchell of Maryland when the demonstrators were being moved there. You should have seen that scene! Again, like an armed camp. Soldiers with guns across their chests ringing the entire building, and dozens and dozens of closed vans—specially hired for the purpose—pulling up one after another to deposit cattle load after cattle load of young people whose only crime was believing in the Constitution. You'd think they were murderers, the way they were being handled. Artillery, heavy guns, helicopters, police, Guardsmen, soldiers, Marines, everywhere. One look and you had to ask yourself—are they putting down an insurgency? Are they preparing for an invasion from Mars? It was that incredible. I have never, never seen anything like it.

As Parren and I got close to the arena we were stopped at

gun point by a liquored-up cop who unhooked the safety catch on his gun and said to Parren, who was walking a little ahead of me, "Where do you think you're going?"

"I'm a Congressman," he said.

"I don't care who the hell you are," he said.

I took Parren by the arm and said, "Look, let's forget it. We're in a dark alley . . . it's not worth it. This man doesn't know what he's doing. We'll go around the other way."

In the crowd we saw a number of people from the staffs of Senators Adlai Stevenson and Ted Kennedy. A few of them came up to us and said, "Pssst, we're here *unofficially*. What do you think we can do?"

"Get the men you're working for to come here," I said. "Or is that asking too much?"

May 4

I was scheduled for two subcommittee meetings this morning, and I decided to show up big as life because I didn't want these guys to get the idea that I was simply in the business of *stopping* government operations. Afterwards I went to the Floor, where before the session everybody was getting up to make their little self-serving statements about the demonstrations in the one-minute speeches for the *Record*. They call this "The Children's Hour."

I sat there listening to these guys, one after another, get up to attack, attack, attack the demonstrators, wailing about how the anarchists had taken over the capital, about how the anarchists were going to destroy the fundamentals of American democracy. They complimented the police, the Army, the Guard, the Navy and the Marines, the leadership of the House and the Senate, the Attorney General and the Administration for putting down the insurrection. These were the most outrageous, reactionary, backward statements you could imagine. Vicious. Ill-conceived. Awful. And I'm sitting there, next to my friend Ella Grasso, burning up.

"Ella," I said, "I can't stand it."

"You know something, Bella?" she said. "They're all against the kids. The whole country. The newspapers, Congress, the Administration, everybody, they're all against the kids. It's disgusting. Any mother with kids knows how disgusting it is. These are *our* kids."

"I know," I said. "I've got to get up and say something before I blow up."

So I started to walk to the front of the House, in a huff, to ask for unanimous consent to make my own one-minute speech. One of my New York colleagues took one look at me and tried to stop me.

"Bella," he said, "why do you want to get into this? You don't approve of the kind of things some of the demonstrators did yesterday, so why associate yourself with it? You have enough burdens to bear."

I said, *"Please,"* and got up and made my speech, completely off the cuff, in which I said, "We may not agree with the tactics of the young people, but we've got to understand why they came here. They're here because *we* have not acted." And I gave it to them hard about the complete disregard for the fundamental rights of these people that the government exhibited, and about how the Congress is not using its power to call off the war.

Although today's "Children's Hour" was an exception, I'd better explain a couple of things to you about this procedure. It's a device these guys use to get their remarks into the *Congressional Record* to make it appear like they're doing something that they're not. Let me explain:

At the beginning of a session anybody can get up and ask for one minute to address the House on any subject and then revise and extend his remarks in the *Record*. Now, what a lot of guys do is simply waive the speech altogether and have their legislative assistant cook up some words to insert into the *Record*, just as if they had actually stood up and gone through a spiel on the Floor—when, in fact, they didn't. Even if they did, except in rare cases, since very few Congressmen bother to come to the Floor for this daily ordeal, they were, in effect, standing there and talking to themselves.

That's only part of it. What really makes the *Congressional Record* so deceiving is this: Say a debate had taken place on the Floor and you missed it. Very often the committee chairman handling the bill will get permission to revise and extend his remarks and ask that all other members of the House be given five days within which to insert their remarks into the *Record* too. So you come back from the Virgin Islands, or the swimming pool, wherever you were, and you get your legislative assistant to write up a little speech and you go and insert it into the *Record*. When the *Record* is published, it looks as if you were actually participating in the debate.

Although I sometimes—rarely, though—use these procedures when I can't get recognized by the Chair or have more to say than can fit into the opening "one minute" or have to be in committee, I'm not too fond of them, as you can tell. First of all, I almost never miss an important debate. Second, if I ask for one minute, I don't waive, I use it.

In the course of the day the police arrested another twenty-seven hundred demonstrators after an orderly march on the Justice Department. At the same time two thousand of yesterday's seven thousand detained prisoners were still being held and being processed out at a very leisurely pace. The great majority were having all charges against them dropped, because obviously they had been illegally arrested in the first place. Not only was there no evidence against them, but in most cases the police had not even made any arrest record. My office spent the entire day taking calls from parents whose children had been jailed, and I myself did a lot of hollering and screaming all over the city to get as many of these kids out of jail as I could.

May 5

Parren Mitchell, Ron Dellums and I agreed to greet the demonstrators at the Capitol steps as they presented us, as representatives of Congress, with a "People's Peace Treaty." Charlie Rangel from Manhattan also joined us.

As we prepared to begin—we only intended to make brief statements, accept the treaty and leave—we noticed a lot of helmeted policemen gathering around the outer edges of the crowd, but we didn't pay much attention. They had been doing it all week. Suddenly one young guy disrobed on a ledge next to the Capitol steps, and as he stood there naked, the photographers went to him and the reporters came to *me*.

"Are you shocked?" they asked.

Of course I was. But all I said was, "It's not my thing."

I resented their trying to make a sick exhibitionist act of one human being the issue of the day.

Charlie was the first to speak. He was great. Then I came on, and I must admit I was a little amused by the fact that here were a thousand violent anarchists sitting so quietly and peacefully and earnestly listening to us. So I began, "Well, I'm glad to see a peaceful assembly of both police and people . . ." Little did I know.

My speech dealt with encouraging these kids to use political power to effect change. "The establishment should kiss you for putting it that way," somebody said.

But the establishment is made up of little men, very frightened. After I finished, Parren got up and spoke, and then we both started to leave. I was due in New York at five o'clock for a rally at Bryant Park.

"Wait a minute, Bella," some reporters shouted to me. "Don't leave. They're going to arrest the kids the moment you do."

"Huh?" Impossible! This was a perfectly lawful, orderly assembly of representatives addressing their constituents from the Capitol steps, a standard practice with plenty of precedent. The police don't have any jurisdiction here. All this was going on while Dellums was speaking.

And then I turned around and lo and behold, the police *were* arresting the people. Not only that, I found out, but they had started arresting them while *I* was speaking, violating not only their rights, but *mine.*

I got hold of James Powell, the Capitol police chief. "This is outrageous," I said. "Why are you arresting them? They only came here because we agreed to greet them and accept the People's Peace Treaty. You can't arrest them. You didn't even give them any notice."

"Yes we did," he said. "We notified them on a bullhorn. And they should have heard it."

"Well I didn't hear it! And if I didn't, how could they? Give them notice now before you make any more arrests."

"It's too late," he said, "we've already begun."

Cornelius Gallagher of New Jersey and Ogden Reid of Westchester joined me in trying to persuade the police, but they still wouldn't listen to us, so I went and found Jerry Wilson, the city's chief of police, and yelled at him. He gave me the same crap. Later I found out that Carl Albert had okayed the arrests. "This is punitive and vicious," I told Wilson. "Nobody even warned these kids. This is outrageous." I started heading for the Congressmen who were hovering around, afraid to come near, as if they would be poisoned and destroyed forever if they opened their mouths. One guy I gave it to was Roman Pucinski from Illinois.

"My God," I said, "the Constitution is being destroyed in your presence. Don't you men believe in the Constitution? Don't you care about civil liberties?" I was trying to remain as cool as I could, but it wasn't easy.

"How are they violating constitutional rights?" Pucinski asked guardedly.

"They're interfering with the right of petition, that's how—for a start."

Meanwhile, the police were getting uptight. One Senator had to punch a cop in the nose just to get through, and Dellums got into a big hassle, saying he was shoved and pushed because he was regarded as a "nigger."

I came back to my office and started calling everybody I could think of to get some redress of the situation. Twelve hundred kids had been arrested. There were some Congressmen I was very annoyed at because they didn't get involved. A couple came to my office to talk it over. What can I say? People make political decisions. The only ones who did get involved were three blacks and a woman, which is a pretty interesting way to look at it. One oppressed group, I guess, has an understanding of another.

I never made it to New York. Dora Friedman, who's an old hand at addressing rallies, read my speech for me at Bryant Park. I got hold of a few ACLU attorneys and we filed a writ for habeas corpus, alleging the illegality of the arrests by police, alleging police interference with petitions for redress of grievances at a lawful assembly. The four of us went to court and Don Edwards of California joined us. There were, as usual, all sorts of legal technicalities and bickering about jurisdictions, and while I was waiting at the courthouse I went into the cellblocks where I discovered an outrageous situation. One group of thirty demonstrators had been jammed in one small cell for thirty hours—without ever having gone before a judge. I came up and told the government's lawyers about this, and they let the demonstrators out. But that's about the extent of the satisfaction I got. The lawyers were still arguing over federal versus city jurisdictions until finally I exploded, "I don't give a damn whose jurisdiction this is in. It's an offense against these people. You've arrested them while they were exercising their constitutional rights. Let them all out!" In the meantime, a three-judge panel of the Court of Appeals had affirmed a lower court ruling that the police had acted improperly on Monday by making arrests without filling in arrest forms and without making specific charges.

We hung around the court until midnight when the judge finally granted that there had been some denial of equal protection, but that our case was premature until those arrested were formally charged.

I was disgusted. "This is a time which required a man and a judge to stand up," I told the judge, "and it was obviously too important a position to put you in."

May 6

Today I came prepared for "The Children's Hour" because I *knew* what was going to happen. Sure enough, they pulled out all stops. They were more vicious than I had ever heard them. One guy got up and said that while he normally believed that all Congressmen should be treated equally, since we were all duly elected, there were some of us who had overstepped our bounds and should be dealt with accordingly. Edith Green from Oregon got up and said she doesn't believe that women have any greater interest in ending the war than men do, etc. She also attacked the kids.

Meanwhile, all this is going on and I'm saying to myself, "Where are the liberals?" I looked around and except for a few of them who weren't making a peep, they weren't there. Nobody defended *me*, the kids, or the other Congressmen involved. It was unbelievable. It was as though *we* had suspended the Constitution, as though *we* had violated the rights of people, as though *we* had kept this war going on. I got up and made my own remarks, accusing Nixon and Mitchell of being responsible for the suspension of the Constitution. "Apparently they feel that it is consistent to use illegal tactics to maintain an illegal war," I said.

I was pretty upset by Edith Green's speech. I don't believe that women should be pitting themselves against each other. I have never done it, and I will never do it. There are too few of us, and we're not each other's enemies, see. So after her speech, I went over to her and said, "You know, Edith, it was a great speech, but I disagree with every word of it—and you are so wrong."

It was a bad day on the women thing all around. In the morning, I tried to get all the women in Congress to attend a press conference to receive "Save Our Sons" petitions from some women in Massachusetts who were requesting a special meeting with Nixon to discuss peace. The only ones who accepted were Shirley Chisholm and Patsy Mink from Hawaii. All the others, including Edith, had sundry excuses.

May 7

Did I tell you what Hugh Scott said this week? A reporter was pressing him about the conditions under which the kids were incarcerated and he said, "Nobody in the Democratic Party was down there except Bella Abzug. She's the only man in the House."

Isn't that interesting? In his male terms, it must mean that I'm the only one who has any guts around here.

We're doing some barnstorming today. Altogether there are some twenty Congressmen on the road. I'm in Cleveland (Charlie Vanik is our host) with nine others, including Henry Reuss of Wisconsin and Don Riegle of Michigan (my favorite young Republican, we're really simpatico), both of whom I really enjoy. Some guys were in Connecticut yesterday. Some of us will be in Pittsburgh Monday, and some others in St. Louis on Tuesday.

Here in Cleveland today I made a speech at the Men's City Club which was televised. I also did a thing in the streets, I spoke to a labor group, to a business group, to a Jewish group, to a city group, to a women's group, to a senior citizens' group, I taped a couple of interviews, and I'm feeling great. Everybody I've talked to—and I mean *everybody*—is against the war, and we're showing it. Barnstorming's paying off. The whole purpose, of course, is to show reluctant Congressmen how the people really feel, and from what I heard a few of my colleagues who shall remain nameless are feeling the pressure, and good.

May 8

I went to a dinner at the University Settlement, one of the oldest on the Lower East Side, tonight, attended by some of the richest Jews in New York, many of whom do social work for the group. I got a kick out of Spyros Skouras who went around introducing me by saying, "This is the Congressman lady. She's for the mahhhhses."

The evening was a revelation. I thought I'd run into heavy backlash because of my defense of the Mayday kids. Instead, a lot of these elegantly dressed people came up to me and said, "Thanks for helping our children."

May 9

Mother's Day. I was determined to spend it with my mother, but from the moment I woke up the phone kept ringing with this person and that person wanting to know something or having to have something done that couldn't wait. At one point an old friend of mine—who should have known better—came and knocked on my door. I haven't seen her in quite a while, and this is how she greeted me: "Bella, the sewers are backed up in Bensonhurst, there are feces all over the street, and you've got to do something."

"I don't believe it," I said. "You come over here like this, barge into my private dwelling on Mother's Day as if I have no rights. Others maybe I'd expect it from. But you? You of all people should know how I'm killing myself."

"Bella, I had to come because I couldn't get you on the phone."

"Bensonhurst! That's in Brooklyn. It's not even in my district."

"Bella, we turn to you because there's no one else." *Those words again!*

"It's got to stop," I said. "Do you hear me? It's got to stop. I can't go on like this."

"Don't you understand, darling? People are turning to you in desperation."

Of course I understand. I'm the surrogate Mayor, I'm the surrogate Governor, I'm the surrogate President. None of these guys are doing what they should be doing, and none of them give the least bit of indication that they're even concerned. In the end I made the calls. Nobody was home, of course, and I gave the woman the numbers and told her to keep trying. In the meantime, I left messages.

It's not that I'm mean or inhuman, but as it is now, I have no time for myself. None whatsoever. I don't even have time to go to the bathroom. I also have had to cut myself off from people as a human being. Actually, sometimes I feel almost entirely unrelated to people. If I allow myself to become involved personally with them, feeling my own needs, my own emotions, then it takes away from the people I'm representing, the people who regard me as their spokesman—the kids, the women and the minorities. What's shocking is how many of these people relate to me in personal terms. I've talked about what I believe in so much that they are beginning to believe in it too, and in the process they have come to believe in me. It's gratifying, don't get me wrong. But it does give me this awful sinking feeling. I know, unlike many of them, that it takes more than magic to get things done. I wish they'd understand that.

The article about Friday's barnstorming in this morning's *Washington Post* had a very cute beginning: " 'Bug something or other,' said the man, trying to recall the name of Rep. Bella Abzug, whom he had just met on downtown Euclid Street. 'Osbug, bellbug, oh, I forget. But I like her. She's against the war and so am I.' "

Finally, later in the day I got to see my mother. She's coming along pretty well, and I was happy to see her in such good spirits.

"Bella," she said. "I hear you're running for President."

"You too," I said. "Of course you were saying that before anybody."

"Listen," she said. "My advice is don't run. Nixon is going to be reelected. You can't beat him."

Later we took her to the French-Roumanian restaurant on Delancey Street for dinner. Helene and Harry and their kids were there too. As a Mother's Day gift we bought Mama a nice dress and shawl, but Martin left them in the car without locking it and they were stolen. That's life in America. A few months ago our apartment was robbed. They stole portable things they could turn into quick cash—a record player, cameras, things like that—because they were obviously dope addicts. We've since barred the windows.

May 10

I've been thinking it's really disgusting how few liberals came out to help the demonstrators last week. You see, they are scared. On the one hand, they want to be considered as having a strong point of view, but on the other, they don't want to associate themselves with the anger and frustration in the country. As far as they're concerned, it's proper to protest only in words and letters. Any other tactic is questionable. Anything more adventurous, and they run.

Oh yes, in small ways sometimes they do show a sense of inner bravery. But the times require a lot more guts than that. They're too damn cautious. The people are way ahead of them.

I had as much at stake—in many ways—as they did in getting involved with these demonstrators. There are a lot of women across the country who look to me for leadership, and many of these women have nowhere near the advanced views I have on the war. Yet I feel I have to bring these women along, even at the cost of sacrificing some of my popularity. This is the difference between leadership and nonleadership.

(Incidentally, *The New York Times* ran an editorial criticizing Edith Green for her speech attacking the kids.)

Something else that's becoming clear: There's no question that the power structure down here is beginning to feel a bit threatened by people like me and Ron Dellums. For one reason, mainly—we're able to trigger a lot of reaction from the outside. What this means, really, is that we reflect what's going on in the country, and they don't.

As for me, it isn't just that I'm different than they are. It's that I come out of a movement of people and not out of some limited hierarchy or club that dictates that you're down here for a career and therefore have an interest in keeping things as they are. They don't even give it a thought that they're supposed to respond to what people are demanding. They're too busy making little deals and compromises among themselves.

I'll tell you what's killing them more than anything else about me: they can't pigeonhole me. They don't understand me because they see I'm multidimensional. I confuse them. They see that I'm a perfectly reasonable human being when they'd like to be able to call me a wild nut. One moment they see me outside with the demonstrators and the next moment I'm inside diligently working within the legislative process. And I don't allow myself to be intimidated by them. I'm as friendly as can be; I talk about the weather, about how I feel, about how they feel, about the problems of being mothers and fathers. I go to committee meetings, do my homework, question witnesses and have a very good attendance record on the Floor. I never lose my cool in debate, I'm consistent, I'm very responsible about not missing votes and so on. This drives them up the wall! They expect me to be totally iconoclastic, without relief, totally scornful, unable or unwilling to function within the arena of legislation—and I'm not. So that's what I think is driving them crazy.

May 11

The proselytizer ventured into hostile territory tonight. I made a speech to the Federal Bar Association, which is made up of government lawyers, and told them that the Administration's use of mass arrests and preventive detention last week constituted a terrible danger to our civil liberties, and I called on the House Judiciary Committee to investigate. I also said that as for John Mitchell's recent statement likening the demonstrators to brown-shirted Nazis, "To those of us who remember the mass arrests and concentration camps of the Hitler regime, it is obvious that Mitchell, not the demonstrators, was emulating the Nazis."

Pretty strong stuff for government lawyers to swallow, but by the time I finished they were asking for more. That's because of the way I handle a situation like this. To begin with, I know I have to win them over, so I adjust my tone and presentation to loosen them up. That means, at least when I start out, I have to be completely spontaneous. Let me give you an example: The young man who introduced me tonight gave me one of those she-needs-no-introduction welcomes and went on to say simply that I was the Congresswoman from the eleventh district in New York.

So when I got up, I said, sounding disappointed, "You're not going to make any comments about me?" I paused, and there was laughter. "Well, okay, but you ought to know that it's the *nineteenth* district, not the *eleventh*. I can see why you have no comments." More laughter. "Anyway, I realize you asked me here to talk about women's rights, but it so happens that I'm not in the mood to discuss the difference in our chromosomes . . ."

They laughed again, and I went on to tell them a few jokes until I sensed they were loose enough to be hit hard with what I really wanted to say. All this is not as easy as it sounds. You've got to plug yourself into the audience, sensing its reaction—something in the waves—and go from there. It's a completely emotional thing with me; I can't explain how I do it, except to say that it's the difference between one who is a natural public speaker and one who isn't. I'm always changing the style, the tone and the nature of my talk to suit the audience so that it will accept what I have to say. At mass rallies, where everybody's already in agreement with me, I try to move them further along. Other times I try to mobilize them. Other times I try to influence them, such as tonight.

Understand something, though: Although I'm always prose-lytizing my audiences, I never change the *substance* of what I have to say to do it, like some guys do. The style may change, but never the message.

May 13

Mary Perot Nichols has printed some real political bullshit about me in this week's *Village Voice*. She starts out by saying that "Bella Abzug's campaign to embarrass Democratic Congressmen who sometimes miss sessions of the Democratic Caucus backfired a few weeks ago." Then she says, in reference to the April 21 caucus, that I berated Ron Dellums "angrily" for not showing, and he told me, "Shut up! You white elite motherfucker."

Well, she wasn't there and she completely missed the point. Ron and I are very good friends, and we joke a lot. We have our disagreements—mostly in terms of approach—because he chooses to use Congress more as a platform, and I as both a platform *and* a vehicle to get things done. Well, I was kidding him, see, and his comeback was purely a joke. There was nothing angry about it, Mary.

Mary's reasons for printing this tale are very evident to me. She has one candidate, and one candidate alone: Ed Koch, and he happened to be abroad when the caucus met.

No matter what Mary suggests, all I'm interested in is seeing that everybody's at the caucus to make sure we have the strongest possible showing against the war.

Shirley Chisholm and I introduced our own child care bill today, held a press conference on it and testified before the Select Subcommittee on Education of the House Committee on Education and Labor. We've been waiting to do this for a long time, having been persuaded to wait by some other people who were trying to put together a broad coalition to get more support. But the bill these other people have come up with is short on emphasizing the needs of all women (it provides services mostly for the very poor), doesn't provide adequately for coverage in small communities and doesn't specify how much money will be needed.

In our bill we ask for a $5, $8 and $10 billion annual appropriation over a three-year period, which even though some guys warn is politically unrealistic, is still far short of the $28 billion we need to institute a universal child care program. We need $8 billion just to provide facilities for children of those women who are *already working.*

Our bill has some essential features: We provide for twenty-four-hour child care facilities; we give the parents a voice; we prohibit sex discrimination in the administration of the program; we clearly establish a formula for moving toward universally available child care, which is vital to make it possible for all women to function totally in society.

What the bill will do to establish the principle of comprehensive child care and at the same time establish an initial priority for poor people is this: 65 percent of all money in the first year, 60 percent in the second and 55 percent in the third will be available to families earning beneath the poverty level. This way the poor won't be neglected and at the same time we'll be establishing the right of all families, poor or not, to use public child care facilities. If they can afford to, of course, I agree they have to pay some fees. But if we make this a "for the poor only" program, we'll end up with segregated nurseries.

Since Shirley is on the education committee, we hope to strengthen the committee bill with provisions from our bill and bring pressure on the committee as it marks up the bill.

Obviously, in terms of money, we're asking for more than we expect to get. But a lot of men have become women-conscious in their voting habits these days, and it's important that we push to the limit. The Nixon Administration right now only spends $500 million on child care, which is barbaric.

This afternoon a group from the Young Americans for Freedom, a reactionary group of kids, came to proselytize me in my office against China's admission to the UN. I like to keep my door open. Even though I don't have time for that kind of stuff, I talked to them at length, longer than most of their friends. It reminded me of a previous experience I had with YAF members during the campaign when they took over the Women Strike for Peace office in New York and locked the staff out. We called in the cops, and since some of the women suspected a few items in the office might be missing, we asked them to search the kids. "We don't know whether we have the right to search them or not," said the cops, who, I believe, were really in cahoots with the kids.

"Okay," I said. So I asked the kids to empty out their pockets themselves.

They did. There was nothing in them. Then I said, "Now, what are you doing here?"

"We came to read a statement as to why we should not withdraw from Vietnam and as to why nobody should support you for Congress."

"So read it, already," I said.

They read it.

"Okay," I said. "You read it. Now beat it, understand? And the next time you want to debate you make an appointment to meet me in the streets or in a public hall, because if you dare come in here again like this, you won't get off so easily."

They left.

May 18

Of all people, I bumped into Richard Ichord this afternoon in the elevator.

"What are you up to?" I asked the chief witch-hunter, as if I didn't know.

"Oh," he said, "just investigating some of your pals."

May 19

Esther, my administrative assistant, quit on me tonight, and I'm very uptight about it. I hollered and screamed at her like crazy. She's decided the job is too tough for her, and I'm too tough. I don't know. She's strictly a campaign worker. She's taken a job to work with the Muskie campaign in New York.

The campaign thing is totally different from running an office, which demands exactness and coordination, which she doesn't have the background for. She's terrific with campaigns, but I've been pretty critical of the way she's been managing the office. Also, from her point of view, I don't think she wanted to be tied to an office, and she hated Washington, especially the social life.

There are no great loyalties among young people today. It's all inward—you know—what one does for oneself first. Sure, I was hard on her. I'm hard on everybody, including myself. Anybody who works with me knows that—they should even expect it because I make it a point to warn them. I make tremendous demands on myself, and therefore I make tremendous demands on others. But for some reason young people, idealistic as they are, need more rest than I do.

There's nothing unusual about Esther leaving, lest you think there is. It happens all the time. L.A.s and administrative assistants always come and go down here. It's very hard to put a good staff together and have it mesh—especially if you're new. It takes time.

Democratic caucus time again this morning. My office worked like dogs to get a quorum, but, as usual, a quorum was called and we were short. I'll tell you these guys are incorrigible. It's funny; some say it's because of Andy Jacobs and others say it's because of me that they're staying away.

May 20

This morning I felt awful about yelling at Esther last night and I apologized to her when I saw that she was practically in a catatonic state. That broke the tension, and I suppose we'll be friendly again.

Mary Perot Nichols is at it again. This week she writes that Shirley Chisholm intends to run for President or Vice President which will "put her into conflict with another prominent lady in politics, Representative Bella Abzug, who is also telling friends that she intends to be a Presidential candidate."

I'm not running for President, everybody knows that. Not that I would make such a terrible President, but, you know, it isn't a reality. I've never said I was running for President to anybody. Shirley—yes—has said she's *considering* it, but how dare Mary Perot Nichols suggest I'm running too.

What's probably burning her up is that everywhere I go

(159)

around the country people yell out, "Bella for President." That's not *my* fault. I always say, "My mother thinks so too," and that's the extent of it. I'm not projecting a candidacy—even for pressure purposes—and furthermore it's ridiculous for Mary to make out that there's some kind of conflict between Shirley and me. I'm very close to her, just as I am to Ron Dellums.

May 22

There was a tremendous response at a hastily prepared rally in Riverside Park at noon to protest a bill in Albany that would destroy the park in order to build a new eight-lane truck highway, another monument to Rockefeller's "Edifice Complex." All the West Side leaders and legislators were there. It looks like we might win this one. People are fed up with the way their communities are being torn apart to make more room for cars, which are the last thing we need more of in Manhattan.

After the rally I came back to the office and had a very upsetting conversation with Betty Friedan, who used to head the National Organization of Women. Gloria Steinem, Shirley Chisholm and I have this major difference of opinion with Betty as to what the nature of a women's political movement should be. She seems to think we should support women for political office no matter what their views, and we don't. I feel our obligation is to build a real political movement of *women for social change*. I don't think we're at the level where we have to fight to get just *any* woman elected, especially if she turns out to be a Louise Hicks.

But because she tends to regard herself as "the" leader of the women's movement, Betty is impossible sometimes. This may be why she's made it appear as if there are all kinds of differences between us. What distresses me most is that I know deep down that Betty understands politics in the same way I do. This is why I can't understand what she's up to. It doesn't add up.

Now, don't get me wrong about Betty, please. All women owe her a great debt because she helped revive the whole women's movement in this country. She stimulated a revolt among the bored and frustrated middle class suburban housewives, and that led to the organization of groups like NOW. She's been part of the "consciousness-raising" among women that's given some foundation for the political movement we're now talking about. All I'm beginning to wonder is if she realizes that forming a political movement is a more complicated thing than giving lectures, writing books, having one-shot demonstrations and press conferences and appearing on the *Dick Cavett Show*. It takes a lot more than that—it takes organizing and a real knowledge of how the political machinery works.

May 23

Just to give you an idea of how hard it is to be a Congresswoman in my district, in the midst of a number of appointments this afternoon I discovered there was a tremendous block party in the Village. And it wasn't even on my drop-in schedule. My office is so overburdened these days they can't keep up with the nitty-gritty. But you've got to know about these things—even if it's impossible to make them.

Late in the day I flew to Washington to address the Day Care and Child Development Council, and I don't know how it happened, but when I walked off the plane my back started to hurt. If you're fatter than you should be, I guess you sprain muscles like that.

So after the speech I went directly to Bethesda to have it treated, and of course my old friends there tried to get me to stay. I told them I couldn't, but the whole thing has made me determined to go on a diet, finally.

May 27

This is a very bad moment. The city's in bankruptcy, the state's killing us, and the federal government isn't doing a damn thing. We've lost every important effort to get some money out of Congress, and with all the cutbacks in the city, the poor people are suffering worse than ever. Revenue sharing, which a lot of guys think is The Answer, hardly excites me. I don't like handing out money to the states with no strings attached, plain and simple. If Rockefeller gets any more federal money, he's not likely to rush to hand New York a fair share. What we need instead are funds directly committed to health, jobs, housing, schools, child care, narcotics, etc.

The source of many of our problems locally—as the state proceeds to systematically kill the city—is Rockefeller, who's turned into a flaming reactionary. He and I are polite with each other, but we're not on the same side, and we never will be.

There's an interesting story about when our paths crossed as we were both campaigning on the Lower East Side, where the people dislike him immensely because he's never built those drug rehabilitation centers he promised, and because he seems largely unconcerned about the fact that their homes are falling down and there's garbage all over the streets. They have so little use for him, as a matter of fact, that when he tried to speak to the crowd, they wouldn't let him. They simply booed him. First he tried in English; then in Spanish. But they didn't want to listen.

So I explained to him: "Governor," I said, "the reason

they won't listen to you is that you haven't ever done what you said you would do to build drug rehabilitation centers and housing, and while their homes are collapsing, you're building a billion-dollar mall in Albany."

"Then *you* get them to listen to me," he said.

So he had me jump on the trunk of an abandoned car, and he followed me up. I told the crowd, "Let him speak. Listen to him, and then we'll answer him."

They did.

Afterwards we had a debate—right there on the top of the car. In the middle of the thing it was discovered that there were some Arthur Goldberg (he was the Democratic candidate for Governor) people in the crowd who were egging everybody on.

Later on Goldberg, not having a lot of guts, apologized profusely for the situation and managed to turn an anti-Rocky day into a pro-Rocky day by dismissing the two middle echelon staffers who were among the demonstrators. I had to fight with the press just to justify my role in it, since the implication was that I was a heckler too. That's politics. The fact of the matter is that I made it possible for Rockefeller to speak in the first place. I'm no heckler, me.

Anyhow, our picture hit the front page of the *News*, and apparently the whole episode made a big impression on the Rocky entourage. Whenever we meet, it's referred to as one of their great days.

Another meeting this afternoon in my New York office on this business of forming a national women's political movement. In spite of some arguing between me and Betty, I think we're beginning to reconcile things. About a dozen women, including Gloria Steinem, Elly Guggenheimer and a few from Rockefeller's Women's Unit, came, and we all seem to want the same thing.

(163)

The movement is now growing in such proportions that it's going to require leadership from a lot of different elements. Furthermore, if we're going to institute a real women's program, which is what this is all about, we need politically-oriented leadership, and I don't think Betty fully understands politics.

You know, it's nice to say that by 1976 we're going to have two hundred women in Congress, but do we want the kind of women who are going to vote for missiles and Vietnam wars? Or do we want the kind of women who are going to put our tax money into housing and health and child care centers and abortion clinics and things like that?

It's a crucial point, and the differences between Betty and me have to be handled delicately. We can't afford a split in the movement under any circumstances. We're going to have a meeting next month in Washington to hash things out and to plan for a really big meeting this summer for women from all over the country.

May 28

The legislature has just passed the vacancy decontrol bill, which ends rent control in New York City while extending it elsewhere in the state. As far as I'm concerned, this is absolutely the last straw. This session of the legislature has been an utter disaster. While New Yorkers have had to stand by helplessly, Rockefeller, the billionaire Governor, Perry Duryea, the lobster wholesaler from Montauk who's the Assembly Speaker, and Earl Brydges, the lawyer from a small town near the Canadian border who's the Majority Leader, have joined together in inflicting one blow after another on the city.

It's disgusting. The legislature decreed inhumane cuts in health services, education and welfare, slapped us with a higher sales tax, imposed an unconstitutional one-year residency requirement for welfare assistance, wiped out thousands of city jobs and has now topped it all off with vacancy rent decontrol, which, in effect, makes New Yorkers prisoners in their apartments. No one will dare move because rents will go out of sight once they're decontrolled.

In his tyrannical attitudes and utter disregard for the needs of the people, Rockefeller is like George III, the British monarch. As a matter of fact, as a reaction to him, there's now a revolutionary spirit in New York City comparable to what must have been felt in the Thirteen Colonies when they rebelled for essentially the same reasons—taxation without representation.

This morning Mim Kelber and I, whose assistance as cothinker I could not do without, had a long talk in my house and we decided, once and for all, that something has got to be done before they destroy the city from under us. And I'm going to do it.

I am going to have a press conference next Tuesday at the end of this Memorial Day weekend to set in motion the machinery that can free New York City and establish it as its own state. We're moving immediately because there's no more time. And we're taking this course because we have to organize the city as its own entity so people can fight together instead of each group fighting for its own little packages, as has long been the case. After all, we're all in this mess together. The legislature oppresses *all* New Yorkers.

Just as we need social change, we need structural change. We've got to bring government up to date. It's insane to try to live under the same governmental structures set up nearly two hundred years ago. We in New York are being denied the basic right of self-government. The city continues to die because the state government has been captured by the reactionaries who have systematically set out to deprive us of benefits from our taxes, and to ignore the needs of the poor and middle income people at the expense of catering to the vested interests of the rich. It's insane; it's stupid. We've got to demand the right to govern ourselves in order to stop it. It's the basic right of self-determination we're going to be asking for, that's all. Do we want to run our own great city, or do we want to let a billionaire Governor, a lobster wholesaler and a lawyer from a small town near the Canadian border run it for us?

The idea to make New York City a state, in case you didn't know, is not original with me. There's been a long struggle for more "home rule," which, although it hasn't focused on statehood, has sought to get us more control over taxes, services and decision-making. Statehood was first proposed by the Mayor of New York in 1861; it was later advocated by such people as William Randolph Hearst and by William F. Buckley in his campaign for Mayor in 1965. Most people, however, will remember the statehood idea as it was first put forth in Norman Mailer's campaign for Mayor in 1969. He gave the idea some pzazz, but not enough people took it seriously.

May 29

My staff is urging me to hold off on announcing the statehood drive. They want me to set up preliminary meetings, investigations and whatnot before I get myself into a full-blown thing. Well, I'm not going to listen to them. As far as I'm concerned, we have a severe problem in New York City right now, and it requires an immediate response.

You see, this is the difference between me and almost everybody else. I'm an activist. I want action—not talk. You can't just sit around and think or talk and expect to get anywhere. It's not that I don't *think*. Of course I do. But my thing is

(166)

doing. I don't go around philosophizing. I go around *doing.* If I permitted myself to sit around and write long treatises and involve myself in philosophical discussions, I'd only get bogged down—just like everybody else. Instead, I move instantly, prepared to take risks.

I can do this, I feel, because I have a sense of where it's at, of where people are, a sense of how people will respond at a given moment to a given thing. And right now most New Yorkers are bursting with anger at what Albany did to them.

Something else too: I know that if I wait on this statehood thing, there are going to be a lot of ideas, a lot of diversions, a lot of counterproposals, a lot of movements and a lot of efforts to mobilize for this thing and for that thing, the end result being that nothing will come off. If some people oppose the idea of making the city a separate state, fine. Let them offer their own proposals. At least we'll get a debate *on the issues.* But in the meantime, since I'm going to go ahead with my plans, we'll have a movement off and rolling. If somebody comes up with a better idea, we'll change the focus—without having to sacrifice the momentum.

See, one of the biggest problems in our society is that we don't have an organized ready-made political movement of a vast nature that can develop issues like this. We have to create one for each new issue. And since this country is of the nature where everybody's always doing his thing to a point where you can't get all the little things together, I'm not going to give this idea time to splinter before it's even formally proposed. I hope my action, in announcing the statehood drive, will have the effect of coalescing different groups of people, some of whom are interested in better housing, some of whom are interested in more jobs, some of whom are interested in cleaner streets, some of whom want adequate sanitation and police protection. I'd like to bring them all into this larger movement for a larger purpose.

Today we prepared a telegram and sent it out to get support

(167)

from other Congressmen, city legislators, community leaders, borough presidents and anybody who we think will help us, in one way or another, to take this idea to the millions of Johns and Janes who are suffering in the city.

May 30

After a very abbreviated rest in Connecticut, I had to come back tonight for a meeting on statehood. I just don't have any time for myself anymore. My staff doesn't understand that I can't permit myself to be beaten over the head by everybody. My scheduler beats me, my staff beats me, my constituents beat me, my friends beat me—telling me I'm beating everyone else. If things go on like this, I won't make it.

May 31

The big press conference is tomorrow, and I spent most of the day preparing. The response to our telegrams has been tremendous.

June 1

My statement began, "Governor Rockefeller and his state legislature have disenfranchised and disinherited the eight million people of New York City." And in the press conference, which I felt was the best one I've had since I've been in Congress, I pointed out some very interesting facts:

There are forty-three existing states with populations smaller than New York City's. Therefore if we were admitted to statehood, we'd rank as the seventh largest state.

New York City's budget is second in size only to that of the

(168)

federal government. The city's current budget is $7.8 billion, but it sends more than $11.9 billion in taxes to the U.S. government and $2.7 billion to the state. For every dollar we give Washington, we get back 12.6 cents. For every dollar we give the state, we get back 66 cents. If we were to retain all the taxes we now pay Albany, we'd have an immediate net gain of almost $1 billion. In addition, we'd have complete taxing authority, including the right to tax commuters who are now free-loading off the city. And as a state, we'd also get a direct and larger share of federal revenues. We'd also gain two Senators.

Further facts: New York City's police department is larger than the entire federal law enforcement force. New York City runs and largely pays for by itself a university that ranks as the fifth largest in the world. In fact, our educational system, our fire department and our police force are each as large as all their counterparts in the rest of the state combined. And yet— we're totally at the mercy of the state. Not only can we not change our tax base without Albany's permission, but we can't even change the working hours of our policemen.

The Governor and the state legislature have kicked the city around to the point where hospital and health services have to be cut, drug addiction rehabilitation programs shut down and thousands of city jobs and vital programs eliminated. The educational system has had to take a budget beating, welfare payments have had to be slashed to 88 cents a day for food, and now the sales tax is going to go up to 7 percent in New York City. In its final gesture of contempt, the legislature doomed rent control for us in the city and extended it to other parts of the state.

Four-fifths of all Americans live in cities, and yet we have to suffer like this? Most of the big cities, like New York, are on the verge of bankruptcy, because all these years the political power in this country—both in Congress and in state governments—has been in the hands of rural, small town and, in-

(169)

creasingly, suburban interests. That's why we should become a state. If we're going to survive at all, we need to bring political structures into harmony with political reality.

Some reporters wanted to know if there was any precedent for a new state being carved out of an existing state. The answer is yes, and it's provided for in the U.S. Constitution. Both Kentucky and West Virginia were once part of Virginia. Vermont was once in New York State, and Maine was separated from Massachusetts.

They also wanted to know the procedure by which we would go about seeking statehood. This is how it works:

First we have to circulate petitions to get the statehood question on the November ballot. This means by September 3, we'll need 45,000 valid signatures, and maybe another 20,000 in case some of the signatures are ruled invalid. The November referendum will then give voters the opportunity to call for creation of a constitutional convention composed of elected delegates. If the voters approve the referendum, delegates are elected. Within forty-five days after their election— which, incidentally, will be nonpartisan—a constitutional convention will be required to convene. Then, once they draw up the new constitution, it will be submitted to the voters for approval. If the new constitution is approved, we must then secure permission from the New York State legislature to create ourselves as a new state, and then get a majority vote in Congress to approve the action.

Complicated it is. But it's also possible, and I think our chances are far better than most people realize—if the vested interests don't get too uptight about the possibility of *real* change. Statehood is the kind of issue around which *all* New Yorkers— no matter what their politics—can coalesce. Just listen to the names of some of the people who've already telegrammed their support: Shirley Chisholm, Congressmen Bill Ryan and Joe Addabbo, Manhattan Borough President Percy Sutton, State Senators Manfred Ohrenstein and Abraham Bernstein, Assemblymen Al Blumenthal, Leonard Stein and Richard Gott-

fried, Councilwoman Aileen Ryan and six other city coun-
cilmen, twenty-two district leaders, and a number of other
prominent citizens and political leaders—whose names are
being added to the list by the minute. The response has been
overwhelming.

I should mention that there have been a few people who say
they disagree with the idea. One Congressman, for instance.

"Why are you against it?" I asked him.

"Because there are already too many states," he said.
Imagine that!

A few others, more sensibly, said they're not sure how they
feel, except that they'd like to include a more diversified area
than New York City in any new state, so that we don't ghettoize the city. I happen to agree with that. I think having Westchester, Nassau and Suffolk counties with us would be
important. But we don't have the authority to start a referendum campaign in the suburbs—they have to do it themselves.
And besides, even if these people want the suburbs in the new
state, they should at least be out and around now getting the
whole process started.

June 2

The statehood campaign is going to be a big organizing job,
and we're going to need lots of money and help. Unfortunately,
I'm terrible at raising money. As a matter of fact, my lack of
fund-raising abilities almost made me decide not to run for
office. See, I can't sell myself *per se*. I can sell my causes, but
only emotionally and politically. I'm not sure I can sell them
financially any more than I can sell myself. But we'll soon see.

June 3

I can't let a moment go by without keeping my eyes wide
open, which I guess is another one of my burdens. Like in the

debate on the space program, the NASA authorization bill. One of the items was $125 million to research a space shuttle system. I proposed an amendment to cut that out of the bill. The reason I did this is because of a report from the Rand Corporation, which stated that the shuttle program will only be cost-effective if we decide to fund an expanded manned space program, which, of course, is the last thing we need at this moment. Anyway, NASA itself has been talking about an *unmanned* space program. If we're going to spend money for science and technology, we should be spending it to wipe out hunger and poverty and clean up the air and water, not to land more men on the moon. They're up to no good with this space program. This $125 million will only lead to $12 billion to institute the shuttle and $75 billion for the whole extravagant program. And if we give them the money to start, they'll turn around and tell us—as they tried to with the SST—that they can't stop after they've invested all that money. Which is baloney.

As you can guess by now, the liberals weren't around, and the ones who were were too tired to do anything. They weren't interested in leading a big attack on the space program. Even the guy who led a similar attack last year didn't want to get involved. So I got only sixty-four votes for my amendment. And that's not even the worst of it: Nobody but me got up and talked against the shuttle. Further proof that the liberals are routed. They're all full of hang-ups. They win one thing like the SST, and they don't have any energy left for anything else. It makes you feel pretty cynical just watching them.

June 4

Our anniversary. It's twenty-seven years that Martin and I have been married, and for the occasion my staff was kind enough to schedule me to have dinner with my family. But we had some trauma before this dinner.

Naturally, whenever your children are involved, there's always a little trauma. Liz had tickets for the theater at 7:30 and Egee had a date at 8:30. Martin, not realizing that they both had to meet their friends uptown, brought us all to a restaurant downtown. By the time the girls realized what he was doing, it was too late to turn around, and the traffic was terrible. So the girls, of course, were all upset, which got us upset, until finally I just said, "Listen, kids, you're on your own. Do what you want. After all, it's *our* anniversary, not yours."

And that did it. We went uptown, picked up their dates and we all had dinner together at the Press Box. So it turned out nice.

Afterwards I had a meeting scheduled at Ronnie Eldridge's house with Dick Aurelio, the Deputy Mayor, and various other Lindsay assistants on the matter of the relationship between them and us on the statehood campaign.

When Mim and I arrived at Ronnie's, nobody—including Ronnie—was there, except for her kids. So I started storming around, talking about the arrogance of City Hall. You can imagine—I was furious. And this was my anniversary yet. Who did they think they were?

Whereupon Ronnie arrived and announced, "The meeting's been canceled."

"What!" I said.

"They've been trying to call you in Washington *and* in New York, and all over," she said. "I can't understand how you didn't know about it."

I got mad and went on to attack her and City Hall, until finally she and Mim calmed me down. So we tried to have a discussion. But Ronnie insisted, as she has all along, that an idea Lindsay has about chartering "national cities" is better than the fifty-first state.

Mim and I left, very discouraged.

(173)

June 6

They beat me today, I must admit. The occasion was graduation at Tufts University in Boston. It was, as I told them, a
graduation with vengeance, too hot a day, too long a ceremony
and too dull a program.

How I got myself into it, I don't know. First of all, I don't
like to do graduations. They're sad. After all, what are these
kids graduating to? And then, I was under the mistaken impression I was to speak at the regular commencement ceremonies of the School of Law and Diplomacy. It turns out,
though, that I was not invited to speak at the regular commencement, but at a special commencement staged by the students
themselves *after* the regular ceremony. Meanwhile, I'm sitting in the sun busting. All I could think was, "Who got me
into this one?" Then a little girl came up to the platform and
brought me a rose—and I forgot the heat for a while.

By the time they got to my speech I thought I would pass
out. When I got up there, I started telling a few jokes—because I had to stir myself up and get some reaction. In the
end, as always, it went well. The speech itself was a tough one,
especially hard on Nixon and the big corporations. A lot of
the parents came up to me later, identified themselves as
conservatives, and then said they agreed with me!

June 7

It must have been the hottest day of the year and I had to
drive in a car without air conditioning to the Concord Hotel
in the Catskill Mountains for a B'nai B'rith women's conference. All to get a Quality of Life Award, or something like
that. I don't know what, I forget. I didn't want to go. I don't
have time to get awards. But my staff insisted I go because it

(174)

would improve my "Jewish" image. Me—improve my Jewish image. Can you imagine? They can't get over that garbage from the campaign.

So sure enough I arrived there and saw this guy handing out an anti-Bella piece of paper about Israel and the Soviet Union. He had the gall to hand one to me. "Don't worry," I said to the guy. "I'm going to take care of these lies—and good."

And that's exactly what I did. I began my speech with a crack about how my mother always used to tell me to go to the Concord to find a fellow, preferably a doctor or a lawyer. "My mother will be pleased when she hears I finally made it up here," I said. That loosened them up. Then, since I had been introduced as living on Bank Street, I said, "I'm not really from Bank Street. I'm from the *Bronx*. I went to *Hebrew* school there and I used to teach *Hebrew* in the Kingsbridge Heights *Jewish* Center there. As a matter of fact, I did my first public speaking many, many years ago in the Bronx when I was a Zionist youth collecting money for the *Jewish* National Fund in *pishkes* in the subways."

I figured I took care of that guy's little of piece of paper about the anti-Semitic Bella Abzug. I demonstrated my *yiddishkeit*, and the audience loved it. Then I gave them a little women's lib and kidded them about their name, B'nai B'rith, which means "Sons of the Covenant." "Isn't it about time that you were called 'Daughters of the Covenant'?" I asked. We all roared.

June 8

I was going great on my diet for the past couple of weeks, but tonight I got agitated and I blew the whole damn thing. I was at a dinner party at the home of Congressman Scheuer in Washington where I fell into an awful discussion with the wife of Ed Morgan, the commentator. She was talking to a group of people about how hormonal changes, menstrual periods and menopause—as well as other physical factors—make it impossible for women to function like men.

"That's a myth," I quietly interrupted her.

"What did you say?" she asked.

"I said, 'That's a myth.' " More loudly, but still low key. I don't like to get into arguments with other women on these subjects. Luckily, Frank Mankiewicz, the columnist, was sitting next to me, and he explained to her that social, psychological and environmental factors have depicted women as the "weaker" sex when, in fact, as a physical reality they aren't.

At this point, Mrs. Bingham—wife of the Congressman—who was also listening, chimed in: "But it is true that women have physical differences which affect their ability to function. It's like, if either a man or a woman has something like hay fever, they can't function, right? Well, there are certain things only women get and they can't function in certain ways because of them."

"This whole issue is phony," I said. "It's not real. Environmental and psychological conditioning have a lot to do with the way people think they must behave with respect to their physical problems, but it's not for real. It's just used as a put-down of women."

I kept trying not to let myself get too worked up, which is why I was stuffing myself with food while all this was going on. Finally, Clayton Fritchey, the columnist, came to the rescue, beautifully, I thought, by saying, "Well, we men *without* our physical limitations haven't done such a great job in running this world, and I'm willing to let the women take it on."

I'm glad I went to the party though. It was fun, and I don't get to relax much these days.

(176)

June 9

We're on the way to organizing the Women's Political Caucus. We had a planning meeting this evening, and even more women turned up than we'd expected. I reserved one of the committee rooms on the Hill and had some food served. Shirley Chisholm and Patsy Mink were there, and spoke. Betty, Gloria Steinem, Mim, Ruth Meyers, Beulah Sanders, Jacqui Ceballos and a lot of other women from New York flew down. Some Republicans and churchwomen were there and, interestingly, Liz Carpenter (Lady Bird's press secretary) came with her daughter. Edith Van Horn of the United Auto Workers flew in from Detroit especially for the meeting, and I was pleased about that, because if this movement is going to get anywhere we're going to have to get working women involved. Also attending were a number of women from NOW's Washington chapter, women from black organizations, religious and social action groups, students from the local colleges. An interesting mix, but not good enough.

There was a lot of arguing back and forth, and we finally agreed that we had to organize a large and really representative initiating conference. We picked a date in July, which doesn't give us much time. But we really can't wait to do this any longer. I have a feeling we're going to do an awful lot of learning by trial and error.

June 11

I had to *schlep* myself to Westchester this afternoon to speak to a Women Strike for Peace luncheon up there, and I was annoyed. I mean, I love them, and they've been very good to me—both in terms of womanpower and money—all along, but they still think they need my personal presence and leadership. They know I don't have much time, especially to travel

(177)

an hour up there and an hour back, and they know I should be using what little time I have to influence people who don't already agree with me, and yet they insist I come to their luncheon. You figure it out. What am I going to tell them that they don't already know?

Besides, it takes a lot out of me to speak to groups like WSP because they *expect* so much. They're never satisfied with a small, reasonable speech. They only want to be moved to tears and passion. And I've been moving people to tears and passion for so long now that I can't do it anymore; it's killing me. They're busting my gut. They don't understand that I'm only one person.

But I can never say no to WSP. After all, I'm one of them and we've been through so much together. So it was a good speech. (I opened: "My remarks today should be very serious. You people already know I have a sense of humor.") When it was over, everybody was all worked up and they gave me a standing ovation. My friend Gil Wolman, with whom I went to Hunter (she now teaches psychology at Queens College), came along for the ride, and on the way home she said to me, "That was all right, Bella."

"What do you mean it was *all right*, Gil," I said. "What kind of remark is that?"

A remark, I guess, one gets from one's oldest friend.

On the way back I also stopped to do a little shopping at Alexander's in the Bronx, and that proved to be pretty impossible. I couldn't move a step without people jumping all over me, "Bella, Bella." One woman stood in front of me, looked me in the eye and said, "*Oy vey's mir*, it's Bella." Another one shouted to her husband, "Louis, Louis, come here quick, it's Bella." It was wild. I swear I could run for anything in the Bronx and get elected. Those people obviously do a lot of TV watching. How else do you explain strangers coming up to you as if they had known you all their lives? But this is the kind of thing that happens to me everywhere, except more so in the Bronx.

June 12

Some TV interviews on the fifty-first state. A ribbon-cutting ceremony for a shopping mall on West Seventy-second Street, right on the corner of the block where Martin and I lived when we were first married. More TV interviews, and a radio program on the fifty-first state. A speech to a conference of health workers. A typical Saturday. Not a moment to myself.

We've still not had that great meeting on statehood with City Hall. In the meantime, though, City Hall has announced that it's setting up a commission to study the possibility of statehood. I only found out about it from reading the newspapers. Protect me from my friends!

All I can say is that if City Hall thinks it's going to take a popular campaign and make it unpopular by putting its heavy hand on it, City Hall is mistaken. We've got our own committee, and we are going to make sure that the drive stays on a grass-roots level. If Mayor Lindsay wants to be a popular hero, let him do popular things. This is the first time I've been critical of him in a long time, and the reason, to be blunt, is that I don't feel he's behaving correctly.

He should have been leading the people en masse to Albany last month. He should have shut down the city in protest before laying off city employees because the state wouldn't approve his budget. He should have been out fighting, not as an individual, but with masses of constituents. He should have loaded them all on buses to the state capital and led them in a protest march. When the chips were down, again he didn't act. He showed us that John Lindsay isn't an activist. Activism requires more than rhetoric. He muffed it. Well, too bad. But you know what the sad thing is? I believe that if John Lindsay were operating by himself and on his own, he probably *would* be an activist. But some of the people he surrounds himself with keep him from being an activist. Lindsay would be a lot better off if he just followed his own instincts and ignored their advice.

They're bureaucrats, these advisers. They don't act; they study . . . and study . . . and study, and then they have a press conference. They've contributed to his problems all along. Right after his election in 1969—in which I served as chairman of the pro-Lindsay Taxpayer's Campaign for Urban Priorities—I *begged* him to set up a special activist branch of government, to be called the Urban Priorities Division. This division, as I saw it, would undertake to organize constituencies in an activist manner to support the things he was for. It was a fairly radical concept, yes, but something the times called for. I regarded this as a campaign promise, but he couldn't see the whole concept. In fact, our fight about this was one of the reasons I decided to run for Congress. I plainly told him, "You're not going to lead the people, so I will."

Now he sets up a commission to *study* the statehood concept, instead of coming right out and supporting it, and therefore really giving it a boost—as the people want and need.

The real reason I imagine he's not so hot about the statehood idea is that the national cities proposal gives him something to go around the country and talk about. He wants to be a national leader with a national platform. He wants to be President. He doesn't seem to understand that if he gets a movement for statehood started in New York City, it could easily be related to the needs of other big metropolitan areas across the country. Even if it doesn't succeed, the statehood issue can be a terrific educational and organizing tactic as well

(180)

as a way of directing mass pressure against Albany. Why can't he see that?

June 13

I marched with Herman Badillo this afternoon in the annual Puerto Rican Day parade. We were both at the head of the line, and the whole way we were greeted by shouts of "Badeyo! Badeyo!" interspersed with "Beya! Beya!"

Earlier in the parade there had been a big fracas between the Young Lords and the police, and there had been some violence, so that by the time we passed the grandstand, the militants were booing Herman. He said he disapproved of violence, and so on. When the press asked me if I did, I thought about it and said, "Well, as long as this country fails to meet the needs of the minorities, you're going to have different tactics of discontent—and this is one of them."

After the parade I was driven out to a Registration for Peace rally in Mineola, which Lowenstein, McCloskey and Michael Harrington had all managed to keep pretty subdued before I arrived. So I pepped it up. The kids went wild with enthusiasm for my speech. In the middle of it, it started to rain and they cut off the power. I continued speaking without a mike. Whereupon Peter Yarrow of Peter, Paul and Mary tried to save me by suggesting he play some music.

"Peter," I said, stopping and turning to him, "I love music. But not when I'm speaking."

June 14

An unusual Monday in the sense that I stayed in New York in order to raise money for the statehood campaign. Although we're getting thousands and thousands of responses, nobody seems to want to give us any money for it—as I had feared. So I sat and phoned all day and came up with about six or seven thousand dollars to run a full-page ad in *The New York Times*. I did everything to get it. I even borrowed. I convinced some people that they'd get their money back in no time because the response to the ad will be terrific. So, hopefully, the ad will end up paying for itself.

Tonight I got myself up in a long dress and big white hat and went to the mock political convention held by the New Democratic Coalition at the Plaza Hotel. One of the newspapers commented that Shirley MacLaine, Candice Bergen and I provided the sexy quality to the evening. Some comment!

What, you might be asking, is the New Democratic Coalition? They're former establishment Democrats turned reform Democrats turned establishment reform Democrats. They're the "outs" seeking "in." I'm a founder of the national NDC and the New York chapter so I ought to know.

Although the NDC had once hoped to, it has yet to become a real people's coalition. They were there first, but in the meantime, some of the main elements of that coalition—the women, the blacks, the young, the Chicanos—are organizing their own caucuses and building a coalition in their own way.

All the bigwigs were at the Plaza tonight, as well as a lot of rich people and hangers-on. The only reason I went is that they told me all the Manhattan Congressmen would be there. David Schoenbrun, the TV journalist and a good friend, acted as the convention chairman and he called on me to make up a big thing about the fifty-first state. But I was thrown because I couldn't decide whether I wanted to be humorous or serious, and as a result I was, sorry to say, neither. I was annoyed. I managed to make some very brief statements about three different subjects in two minutes, and then I walked out. The whole thing was silly. I felt like a fool.

June 16

No quorum again at the Democratic caucus. I had decided not to organize for this one, though, because a vote on the Nedzi-Whalen Amendment, which would prohibit the use of military procurement funds (for new weapons) in Vietnam after the end of the year, is coming up for a vote in the House tomorrow. I don't want all the liberals to pounce on me and say, "She's interfering with our chances on Nedzi-Whalen," so I laid low.

Anyway, all that happened today is that they decided that next month they're going to hold a special meeting to see what they're going to do about the fact that two items—mine and Andy Jacobs'—are tying up the caucus. In other words, they're going to hold a caucus on the caucus, because there is no caucus. The minute they come in, they call a quorum, and that's it. So it should be interesting to see what they're going to do to us.

Nedzi-Whalen will be the first time the issue of setting a date for United States withdrawal from Vietnam will be put directly to a vote in the House. It's an amendment to the $21 billion military procurement bill that would get our troops out by December 31, 1971—with a lot of "ifs" and "buts" attached. But weak as it is, it doesn't have a chance to pass, so I've been trying to figure out all week what I could do to dramatize the issue so that it just doesn't get voted on and lost in oblivion. What I've been doing is attempting to bring together a group of people to join in trying to tie up the House over the Nedzi-

Whalen Amendment so that we'll have time to build up a ground swell of popular support.

Before I go on any further about this, let me give you some background, because it's important. Unlike in the Senate, where almost endless and unrestricted debate is possible, in the House we are not free to raise issues as we want and debate them when we want. Every major piece of legislation that is brought to the Floor of the House is done so only at the whim of the all-powerful Rules Committee. It goes from the committee that "marks it up" directly to the Rules Committee, where it gets a "rule." They decide whether it will be debated for one hour, for three hours, for two days, with amendments allowed, without amendments allowed, with points of order, without points of order and so on. Even when amendments are permitted, you can only talk for five minutes for or against. Do you follow me? What I'm saying is that the Rules Committee—which is dominated by Southern reactionaries—dictates what bills come to the Floor, when they come to the Floor and how they come to the Floor. Also, all amendments and all debate must be "germane" to the item under consideration. Of course, anything they don't want to hear is ruled "non-germane."

If the House were like the Senate, it would be possible to bring certain matters into the public arena (through extended debate or filibuster) in order to develop support and pressure from the public. But since we don't have that power, what I've been looking for ever since I've been here are means by which we can tie up the House for as long as possible, and thus dramatize the issues at hand. I don't want to tie up the House simply for the sake of tying it up. I'm not a traffic cop. I'm only interested in tying up the House in situations where I think it's necessary to bring a special issue to focus. Such as Nedzi-Whalen.

Okay, so how do you do it? First of all, and most important, you need a core unit of about forty members to cooperate with

you. They aren't easy to find. A lot of the men around here—
I should say most—feel that if you're unable to win a majority
vote on an issue, why waste your time in tying up the House?
They believe that doing so might be counterproductive, maybe
even scare away votes. My theory is that it's not counterproductive or wasting time at all, because by tying up the House
you're *buying time* to allow pressure to build from the outside.
It's the old fundamental conflict: to compromise or not to
compromise. I feel that if you push and push and push without
compromise for the right position, then you're serving the
function of drawing attention to the politicians who are acting
outside the public interest by supporting legislation that
ignores the needs of human beings. Whereas when you compromise with these guys, you let them off very easily, because
most people never find out what they did and therefore they
can't be held accountable.

Okay, so say you have forty members willing to cooperate,
then what do you do? Well, what virtually makes it possible
for the House to function at all is the long-standing tradition
of agreeing to "unanimous consent" in doing away with certain time-consuming procedures and practices. So if we as a
unit decide we aren't going to give our unanimous consent
and waive these procedures, we can tie up the House, let me
tell you, and good. I have a list of forty-eight tactics to delay
proceedings, such as calling quorums, objecting to dispensing
with the reading of bills, demanding the reading of the previous day's journal (which is similar to the minutes of a meeting), objecting to every single "unanimous consent" request,
asking for roll call votes and so on.

Unfortunately, we're not really prepared yet to try some of
these things out on Nedzi-Whalen tomorrow. Mainly, we
didn't have enough time to recruit and orient enough members. Also, some of the pressure groups we called in to help
us are not ready yet either. But anyway, we've laid the ground-
work (it's a bipartisan effort, incidentally), and we might try

our tactics out when the authorization bill comes back from the Senate-House conference later in the session.

June 17

In the course of this great debate today on Nedzi-Whalen the Democratic leadership showed itself for what it is—totally bankrupt. Carl Albert made a speech about how we can't humiliate the nation or the President in the eyes of the world, and therefore we must not differ with him on foreign policy. It was the old stuff about how party differences must end at the shoreline—so awful, really, that I booed. In the end we got only 158 votes for the amendment. Very discouraging. But to be expected, I guess.

The liberals? Oh, they were thrilled because this was the first time the House ever voted on the war at all. They were congratulating themselves all afternoon on their progress. Imagine that. Now that *The New York Times* has published its first installments of the Pentagon Papers—and the government is attempting to suppress them—we all have come to realize very clearly that the Tonkin Bay Resolution was a frame-up and a conspiracy by the President against the people and the Congress—and the liberals think they're making progress by being defeated on Nedzi-Whalen.

Not only have I found ways to *tie up* the House, but I've just discovered a way to force it *to act* too. I found out how to get a resolution through committee and onto the Floor, by-passing the Rules Committee, within seven days! It's called a "resolution of inquiry," and it is rarely used. In fact, it's only been used maybe a dozen times in this century, most recently in 1950 and 1965.

Here's how it works: You write up the resolution and you

can direct it to the President or a cabinet member, asking that they produce for Congress certain facts that exist with respect to a particular event or situation. The resolution is *privileged* —that's the amazing part about it—which means that it must be sent immediately to committee and reported out either favorably or unfavorably within seven working days. If it's passed in the House, the executive branch then has fifteen days to come up with whatever you're asking for, and even if it doesn't, it's a good way to force a debate.

It's a way of holding the government accountable, maybe the only way. In Britain the government has to come down in front of Parliament every day to explain its actions, but here the President never answers directly to Congress. He answers questions only at a press conference—when *he* feels like calling one. Even then he rarely gets a tough question, and no one disputes his answers.

Now that I've discovered the resolution of inquiry I'm putting one together to demand the Pentagon Papers. I plan to introduce it Monday (June 21), and in the meantime I've sent out a "Dear Colleague" letter asking for support.

June 18

I flew to St. Louis for a conference of the Interstate Association of Commissions on the Status of Women, and when I walked off the plane, it was like walking into an oven. Mississippi all over again. I had forgotten that terrible heat.

Since a lot of the women—they were from all over the country—were middle-aged and very straight-looking, I was kind of scared at first. I think they expected me to be a tough babe, so I cooled it a bit and gave them a good speech, which was stronger on the issues than on philosophy. I talked about what discrimination means to women in terms of money. We earn an average of $60 for every $100 earned by men, and women with college educations earn only $114 more a year than men with eighth grade educations.

Among the unusual people there was one woman who was Spiro Agnew's speechwriter. Would you believe it? Also Barbara Franklin, who's the President's woman on women. I asked Betty Friedan about her. "She's so naïve," Betty said, "it's pitiful."

In yesterday's *New York Post* columnist Pete Hamill ran the results of a poll he took a couple of weeks ago. One of his questions was, "The next Mayor of New York should be . . ." Well, guess who won it? I beat Lindsay by .2 of 1 percent— all in write-ins. How do you like that? Nice, but Pete Hamill's crazy if he thinks I'm going to run for Mayor.

June 19

Voter registration rally in Central Park for the eighteen-year-olds. Between the music and the heat I almost died. But not before I made a sharp pitch to my young friends to come into the political water with me.

June 20

Introduced as "the Congresswoman for the whole United States" at a voter registration rally in Brooklyn.

June 21

Candidatitis! I guess when you're running for President there are no holds barred. I'm talking about Pete McCloskey. Even

(188)

though he's a good friend of mine, he did something this week that I regard as a little pushy, says pushy Abzug. First he agreed to co-sponsor my resolution of inquiry on the Pentagon Papers, and then he turned around, unknown to me, and announced to the press that he was going to introduce his own resolution of inquiry demanding the Pentagon Papers. Well, Pete McCloskey didn't even know what a goddamn resolution of inquiry was until he read my "Dear Colleague" letter. So how do you figure it? You want to know what he says? He says he's directing his to the Secretary of State while I'm directing mine to the President. Fine distinction.

"You did a great service for us, Bella," he said. "*You* found this precedent."

I must admit I'm a little stunned. It's not usually my kind of thing to push into another guy's terrain.

I'm putting together another resolution of inquiry in which I'm asking for three studies, all known to have been conducted by the Pentagon, and all on the economy and the workings of the South Vietnamese government, its election plans, etc. I'm also asking for known United States plans to keep a residual force in South Vietnam indefinitely. I'm very curious to see what the response is going to be to these resolutions, since they can't be ignored.

June 22

I'll tell you right now: This is a day I'm going to have to explain to a lot of people for a long time to come.

Nixon's so-called welfare reform provisions came up for a vote as part of the Social Security bill, which increases Social Security benefits 5 percent and ties future benefit increases to

(189)

the Consumer Price Index. Even though these Social Security increases are inadequate, it's obviously all they're going to give us, and so I'm in favor of them. But because it was impossible to vote for the Social Security increases without also voting for the welfare reform, which I'm against, I found myself in a tough spot. In the end, I voted *against* the bill.

Let me explain how it happened. There were three major votes, actually. In the first we tried to strike the Family Assistance Plan (the welfare reform) from the bill. This plan of Nixon's guarantees a family of four a pitifully low annual income of $2400. That's lower than some states, like New York, are already providing! I, along with various members of the Black Caucus, had introduced our own bill with a $6500 minimum. Nixon's plan, unlike ours, also has a number of very onerous provisions, such as requirements forcing women to work in order to get benefits. He wants to make it so women won't be eligible for welfare if they turn down jobs at the same time that he's only willing to spend a half a million dollars for child care. Absolutely outrageous. Since a very large proportion of women on welfare have been deserted by their husbands and left with large families to support, you tell me how they're supposed to work if we don't give them a place to leave their children.

In trying to get these onerous welfare reform provisions out of the Social Security Act, we were beaten down, 234-187. So then we tried to get the whole bill sent back to committee. We lost that one 221-158. Then, finally, when the bill itself came up for a vote, in voting against it, I found myself in a weird coalition of blacks, liberals and reactionaries (who didn't want an income floor at all). We lost, 288-132.

I guess the more political thing to do would have been to vote for the bill so the elderly people wouldn't get the idea I was against raising their Social Security payments. But all I can say is that if my future depends on what I did, so be it.

You have to do these things to show people that you're going to stand up and fight not only against the war, but on other important issues, like this one, too. So that's the thing. Afterwards, I came back to my office and called Mim in New York. I sensed that she was upset by what I did, and I tried to explain to her that I just felt I couldn't abandon the blacks and the women in this country on a matter like welfare, no matter what the personal consequences for me.

June 26

With a public press conference on the steps of the Forty-second Street Library, we formally kicked off the statehood drive at noon. I signed the first petition.

The full-page ad for the fifty-first state campaign ran this week in the *Times*, but I'm a little disappointed with the results. We still haven't been able to raise the money we need to conduct the kind of campaign we'd like. I think one of the problems was that the ad ran too late. It comes three weeks after the initial press conference, it's summertime, many people have gone or are going away, and it's difficult in these circumstances to sustain the enthusiasm we started out with. Also, we're not getting the kind of cooperation we expected from various groups around town. Even though there are a lot of elements who agree with us, not many of them have chosen to get involved in the nitty-gritty. This, I guess, is always the problem in putting a movement like this together. While it's been sponsored by umpteen numbers of legislators and private citizens, and while it has the support of all kinds of people in the community, when it comes down to raising the money and doing the work we're left feeling shortchanged. My New York office is the headquarters, and my staff is doing most of the work in getting the petition drive underway. They say the phone calls are driving them crazy. On the other hand, they're getting hundreds of volunteers, a lot of whom have never been involved in anything political before.

We are also getting a little assistance from some very unlikely quarters. The other day, for instance, the City Council of Buffalo passed a "good riddance" resolution supporting our drive.

June 27

I'm tired, irritable and exhausted from a brutal weekend. They're killing me with this heavy weekend scheduling, and it's beginning to add up to a terrible wearing-out process. And the worst thing is that I don't think anybody—staff or constituents—realizes what I'm doing to myself.

For instance, this weekend, from the moment I got off the plane on Thursday night until now—Sunday night—I haven't had two free minutes to myself. There was a meeting on the statehood drive, a meeting at St. Patrick's Police Athletic Association in Little Italy to help set up a day care center, a meeting of a group of tenants in Knickerbocker Village, a middle-income housing project, who are up in arms about rent increases, the statehood drive kickoff rally yesterday, a television interview, a meeting with the Bowery Renewal Committee, a block party in conjunction with the Fordham summer program, an Open Air Fair in Clinton. And that isn't even half of it when you consider the telephone calls and the appointments in my office.

In the midst of it all some people were trying to get me to go out to Great Neck, Long Island, to raise money for barnstorming. Even though I had not committed myself, they put my name on the program and publicized the fact that I was going to be there. This is not the first time I've been trapped like this, and so I decided, once and for all, to call a halt. I didn't go.

June 28

In the morning I testified before the Armed Services Committee on my resolution of inquiry demanding the Pentagon Papers, but I couldn't get anywhere with those guys. They're all taken up with the fact that Nixon has announced he's going to release the documents to Congress.

It would be funny if it weren't so outrageous. While Americans are reading excerpts from the Pentagon Papers in the daily press, Eddie Hébert is busy setting up what he calls "special security" with the White House before any of us in Congress can see these precious documents.

First, the White House said, he has to find a room that's safe enough. Then the "papers" will be brought over under armed guard, and Hébert's going to allow us the privilege of sitting alone, one at a time, in a locked room to pore over forty-seven volumes on the condition that we don't take notes and don't talk about what we read. What a farce!

June 30

The Nixon ploy was enough of an excuse for the committee to decide to report back adversely, 25-2, on my resolution, and so the House voted this afternoon to table it. But at least 111 others voted with me against tabling, which shows that a lot of the Representatives here are really shaken up by the disclosures. The old-timers tell me that this was an amazingly good vote—especially on a resolution offered by a newcomer. They're also impressed by the resolution of inquiry tactic.

July 4

My family and I are in California for the weekend for my nephew's wedding. Even though I'm determined to keep this trip strictly a family thing, Lowenstein has been trying to pin me down for a big beach-in registration rally. I just found out it's been canceled, thank God, because I probably would have gone. Still, they wanted to know if I'd go to the beach anyway with McCloskey and help register the eighteen-year-olds. But Martin and my daughters wouldn't allow it. So I said no. Besides, why should I? I'm not running for President. McCloskey is. Let him run up and down the beach.

July 6

More than seven days have passed and Eddie Hébert has not had his committee report out on my second resolution of inquiry on Vietnam, because he doesn't feel it's privileged. His reason, which is bunk, is that I'm asking for opinions, not facts. I now have the right to bring it up on the Floor myself, which, curiously enough, is what he's been urging me to do. He says that once I bring it up, he'll ask for a point of order that the resolution is not privileged. But since he's so full of charm and democracy he promises to give me the hearing— not now, but at some future date.

So he's been bugging me and bugging me about when I'm going to raise the issue on the Floor. Finally, today, I asked him, "Eddie, why are you being so pushy? If I'm not pushing, why are you pushing?"

You know what he said? That he's afraid I'll sneak it in one day when he's not around and therefore not able to make a point of order. Since he's spent his whole goddamn career being sneaky, he figures I'm sneaky too.

"I assure you, Eddie," I said, "that being sneaky is not my style. So for your information—I'm going to bring it up on the Floor tomorrow."

I got the Floor, made my general statement as to why the resolution *is* privileged, and Eddie got up and made his point of order, and I got up to answer his point of order, when, lo and behold, I was *double-crossed.* Carl Albert started reading his prepared answer, in which, of course, he agreed with Hébert's point of order.

In case you've ever sat down here in the gallery and watched the House in session, you might have gotten the impression that the Chair listens to both sides in situations like this. That's not the case at all. It's all oiled and greased beforehand. Before I opened my mouth, the parliamentarian had prepared an answer to kill me. It's utterly fraudulent; there's no real debate, no real argument. And Carl handles it all very suavely. When I wanted to answer Hébert's point of order, Carl made believe he didn't see me, and went on, unfazed, to read the ruling.

So I did something that's practically unheard of. I stood up and said, "I appeal the ruling of the Chair." Whereupon the House almost fainted. *Nobody* appeals the ruling of the Chair. To make a long story short, that didn't do any good either, but in appealing I was able to demonstrate my displeasure at how the thing was all rigged against me.

A McCloskey resolution of inquiry requesting information on the clandestine war in Laos also came up for a vote on the Floor this afternoon, and he lost by about the same margin that my Pentagon Papers resolution did. He had a series of two other resolutions which came up too, and both were also tabled. He didn't put up much of a fight. He does things like that. He doesn't go all the way. I don't know the reason; maybe it's because he's a Republican and he feels he has to relate to the party at least a little.

Incidentally, on a personal level I get along with Pete very well. He's an interesting man, and I think he usually shows a great deal of courage, with a Marine kind of fortitude. In the past, however, he's not been too good on the woman questions (he voted against the Equal Rights Amendment), and I find him voting with the Administration on domestic matters a little too often. On the war issue, of course, he's strongly, strongly committed, and I think what he's doing is enormously helpful. But beyond that, to tell you the truth, I'm not too clear where he stands.

July 8

There are two politicians I'd like to have on my side who've both come out against the fifty-first state. The shame of it is that I believe both have done so for reasons that are purely political.

One is Herman Badillo. He came out against statehood when he was trying to become a candidate for Mayor the year Norman Mailer ran. Now, again, feeling boxed into that position I guess, he says he's still against it. The reason he gives is that he's afraid statehood will only ghettoize the city. He fears factories, jobs, the middle class will all move out. So okay. What he would like, then, is a new state that includes the suburbs. Well, I'm all for that. But you have to give the people in the city the choice of statehood to begin with. And while you're starting the movement, you can be working at the same time to modify it. What you don't do is criticize it outright— as he has done, for reasons, I'm sorry to say, that seem more political than fundamental.

And then there's Manny Celler. He's come out against statehood too, which is ridiculous in light of the fact that some years ago he was a proponent of it. Why he changed his mind, God knows! Maybe because he's head of the New York delegation and somebody said to him, probably Rockefeller, "We don't want to have anything to do with it." I hate to have to say that about Manny. Not that he plays ball with Rockefeller—he doesn't—but he's an "elder statesman" type, and sometimes, I guess, he figures you just don't rock the boat. He's come a long way on lots of issues, but he's dead wrong on this one.

July 9

Ed Koch called a meeting today on home rule. Because I had my own meetings in connection with the economic development programs on the Lower East Side, I didn't go. Instead I sent a representative. From what I understand, it was a nothing meeting. What Koch is up to is evident. He doesn't say he's opposed to the fifty-first state movement, but at the same time he's trying to put together a coalition to press for home rule. Home rule is an old and generally timid concept. Hardly anybody gets excited about it anymore. For years we've been trying to gain more local control, which is what home rule is, but nobody's gotten anywhere because the courts have consistently limited us.

I had to drag myself back to Washington tonight for a preliminary meeting of the convenors of the National Women's Political Caucus, which begins here tomorrow. As luck would have it, after I got on the plane with Sarah Kovner and Amy Swerdlow, an old friend from WSP, it was delayed an hour and a half or more (the usual efficiency of our great airlines). The meeting started at eight; I originally figured on arriving at nine, but I didn't get there until about ten-thirty.

Actually, I didn't miss much because the meeting was about the procedures we'll use to conduct the caucus. Although these are the kinds of things everybody worries about at the outset, they never turn out to be significant. The really significant thing we're doing in bringing women here from all over the country is formally establishing ourselves as a nationwide political force with goals to double and triple in the immediate future the number of women in political office, as well as to have an impact on the 1972 political conventions and platforms.

Once the meeting on procedure ended, some of us gathered in Gloria Steinem's hotel room and talked about the necessity to create as broad a movement as possible to include Republicans, Democrats, feminists, women from the consumer movement, women from the civil rights movement, women from all minority groups, young women and housewives. We also agreed that the caucus would have to commit itself not only to issues directly relating to women and sexism, but to establishing a national program of priorities against war and racism and poverty.

It wasn't all serious talk though. There was lots of chitchat. Women kept dropping in and out of the room, which got to be pretty crowded at times. One of the intriguing women there was Shana Alexander, the editor of *McCall's* magazine, pretty and very ladylike. She hardly said a word. Later she explained she was new to politics. She's going to have to learn fast.

July 10

After an early appointment at the House Beauty Shop, I arrived at the conference at about ten o'clock. This was the plenary session. It was very impressive—there were women from all over the country—California, Texas, Alabama, Kentucky, Michigan, not just New York. In addition to me, there were a number of other keynote speakers, including Betty, Gloria, Betty Smith, a Republican from Wisconsin, Fanny

Lou Hamer, Paula Page of the National Students Association, and Evelyn Cunningham, who heads up Rockefeller's women's unit.

I said it in my speech, and I'll say it again here, this was truly a historical meeting—easily as significant as the first little convention for suffrage in Seneca Falls more than a hundred years ago. The presence here in Washington of three hundred women from twenty-six states serves notice to everyone that women will no longer accept second or last place—politically, socially, economically or humanly. And though we may, as a unit, have some trouble working out our organizational and tactical problems, there is one thing that we're all in perfect agreement on: women should be fully represented in the political power structure as both a matter of right and a matter of justice. At the same time, I don't think any of us intend to replace the *male*, white, middle class elite that runs this country with a *female*, white, middle class elite.

From my speech: "I believe very deeply that the hope of an effective women's political movement lies in reaching out to include those who have been doubly and triply disenfranchised —reaching out to working women, to young women, to black women, to women on welfare—and joining their strength together with millions of other American women who are on the move all over this country demanding an end to discrimination and fighting for their rights as full and equal citizens.

"I am not elevating women to sainthood, nor am I suggesting that all women share the same views, or that all women are good and all men bad. Women have screamed for war. Women, like men, have stoned black children going to integrated schools. Women have been and are prejudiced, narrow-minded, reactionary, even violent. *Some* women.

"They, of course, have a right to vote and a right to run for office. I will defend that right, but I will not support them or vote for them."

After the plenary session we broke up for a series of workshops: political strategy, structure, issues, party platforms, conventions, candidate criteria, grass-roots organizing—each of which I dropped in on to be helpful where I could.

In the course of the day's events things got very lively, and by evening separate caucuses were popping up all over the place. The young people felt they didn't have adequate representation on the nominating committee, and so I had to see to it that they got some. The black women organized their own separate caucus to demand a strong commitment against racism from the entire caucus—which they got easily. There were some young radicals who wanted to be sure that we all shared a sufficient commitment against the war. They, at first, were thinking of taking over the platform, as radicals have a tendency to do sometimes, but that was straightened out too. I played a role in convincing them that they would have plenty of opportunity to speak their minds, and they did.

By the end of the day I was very gratified. The overwhelming majority of the caucus was not only embracing the purely feminine issues, but extending itself to taking positions as women in the total society too.

July 11

We wound up the caucus by selecting a twenty-one-member steering committee to coordinate the future work of the group, by announcing certain goals for women's political power, and by agreeing on certain guidelines that we will use to determine our support for women candidates running for office.

The steering committee, of which I am a member, has seven blacks, one Indian, eleven Democrats and two Republicans. Fanny Lou Hamer of Mississippi, a woman of great dignity and natural eloquence, received the highest number of votes, and I came in second. Shirley Chisholm, Shana Alexander,

Betty Friedan, Gloria Steinem, Mary Clarke of Los Angeles WSP and Olga Madar, a vice president of the United Auto Workers, were also elected. Olga, incidentally, is a great gal. Tough and practical. Since, in all, there is only one woman under thirty and no Puerto Rican or Mexican-American women, we agreed to add four new members from these groups in the future.

As immediate goals, we intend to elect women to office at all levels of government; we intend to insist that women comprise at least half the delegates to both political conventions next year. We intend to work for the enactment of the full feminist platform, and we intend to call a full-scale National Women's Political Caucus for sometime early next year.

We decided, as I mentioned yesterday, on an absolute prohibition on supporting racist candidates of either sex. In addition, we adopted a number of less rigid guidelines, which we hope all women candidates will adopt. They include:

Support of the passage of the Equal Rights Amendment without any crippling riders.

Enforcement of all existing and proposed antidiscrimination laws, plus the important addition of a "cease and desist" clause to the Equal Employment Opportunities Commission. This will enable the commission to move immediately and with simplified procedures against employers who discriminate against women.

Adequate housing and medical care for all Americans.

Elimination of the many tax inequities that affect women and children.

An end to discrimination against women, especially women who head fatherless families and welfare mothers.

Repeal of all laws that affect a woman's right to decide her own reproduction and sexual life.

Fair treatment of working women, including full tax deductions for child care and household expenses; maternity leave and voluntary parental leave for childbirth; change in the Social Security system to end discrimination against families with working women; and an end to the economic and social degradation of women, whether by employers or by unions.

An immediate withdrawal from the war in Indochina, and an end to the use of physical violence as an acceptable way of resolving conflict. Also, an end to the use of repressive measures against individuals advocating social change.

There are some things I want to make clear about this caucus, because I can't tell you enough how significant it was. Some people are under the mistaken impression that we're putting together a women's party. That's wrong.

Instead of organizing a political party, we got a fairly diverse group of women together to come to an agreement on an overall statement of goals and guidelines. We took a realistic look at the situation. We don't have a chance to elect a woman President in 1972, and we all know it. On the other hand, we realize that if we aren't diverted by tokenism, women have a great chance of gaining the political power they've long been denied.

Without getting scientific or psychological or historical about it, it's long been my judgment that women have been at the forefront of social change. When we first got the vote, we used it to clean up the sweat shops, to clean up the horrors of child labor, and so on. Then we got sidetracked. Instead of carrying forth Carrie Chapman Catt's notion that women should organize as a political movement, the movement became *nonpartisan* and followed the League of Women Voters route. So between their nonpositions and Madison Avenue's assigned stereotype of women as flowers in the home who can be sold all kinds of products to beautify themselves, and Hollywood with *its* awful stereotypes, women were sunk. Up until now, we've been laboring under the concept of women as appendages to men and children and subjected to constant

(202)

brainwashing by Madison Avenue, Hollywood, TV—and the descendants of John Adams who know when they have a good thing going.

We now see the concept changing because the women's movement, which renewed itself several years ago as an intellectual revolt of the bored middle class housewife, has grown into a broad movement seeking complete economic, social and political change in all arenas. It's like the black movement, which started out over the right to a seat in the front of the bus and then extended itself to pursue for the black people their rightful piece of the whole system.

The women's movement, like the black movement and the movement of the young people, comes at a time when the system is not responding to the largest numbers of its people. This puts all these movements in a very critical perspective, because out of all this ferment the last thing we can realistically expect is for things to remain the same.

As I see it, either these groups get what's rightfully coming to them—which means that the political, economic and social systems will have to be overhauled—or those who are resisting these groups will move the country to the right in order to repress them and move the clock back. Because constitutional government is suffering a breakdown, because a war is being fought illegally and without the consent of the people, and because the economic system is being seriously questioned, all movements for social change have a greater chance to succeed—or fail—than ever before in the history of this country. There's no in between. Either the society is going to move forward by accepting radical change or it's going to move backward by sustaining itself against the will of the large masses of people.

This moment in history requires women to lead the movement for radical change, first, because we have the potential of becoming the largest individual movement; second, because our major interests are in common with other oppressed groups; and third, because we've never had a chance to make mistakes in government and so we have no mistakes to defend. Men have made the world the way it is.

And that's what this women's caucus was all about. We're going to run for office. We're going to have our say about convention representation, party platform, policies and candidates. We're going to insist that those people who run for office not only support our women's program, but commit themselves to turning around the emphasis of this government from war and the military to the needs of health, housing, education and jobs.

Oh, it's going to be tough. That I can tell you. There are a lot of women whose competing views and competing interests we're going to have to work out. The caucus helped us to get started. This movement needs all kinds of leaders from everywhere, because neither I nor Betty nor Gloria nor Shirley is going to make the movement by herself.

Power fights, unfortunately, are inevitable. We've got to realize that. Some people who haven't been active in the movement until recently are going to show up and want to become its leaders. Some people will try to attain power by attacking those women who already have it. These things happen—it's human nature—and we've got to be prepared. My role, as I see it, since I am the only woman who's ever successfully run for national office on an essentially women's rights–social change program, is to help give the entire movement the kind of guidance and perspective that nobody else is qualified to do. They're especially going to need practical advice on the detail stuff—how to get women involved in the delegate selection process, how to relate to the political parties, the primaries, etc. It can be tedious, but if we mean business we have to be on top of everything.

July 12

Flew to Wichita, Kansas, for a speech at the Wichita State University. Republican territory or not, the response was tremendous from an audience filled with young people, women, working people and professional people. They were all obviously much in agreement with what I had to say.

Very often Betty tries to make believe that she's much broader than I am when it comes to relating to diverse groups. She seems to feel I'm not interested, for instance, in incorporating Republicans, or any group that disagrees with me, for that matter, into the women's movement. Obviously, that's not true. Why else would I go to a place like Wichita?

I don't believe in organizing the already organized. I believe in spreading the message. And the message I take to Wichita and wherever is that I will do the honorable and credible and decent thing always in finding a way to institute programs that will benefit the largest numbers of people. That, I suppose, is what people mean when they say I'm an urban populist.

If you talk to them straight, people, whether they're in Wichita or New York City, will listen and relate and try to understand.

July 13

We're in trouble again on the Equal Rights Amendment. It's come out of the Judiciary Committee crippled with the Wiggins Amendment, which permits protective legislation, abortion laws and almost any other form of discrimination to be retained by states under the umbrella of "health and safety." There's also an amendment that prohibits women from being drafted. These are the very things the Equal Rights Amendment was meant to do away with!

So now we've got a big fight on our hands. First, we've got to get an "open rule" so that the amendments can be voted on separately. Next, we have got to get a firm commitment from every Representative to vote for the Equal Rights Amendment *without* the amendments.

Sixteen thousand letters went out to women all over the country from my office today, alerting them to what's going on. By the time the amendment is up for a vote, we'll have every Congressman swamped with phone calls, letters and personal visits to assure ourselves that we get out of this Congress an equal rights amendment that really is an equal rights amendment, not one like Judiciary has reported out, which only tries to reemphasize that women are not and will not be equal. Believe me, we're going to fight this one right to the end, and any guy who votes against us is going to be held accountable in the next election. That I promise.

July 14

We got some characteristic reaction from the White House on the Women's Caucus. Secretary of State Rogers brought the subject up when he and Nixon were getting their pictures taken with Henry Kissinger, who's just back from a "fact-finding" trip to Paris.

Kissinger, smiling, said he heard Gloria Steinem was at the Women's Caucus.

"Who's that?" the President asked. (He doesn't read the papers, so how would he know?)

"That's Henry's old girlfriend," Mr. Rogers said jokingly. Then Rogers mentioned a photograph of me, Friedan, Steinem and Chisholm, which one of the wire services had circulated.

"What did it look like?" Nixon asked.

"Like a burlesque," said Rogers.

"What's wrong with that?" asked Nixon.

Isn't that something? Obviously, these guys are accustomed to viewing women in terms of flesh shows. It's insulting, I must say, but hardly surprising.

I issued a press release attacking Nixon and warning that the women's political movement was no laughing matter. I also included a statement by Gloria, who said, "I am not now and never have been a friend of Henry Kissinger's."

July 16

The big news is Nixon's announcement that he's going to China, and I had an interesting discussion with Eddie Hébert today about it. "Now guys like you have an opportunity like you never had before to be great statesmen and great Democrats," I said. "Are you going to let Nixon outdo us? He's going to go to China and normalize relations between two great ideological enemies, and he's going to come out looking like the great peacemaker. We Democrats have got to put him on the spot. We've got to insist he set a date to withdraw from Vietnam before he goes to China. And you, Eddie, can be a great Democrat, believe me, if you do something now."

"Why that's the greatest compliment anybody's ever paid me," he said.

"What compliment?"

"You called me a Democrat."

Later in the day, back in New York, I gave a brief speech to about two hundred older Girl Scouts—who are between sixteen and eighteen years old—and afterwards a few of them came over to me and asked if I was married.

"Yes," I said.

"Do you have daughters?" they asked.

"Yes."

"Then why didn't you bring them with you?"

"Well, do your mothers drag *you* everywhere they go?" I said.

July 17

You remember Manny Celler's old arguments against the Equal Rights Amendment, to the effect that women have always been unequal since Adam and Eve? Well, he's brought them up to date. He's now telling people, "Why, women weren't even at the Last Supper."

So I took him aside and said, "Listen, Manny, I want you to understand one thing: We may not have been at the last one, but we sure as hell will be at the next one."

July 18

Sorry to have to say it, but we're having a little difficulty with the fifty-first state campaign. It's summer and a lot of people are either out of town or sweltering unenergetically in the heat. We have less than a third of the forty-five thousand signatures we will need by September 3 to get on the ballot. Considering legal problems, challenges and technicalities, we had been hoping for at least sixty-five thousand signatures. The major problem has been that we just don't have the volunteers to circulate the petitions. They flocked in at first, but if it's a hot day they don't show.

Another problem is that I have been the only one to give the movement major leadership. And when it comes to raising money—which is what we need, and a lot of it—I'm awful.

The ironic thing is that I can organize causes for other people, elections for other candidates, things like that. Such as in the McCarthy campaign in 1968. The history books will have little to say about me with regard to that campaign, but it's a fact that I had very early input into it with Al Lowenstein. I got no national recognition at the time because I didn't seek it, just as I don't seek it now. But now it just comes. A lot of people are silly enough to believe that I just sprang up out of nowhere. As if suddenly, overnight, I just developed this personality. I mean, I always had it.

What amuses me are those people who say, "My God, here's this woman who just happened on the scene, and every day she's on television and in the papers. She must spend all day figuring out how to do it." Wrong! I spend all day figuring out how to beat the machine and knock the crap out of the political power structure—and that's how I do it.

July 19

Even though I beg my staff to keep the weekends free, there's always something to tie me up. It's impossible. All weekend I was busy with the fifty-first state campaign, with getting the young people out to register to vote, running all over the place. Why can't I have my weekends free like everybody else?

One good thing: Bob Tendler, the president of the Village Independent Democrats, has agreed to take over the campaign, and things are livening up already. I've also asked Bob to join my staff in the fall as community organizer. He's a very committed guy, and a terrifically hard worker.

July 20

And so today we had the big Democratic caucus on the caucus, called by the leadership because Andy Jacobs and I have been tying up the caucus all year long. The leadership says the reason they haven't been able to get a quorum in the caucus is because of us, which is nonsense, of course. Historically, they've had very few quorums in the caucus. And, as a matter of fact, more people than ever before have been coming to the caucuses this year because we've been organizing them to come.

In the last few months there have been some stories circulated by my liberal friends that I'm counterproductive to the cause of peace because I won't let the caucus get into any other issues until it goes on record to support a December 31 withdrawal from Vietnam. Well, that's nothing but sour grapes. The fact is, great liberals that they are, they're not doing anything to get the issue of peace heard. Besides, the *moderates* (Sam Gibbons, Sparky Matsunaga, Ed Boland, Jack Bingham, Bill Anderson, etc.) who introduced the Vietnam disengagement resolution the first time aren't saying I'm counterproductive. So it's obvious that certain unnamed liberals are just attacking me to justify their inaction. They think that by tearing me down their constituents will forgive them for failing to be activists, like I am.

I mention all this because I was the only one who made any kind of a fight in the caucus today. All the other liberals gave in without a squeak. My recommendation to the caucus was that we do away with the idea that you need a majority to have a quorum, as on the Floor. That's logical, isn't it? If they didn't keep calling quorums, we could act.

But little do they listen to me on these matters, so they went ahead and solved the problem in the most undemocratic and most outrageous manner possible: They gave the chairman the power to cancel, or adjourn, at his whim, up to two caucus meetings in a row. And they gave him the power to determine by himself the order of the items on the agenda.

In effect, what they did is take the power away from the people in the caucus and give it to the chairman.

July 21

I had the honor of becoming the first woman member of Congress to be invited to address a luncheon of the National Press Club, which until recently excluded women from membership. I noted that fact at the end of my remarks when they presented me with the traditional gift they give to speakers—a necktie with the club's seal on it.

"I haven't worn a necktie since my bar mitzvah," I said.

This is a very WASPy club, I want you to know. I doubt they even got my joke. One guy came up to me afterwards and said, "You know, everybody says you got a Brooklyn accent, but I don't think so."

"Well, that's because I'm not from Brooklyn," I said. "I'm from the Bronx."

July 22

In case anybody is wondering whether the Women's Caucus is having any impact: The Republican Party's Committee on Delegates and Organizations has recommended that half the members of each state's delegation to the convention next year be women. In 1968 only 17 percent of the delegates and alternates were women (13 percent in the Democratic Party).

Of course the battle is still far from won. This is only a recommendation to the state delegations. It is not binding. The Democratic Party already has in effect binding regulations that require delegates to be representative of the party makeup in their states as regards race, sex, age and so on. There's going to be a lot of fighting about this at the national convention in Miami Beach, I assure you, because we're going to be demanding that every state delegation have its proportionate share of women, which means at least 50 percent.

I was in the District of Columbia Superior Court today to testify in connection with the Capitol steps demonstrations last May. Since the statute says you can't gather on the steps unless you're orderly, the government was trying to prove that the crowd was unruly. So when I was on the stand, the government lawyer asked, "Did you rush up the Capitol steps with the demonstrators?"

"Rush up the steps?" I said. "Those are a lot of steps. I don't rush up to get to the top. I walk up them very slowly and I hope that I get to the top."

"What happened after you addressed the crowd?"

"They applauded," I said. "Thank heavens."

And I went on to explain that the occasion, in terms of how the crowd behaved, was no different from when I was sworn in on those steps, and that it was no different from all the times when I, as a citizen, had been on those steps to petition Congress. My testimony, I kind of think, killed the government's case. In effect, we won not only the cases relating to the Capitol steps, but most of the cases relating to the entire week of demonstrations. Most of them were simply dismissed. Which only goes to show that we were on the side of the law and the government was on the side of the lawless.

You'll be interested to hear that the first thing the caucus chairman, Olin Teague, has done with his new powers is to cancel this month's caucus.

July 23

Every day my staff and I are, in one way or another, working with problems in the district. I would say that we run in my New York office a larger service operation than any other Congressman or Congresswoman in the country. So far this year, for instance, we've listened to and tried to help nearly two thousand individual constituents on problems ranging from an overcharge on an electric bill to an unfair draft classification. We'll do whatever we can for anybody who comes in and asks.

Usually my staff handles most of the individual requests, but when it's necessary I intervene myself. For instance, the state announced not long ago that it intends because of budget cuts to close the Gouverneur State School for the mentally retarded, which is located in my district. The 194 brain-damaged children who now live at the Gouverneur facilities were to be transferred to Willowbrook on Staten Island. But the parents of these children, and the community, began fighting the closing, and they contacted me. They feared that their children will not get nearly as good care at the Staten Island facility, which is already overcrowded, and they don't want their children so far away that it would be impossible to visit them as often as they now do. So I wrote a very strong letter to Rockefeller, and we followed up with phone calls.

Today news came back that a decision has been made to keep the facility open for at least another year. It's a temporary victory, to be sure, but there are a lot of parents who are feeling very relieved tonight. But I can't stop thinking it's so crazy, the whole system. They cut the budget and who do they make suffer? The poor and the sick. Anyway, now we've got a year to come up with a permanent solution.

These are the kinds of things I do in the district. Let me tell you about something else that happened a few weeks ago. There are a huge number of Puerto Ricans in my district. It's important for their children that schools offer bilingual programs. On the books there are provisions for federal funding of bilingual education, which is designed to use the child's first language as the medium for instruction until his competence in English permits the use of both languages. Well, a school district on the Lower East Side made an application for these funds, and for complicated technical reasons having to do with the proposal it devised, the bid was rejected. When the matter was brought to my attention, I intervened directly with the Office of Education. I gave them such a tongue-lashing on the phone that they sent one of their top officials flying up to New York to meet with the district leaders and Mim. They officially agreed to help the district revise its proposals so it would qualify to receive the funds. Now, I found out today, the district is not only going to get the $100,000 it originally asked for, but another additional $75,000. How's that? Also, two other school districts in my Congressional district are going to be getting federal grants too.

July 24

For the past couple of days I've had a pesty reporter from *Time* tailing me all over the place, and I'm getting the feeling that I'm really gonna get it, and good. It's my death knell. I don't know how to get out of it. I called Gloria Steinem and some other friends who know about these things, but they all said, "No way out." The same guy has done a hatchet job on Gloria for a future issue of *Esquire*. So I've got to talk to him. I guess I knew this was going to happen—one time or another. I mean, all that good publicity can't go on. Howard Brock, who handles the press for me in New York, wants me to be calm and cooperative. He should know better.

July 26

I've been having some interesting exchanges with Eddie Hébert the past couple of days on the Mansfield Amendment to the draft bill, which is in conference.

"Eddie," I've been saying, "here's your moment. You can

(214)

set a date and be a hero. You can't bring the bill back without a date."

"Bella," he says, "don't worry. We're going to do something which will satisfy you . . ."

"Eddie," I say, "but will you have a date in it? We need a date. You can be a hero."

"Bella . . ."

"Eddie, the whole country wants a date except you and [John] Stennis [chairman of the Senate Armed Services Committee]."

July 28

We passed another Public Works bill today, 375-27. Nixon, more concerned with making himself look like a fiscal conservative than with providing jobs for those who have been forced into unemployment by his economic policies, vetoed the first bill we passed three months ago.

While the bill we passed today was not as good as the original, the qualifications for designation as a "special impact area" were broadened and simplified, thus making it easier to deal with urgent problems of poverty and unemployment in such areas as the Lower East Side. Also, the anti-sex discrimination provisions I added to the original bill—which give women the same right to jobs, employment and other benefits provided for in the bill—were written into the new bill, and passed along with it. So we seem to be getting somewhere.

July 29

In the last few days I introduced two pieces of women's legislation that I think are pretty significant.

First, a bill that would prohibit the federal government from designating in any records, correspondence or documents the marital status of an individual. Since the male prefix "Mr." is unaffected by marital status, we want the same kind of designation for women, something like, say, "Ms." If not that, we want the prefix eliminated altogether. There's no justification for idle curiosity about whether a woman is a "Mrs." or a "Miss." Women have to be treated as individuals—not wives of individuals. Besides, designations like "Mrs." and "Miss" only tempt an employer into discriminatory practices. If a woman is married she's discriminated against in terms of promotion and responsibility, and if she's not married she's discriminated against on the grounds that she might get married and leave her job.

The second bill would authorize abortions and sterilizations in military facilities without regard to the law of the state where the facilities are located. This bill is designed to knock down the President's stupid order to the contrary.

Between keeping tabs on the conference report on the Selective Service bill and on my resolution of inquiry, which is long overdue, I've been in touch with Eddie Hébert on an almost daily basis. So Parren Mitchell said today, "I don't know, Bella. There seems to be a lot of fraternization these days between you and the military-industrial complex."

July 30

They beat us by three votes this afternoon in voting a $250 million loan guarantee to the Lockheed Aircraft Corporation, which only goes to show you how this House jumps to the needs of the big corporations—or more correctly, the big banks supporting the big corporations—while legislation to feed the hungry, to house the homeless and to employ the jobless lingers around here for years. Two hundred and fifty million dollars at the snap of their fingers! Do you know how much money that is? It represents two and a half times what the Administration has requested for air pollution programs next year; it's twice what Nixon has budgeted for highway safety; it's two and a half times what has been requested for cancer research. Can there be a more stark comment on our misplaced national priorities?

The statehood drive has been hit below the belt in a report issued by a group called the Citizens Union. According to the report, which was written by an assistant professor of political science at Baruch College, New York City is a dying metropolis with a shrinking tax base which won't survive without the help of Albany. It's an awful report, very misleading and based on secondary sources and faultily interpreted data.

This talk of a shrinking tax base is nonsense. New York City has one of the richest concentrations of wealth in the world. The real estate value of property for taxable purposes alone has doubled in the last ten years. By any indication, the city has a great future as an employment center, as a social center, as a cultural center. To try to take some figures (you can do anything with statistics) and make it look otherwise is ridiculous.

The report seems to imply that we think statehood is The Solution to the city's problems. I never made that claim. We're in problems up to our neck in this city. The only claim we're making is that as a separate state we'd fare better than we're faring at present. We'd be able to keep more of our own tax dollars, and at the same time strengthen our links with the federal government and enlarge our capacity to enter into bistate and regional compacts. Statehood is not an isolationist concept either, as the report also suggested. Thirty percent of wages earned in the city are earned by nonresidents who live in suburbs that have, in effect, become economic satellites of the city. They have as much a stake as we do in the city's survival, and in fact, they're developing many of the same problems we have, and I think eventually I'd like to see them as part of our new state. The ties between city and suburbs—even though existing governmental structures pit us against one another—are very strong. After all, we're all in this together.

This Citizens Union report is a little hard to figure out. Usually they present both sides on controversial issues, but here they assigned one woman who is against statehood to write a report and never made an attempt to present the other side. The big question in my mind is: Who are the people who are really behind this report? There are plenty of vested interests, like the landlords, who want to keep things just as they are. And, unfortunately, there are a few politicians who don't like the fact that once again I came up with a proposal that was both popular and meaningful.

July 31

A private fund-raiser for my campaign deficit was held tonight in Westport, Connecticut, in an unbelievable house which seemed to me to be on a peninsula of its own. It was the home of Miriam and A. B. Rosen, very generous and charming people. I'd say about 150 people were there, an assorted group of actors, executives, journalists, advertising people, doctors and lawyers and their wives. All in all, they raised a nice little sum of money for me, which is unusual. We made the deficit a little smaller, but it's still there.

Actually, I hate these things. I can't help but feeling as though I'm begging for my supper. All my life I've been an independent person who's made her own living, just as my husband has made his own living. I'm not accustomed to asking people for money or anything. That's the misery of this political business. Campaigning for office has become an outrageous marketplace where the rich can run and the poor and the in-between can't—not without putting themselves in debt for the rest of their lives, which is exactly what I've done.

August 1

Well, Shirley Chisholm's made it public: she's considering running for President, and she has supporters testing the climate in more than half the states. Very interesting woman, Shirley. Wants to be varied in her approaches. Likes to do the unexpected. She believes, as I do, in building the new coalition to change the Democratic Party, and if our hopes materialize we're going to have a lot of clout in 1972. What she's concerned about, as I am, is that we get a good candidate, not just an acceptable, tired old liberal.

While the Women's Caucus is not in itself ready yet to support any particular candidate, Shirley—and we've had a lot of discussions about this—feels that as an individual she should undertake a symbolic campaign to show that a woman should be considered for President. She's told me that if she can raise the money, she'll run in certain primaries, notably Wisconsin.

As far as the Caucus is concerned, most women who've spoken out on the subject feel that if we were to launch a candidate at this point—even for pressure purposes—it would largely be a diversion of our energies. We want to get strong caucuses organized in each state. We want to concentrate on pressuring the conventions for proper representation of women and other disenfranchised groups, and getting women to run in local, state and Congressional elections. This is the building-up-from-the-grass-roots approach—setting reasonable goals and objectives which, once attained, will inspire more women to join us. Shirley understands this, but she's always operated as an individual to a large extent. So have I, of course, but I usually try to relate to groups more than she does.

August 2

The draft bill is back from conference, and pretty much as we expected the heart and guts have been ripped out of the Mansfield Amendment. They've changed it so that instead of its being binding on the President, it's simply an expression of Congressional views that a date should be set for withdrawal. But it doesn't specify when.

Instead of allowing the conference report to come up in the regular course of business, in which case we can start some obstreperous activity to delay the vote, the leadership has decided to get a "rule." This means they could make us vote on it on a completely take-it-or-leave-it basis. All they have to do is give us a rule where we can't debate individual amendments separately. Because I have a feeling that this is what they have up their sleeves, I wrote a letter to William Colmer, who is the Rules Committee chairman, and asked that he make it possible for us to give this report "the fullest, most open consideration that we can give it." But a lot of good my letter is going to do. Just watch.

Whatever happens, I expect I'll have to do a lot of screaming. So wouldn't you know it? I've got a case of laryngitis. I can't talk.

August 3

All last month I sat through some pretty interesting hearings on water pollution conducted by my full Public Works Committee, and I came away convinced that the problem is one big bamboozle. There are at least fifty thousand polluters in this country who are getting away with murder. There are some laws, but they're not enforced. All the money, or at least a good deal of it, that has been appropriated to fight pollution has gone for personnel and for things like treatment plants, which only make it easier and more respectable for polluters to continue to pollute. Most of the polluters are corporations, and one has to assume that the Nixon Administration is not about to make life too difficult for its big business pals.

Meanwhile, the level of water pollution we've been forced to tolerate in this country has become unbearable. Human and industrial waste is dumped directly into streams, rivers and waterways to the point where it's a health hazard just to be near a body of water in some areas. I found out that one river in the Middle West has become a fire hazard because of all the chemical pollutants floating in it. Everywhere you see a body of water anymore it seems to have become a dumping ground for waste. It's horrible.

So I decided to introduce my own water pollution bill, which I did today. Besides tripling the appropriation to $30 million to state and interstate water pollution agencies, the unique thing about my bill is that it would impose heavy "user charges" to force polluters to pay to clean up their own waste. Because of our upside-down way of looking at things in this country, it's now the taxpayer who's expected to pay for such things as sewage treatment plants.

The point of the bill is really to make polluters pay for their crimes against nature. Selfish economic interests, like the not unrelated selfish military interests, have made life miserable for all of us on this planet, and in this country. And, in the final result, we're not going to get anywhere until we change our idea of who's entitled to what in this society. So that's why, along with everything else, I've decided to make a big deal about water pollution.

Don't get the idea that my bill is going to solve anything

though. We're never going to solve the problem of pollution in this country until we demand a change in the whole method of production, along with a lot of other fundamental changes.

Laryngitis or not, this was my day for taking on Wayne Hays from Ohio, a mean, mean character who's always attacking everybody personally on the Floor. I figured that a bully deserves to be bullied by a bully, and so I couldn't resist my calling.

Here's how it happened: When an amendment to the foreign aid bill was offered which would cut off military aid to Greece, Jim Burke from Massachusetts got the Floor and objected strongly, talking about the greatness of Greece from way back, and what an example for democracy Greece has been throughout history. When Jim sat down, Hays—who, although usually a reactionary, is on the liberal side on this issue—got up and said, "I compliment the gentleman on the well-phrased statement he just made, but it does not quite hit the mark." As if to say, "That was a well-written speech, Jim, which we all know somebody wrote for you, but you're wrong anyway." An under-the-belt attack; all Congressmen have speeches written for them. Hays then went on to say that Burke's argument was "unadulterated baloney." The two had some nasty exchanges and it got to the point where Hays wouldn't even yield the Floor to Burke. "Sit down and be quiet," he said.

A while later Ron Dellums got up and proposed an amendment of his own to cut off aid to Brazil and Portugal because of the torture of political prisoners in those countries.

This time Wayne Hays gets up and reads a press clipping about Dellums from a Milwaukee newspaper, which said, "Representative Ronald V. Dellums, Democrat of California, says he thinks that most Senators and Congressmen are mediocre and prima donnas who pass legislation that has nothing to do with the reality of misery in this country." Hays turned to Dellums and said, "Did the gentleman make that statement?"

"Yes," said Dellums. "Do you want me to explain it?"

"No," said Hays, "I don't need you to explain it. I just wonder if you then want a bunch of mediocre prima donnas to pay more serious attention to your amendment?"

"If you don't," said Dellums, "then my statement has even double merit. I would simply say to you that they go around strutting from their offices to the Floor of the Congress and do not deal with the human misery in this country."

"You may strut around from *your* office to the Floor and to God-knows-where—apparently to Milwaukee—but I do not measure, as my father used to say, everybody's corn in your own half bushel."

After this mean exchange Wayne came to the back of the room where I happened to be sitting with some other people, including Jim Burke.

"You know, Wayne," I said, "I think it's pretty crummy of you to go around attacking people personally on the Floor. It's one thing to disagree with somebody, but why attack them so viciously?"

"Well, Jim and I are old friends, we don't mind," he said, nodding to Jim Burke. "Right, Jim?"

"Yeah," Jim said.

"Okay," I said, "Jim might be able to take care of himself. Both you guys have been around here God knows how long. But here's Ron Dellums. A freshman, right? Trying to get an amendment considered, which is hard enough in the first place, and you have to get up there and heckle him about something he said out in Milwaukee. You may have a right to criticize him for it—but not the way you did. You're always attacking people personally. Like a bully."

"Well, I may do it to you one day yet," he said.

"You know what, Wayne?" I said. "You start up with me and I'm not sure you're going to get the best of it."

(223)

August 4

I had a meeting with a delegation of Soviet women in my office. We brought out some sherry and I asked them, since I think it's important for women of different countries to have these kinds of exchanges, what it was like to be a woman in their country. They said that women make up 35 percent of the local governing councils, that 31 percent of the Supreme Soviet is female. As we got going, though, they hinted at some problems they were having in reconciling the roles of woman as producer, mother and wife.

"Oh," I said, "you have some of the same problems we have. You might be at a higher stage of development in these matters, but apparently you've still got male chauvinists over there too." They chose not to answer.

As they were leaving I said, "By the way, we don't like that big SST you've got over there."

"Why?" they asked.

"Because a lot of guys here think that because you've got one, we've got to have one too."

They looked puzzled. "Some of us would rather compete with you on child care centers," I said.

What a day to have laryngitis! They screwed us up and down the line on the Selective Service conference report. They gave it a rule that prohibited us from raising points of order and from voting separately on the individual amendments. Between those who opposed the bill because it doesn't provide for the kind of military pay raises that will lead to a volunteer army, and those who are upset by the emasculation of the Mansfield Amendment, and those who are opposed to the draft in principle, we had enough votes to defeat the conference report. But we couldn't vote on the individual parts of the bill. We were given a choice only to take it or leave it, and naturally, they took it, 297-108.

And me? Was I frustrated! I passed Eddie Hébert a note that said, "Since I can't talk, would you please give me time to whisper?" He laughed. I was serious.

August 5

I can't stand the laryngitis anymore, so this morning I went to Bethesda to see a specialist about my throat. The diagnosis is that I have a nodule, which if it doesn't clear up, I'm going to have to have removed. That's all I need. Two weeks out of commission. Anyway, the doctor said it wasn't urgent, so I can put it off at least until after the recess which starts tomorrow. Martin and I are leaving for Israel and Europe Sunday for a couple of weeks.

The doctor was very funny. "I always thought you were a woman of the people," he said. "But it turns out you're a plutocrat just like the rest of them."

"How come?" I asked.

"Well," he said, "yesterday I got a message that I was to be here at eight thirty this morning for a command performance. Mrs. Abzug will be here, they told me. I told them I couldn't make it here at that hour because I was scheduled to teach a class. A half hour later the Admiral's secretary called me back: 'The Admiral says you better be there,' she said."

"You listen to me, Doctor," I said. "I had nothing to do with that."

"Oh, I know that," he said. "But still, your whole image is shattered in my eyes."

Saw Wayne Hays on the Floor. "What happened to your voice, Bella?" he said. "I think it would be a good day to make some remarks about you."

"That wouldn't be very sportsmanlike, now, would it, Wayne?"

"Who said I was sportsmanlike?"

"Spoken like a true scoundrel, Wayne," I said.

August 6

I went to a press conference in New York called to oppose the new fifty-cent fare they're now trying to pass off on us to ride buses and subways in New York City. I said if they put it through we should have a fare strike.

"Isn't that illegal?" a reporter asked me.

"What's more illegal?" I asked him. "Stealing pennies out of a poor man's pocket? Taking food out of his child's mouth? Taking the clothes off his family's back? Or urging him not to pay an outrageous fare of half a dollar every time he rides the subway?"

September 1

Back from our vacation. Although we spent a few days relaxing on the beach in Yugoslavia and a few days touring Copenhagen, the high point of the trip was the week we spent in Israel. We hadn't been there since 1959, mainly because I got very sick when we were there that time. I got such a violent bacterial infection that they thought for a while I had paratyphoid. It incapacitated me on and off for about eight months afterward. You might say it was a rather unusual act of political courage for me to go back there again this year, but we were very curious to see how things had changed.

Our trip this time was, of course, a little different. We were avid tourists in 1959. We rented a car and hired a driver, because we were determined to go swimming in every body of water in the country, from the Jordan River to the Mediterranean, from Lake Kinneret to the Red Sea. I remember that our guide, when he realized what kind of people we were, told us he had to go back to Tel Aviv before he took us any-where.

"How come?" I asked.

"Well," he said, "I have to get my bathing suit and my gun. My bathing suit because there have never been any tourists like you before, and my gun because you want me to take you places where we're likely to get shot at."

This time we visited all the occupied territories—the West Bank, the Golan Heights and so on—and the ironic thing is that our guide didn't have a gun, or need one. Certainly it's one of the most unusual occupations in history. You can drive through all the Arab towns and villages and never see an Israeli soldier.

When we weren't off exploring the country, I had a number of appointments with various government officials. I wasn't able to see Golda Meir, but I did have an appointment arranged with Yigal Allon, the Deputy Prime Minister. Unfortunately, his brother died the day the appointment was scheduled for, and we never met. One of the most interesting meetings I did have was with a high official in the Ministry of Foreign Affairs. At first he annoyed me a little because he seemed to be talking only in the most general way about the serious problems of Israel. Then I realized it must be very difficult for officials from another country to discuss their real plans with an American Congresswoman, so I couldn't expect too much. And the more I think about it, the more I realize this guy was unusually frank and honest, considering the circumstances. I came away with the distinct impression that there was real hope for some kind of negotiation between Israel and the Arab states, and that the Israelis were disappointed that Joseph Sisco from our State Department wasn't more effective in arranging it. In all, I enjoyed the whole discussion with this official. He was a very bright guy who indulged in a bit of dialectic Talmudic reasoning, as most Israelis do, and as I suppose I do now and then.

During our visit we attended a dramatic emergency meeting of the Knesset (parliament) called specially to deal with a doctors' strike. As I was coming out of the Knesset building, some young Americans spotted me, raised their hands in clenched fists and shouted, "Bella! Bella!" Fist-raising is a symbol of young people who are seeking change in society and who want to show their strength and unity. It's not, as many people think, only a symbol for black power. All the kids do it. If you've ever seen me at a rally, they're always raising their fists and giving me the V peace sign, both of which I return. I don't usually go around raising my fist, but to young people you've got to understand it's a form of greeting, a way of saying hello. And what's nice about it is that it signifies camaraderie and togetherness.

When I was sitting in the Knesset I noticed, to my surprise, that only 8 of the 120 members were women. One evening I met with some of the most outstanding women in the country and challenged them on this. The reply I got was that since women in Israel in fact *have* equality they don't have to prove it so much. I can't say I bought that argument—retrogression sets in if you're not at it all the time—but, on the other hand, I guess when a country has a woman prime minister it's the greatest evidence of acceptance of women that you can have. So the problems of women in Israel are not as great as they are here.

I was kind of surprised, though, to find that their child care system was not as fully developed as I had thought it would be, although far more advanced than ours. I was told that there are a hundred thousand working women with children in Israel, but space for only fourteen thousand children in day care facilities. However, the Ministry of Labor has made a major commitment to the construction of more facilities, and in two years they expect to have at least another fourteen thousand places.

Besides visiting child care centers, hospitals and absorption centers for new immigrants, I had meetings with the Ministers of Absorption and Health, numerous journalists and a representative of the Israeli Defense Forces—all very informative and interesting.

Just as I was about to leave Israel I received a call from the American Embassy and was asked if I would address the staff. That was an experience not to be believed. I went there and spoke to them as you would speak to people who have been away from their country for a number of years. I tried to explain, in the way I see it, what was happening with the Nixon Administration, the never-ending war, the disastrous state of the economy, the women's movement, the youth movement, etc.

They were stunned.

Afterwards there were a number of fascinating questions. To one I replied that it was my view that the United States should give foreign assistance only to democratic countries.

"Well, how do you determine if a country is democratic?" I was asked.

"I would imagine if I were a member of the State Department I would have some difficulty making that determination," I said. "But if I weren't a member of the State Department I would have no problem at all."

While I was away a number of interesting things happened. The article in *Time* came out. I was scared to death of that young man who was doing it, and although a lot of people think the article was favorable, it got me very angry. I don't want to read any more articles about how I use four-letter words. I don't use four-letter words, and that's it! Well, anyway, not to the extent they say I do, and *never* in Congress. And I'm also tired of all this business about my famous "staff problems." That's pretty outrageous and silly stuff. Plenty of freshmen don't have the same administrative assistant they started out with, and they changed theirs *before* I changed mine. Everybody has a little trouble putting together the right kind of staff, including people who've been in Congress a lot, lot longer than I have.

Oh yes, I sent John Lindsay a postcard from Denmark. "Great vote from Europe," it said. "Regards to Mary." I had known he was going to switch to the Democratic Party, of course. It was not news to me. I could have clocked it, time, date and place. But what interested me was the overwhelming response the switch got in Europe.

I'm glad Lindsay's a Democrat now, but my feelings aren't clarified about whether I think he should run for President. Lindsay considers me a good friend, and I consider him a good friend. He endorsed and supported me; I endorsed and supported him. Not only that, but I worked in his campaign to bring in the grass roots, or as somebody once said, "the weeds."

But I don't think the man has shown enough activism to justify his running for President. My friends at City Hall would be very aggravated at my saying this. They would answer, "So what have the other candidates done?"

All I can say to that is that the other candidates haven't done anything either. McGovern, of course, has very good positions on the issues, but he certainly hasn't put a flame under anybody. I'm looking for a candidate who's got the capacity to give people what they're desperately searching for —leadership. I want somebody who will attack the military, the concentration of corporate power, the plight of the cities, the continuation of the war, who will attack Congress for not stopping the war, and who in the process will build the coalition I've been talking about all along. I want an activist candidate.

It's true John Lindsay is a great liberal. He feels. But he has yet to prove he's an activist. And he also gets very uptight when you disagree with him. That must be his social background and temperament, which he would do well to get rid of. I don't know though. I suppose he's only got what he's got. I can't expect him to act like a Russian Jew.

So whom will I support for President? Let's say that if either McGovern or Lindsay changes his *style* and *approach*, I'd be inclined to support either one of them. But only if.

September 2

Well, we made it. This afternoon I delivered to the City Clerk the petitions calling for a referendum in November on statehood. We were able to get a total of fifty-five thousand signatures—ten thousand more than required, but ten thousand less than we had been hoping for. Now begins the process where the Clerk checks the validity of the signatures. This should take a month or so.

This whole movement has been gratifying and disappointing to me at the same time. On the one hand, I really feel moved by the hundreds of volunteers who devoted themselves to this project, and in the end did a magnificent job. On the other hand, we were unable to sustain the initial enthusiasm from when I first announced the drive. Summer is a bad time for a major campaign. Hopefully, we'll pick it up again once we get on the ballot.

September 12

I just spent a week in the hospital suffering from pneumonia. I was afraid this would happen, because when I left Israel I had a very bad cold. But anyway, I feel better now that I'm out of the hospital. It was a wild scene. I was getting so many phone calls and visits that I was exhausted each night. Friday, for example, Zohar Karthy came by with two women from Bonds for Israel. Zohar is a young, very attractive Assistant Minister of Labor in the Israeli government who's heading up the movement to provide more child care centers. The Israelis have a different problem from ours. They have a labor shortage, and so they're actually encouraging women to go to work. Zohar told me about one Druze village where the government built a pantyhose factory especially for women. And then, of course, they built a child care center for them.

There was a policy council meeting of the Women's Political Caucus scheduled for that night, and a lot of women dropped by to see me first. I hated missing it, but what could I do?

Suddenly, since I've been back, there's a lot of talk about the upcoming redistricting, about how I'm going to be "redistricted out of office." Nothing will probably happen until early next year when the state legislature takes formal action, but there are a couple of things I want to clear up here about the whole matter, since a lot of people don't seem to understand it.

First of all, talk that I'm going to be redistricted out is nonsense. What's going to happen is that Manhattan will lose one of its four seats in Congress, and that means the districts will have to be cut up differently than they are at present. Once they start carving, they might come up with, say, a new district which is made up of part of my present district and part of Ryan's or Koch's. In that event, it will be neither their district nor mine. It'll be up for grabs.

The point I'm trying to make is that the territory I now represent will be in *some* district, and probably two districts. It's not going to disappear. Since in New York you don't have to live in the district you represent—although at present I do —I can look at the new districts and pick the one I want to run in. Koch and Ryan will have the same option.

Whatever happens, the primary is going to be the toughest fight I ever got into. It's a shame, really, that a person has to face a meaningless primary, but what can I do? I'll tell you something else: Although a lot of people are convinced I can beat anybody, anywhere, anytime, I, quite frankly, am not so sure.

September 13

Well, we finally had something of a day in the House. By a vote of 356-49, we voted to repeal a law on the books since 1950 which gives the government authority to put suspected spies and saboteurs into detention camps during wartime and times of insurrection. Even Nixon supported repeal. Before the vote was taken I was kidding Eddie Hébert that this was one time we could both be on the same side of an issue.

"No, we can't," he said.

"Why?"

"Because that damn fool Ichord's got his neck way out on this one. He's on my committee, and I have to support him."

They stick together like flies, those guys.

There are two routes between my office and the Capitol building—one through the tunnel and the other up on the street. I don't like the underground route because it makes me feel like a rat in a maze, so when I get a chance I take the street. Sometimes, though, when I'm on my way back to the office, I'm very upset and involved in my thoughts from what happened on the Floor, and once, without looking, I walked into the middle of the street with the light against me. I nearly got run over. The traffic cop was hysterical.

"Ah, it doesn't matter," I told him. "Nobody'll miss me anyhow."

Ever since that incident he watches me like a hawk. He

actually stops the traffic for me. The men around here insist he only does it because I'm a woman. It's just like when we line up to vote in the well, and they recognize me first. The men say I'm taking advantage of being a woman; they try to tease me about how I'm not "liberated," and should tell the clerk not to recognize me first.

I always have the same answer: "I take any advantage that comes." Besides, women are entitled to reparations.

This is the first day back here since the recess, and everybody's telling me how great I look. And they're right! I still have some of my tan and I've lost some weight. My hair's been set and I happen to be wearing a new dress which is very becoming to me. It's really something how all the men notice these things. I've been trying to tell them the only reason I look better is that I just had a week's rest in the hospital.

"What was the matter?" asked Otis Pike.

"I had pneumonia."

"You should have it more often," he said.

My office is getting into better shape. Margot Polivy, a young FCC lawyer, is taking over as administrative assistant, and Eric Hirschhorn, who's been working in Albany for a group of liberal assemblymen, has already started as my legislative assistant.

September 14

I introduced another resolution of inquiry, this one directed to the Secretary of State to furnish all communications between his department and the U.S. embassy in Saigon and Messrs. Thieu, Ky and Minh with regard to the upcoming Vietnamese presidential elections. To everyone knowledgeable about Vietnam, except this Administration, the very thought of "free" elections has been ludicrous from the outset. And I want to

(234)

find out just what Nixon is doing to cover this up. As I said on the Floor, "Perhaps such revelations will stir this body to the action necessary to end once and for all—now—this interminable and senseless war." At the very least, I think it will help us get the 218 necessary votes to cut off funding for the war. Between now and the end of the session, I figure we'll have six or eight opportunities in votes on defense authorizations, appropriations and conference reports to do just that.

I ran into the columnist Mary McGrory after a National Democratic Coalition panel on foreign policy this afternoon, in which I had gone into my thing about women, the male power structure and the military-dominated society. "Bella," she said, "I want you to know I disagree with what you're always saying about how women are going to change things. There's not another woman in Congress who's doing anything but you." I told her it will be different when the Women's Political Caucus gets going. Some of the women in Congress are no better than men, because they're all products of the male power structure. They come in, replace the men, act the same way as men, and do their bidding. They don't come out of a movement for social change.

But she said, "You're the only one, Bella. You're great. You're the only one who cares, who knows, who feels. And I'll never buy that women's political power stuff you talk about. You'll never convince me." And on and on she went. I couldn't stop her, I don't know what got into her.

September 15

Everybody's talking about the tragedy at Attica, and the absolutely horrifying things that happened there. What they don't seem to understand, though, is that when people, like the Attica prisoners, have ineffective means to redress their grievances, they feel compelled to resort to illegitimate tactics to resolve them. It's evident that the vast majority of the prisoners' demands were valid ones—twenty-eight out of thirty were accepted without hesitation. One of the two remaining—that of amnesty for the prisoners—would never have been necessary had prior attention been given to the urgent matter of penal reform.

Now we hear that the state is going to conduct an investigation. Isn't that ridiculous? This means the state is going to investigate itself, despite the fact that the Governor and other state officials may themselves be highly culpable for both the conditions that led to the revolt of the prisoners and the murderous handling of the rebellion itself.

Whoever caused the deaths at Attica has got to be brought to justice. That's why I'm urging Manny Celler, who's chairman of the House Judiciary Committee, to conduct an official Congressional investigation. And just so, in the meantime, we don't have another awful tragedy like this on our hands, I'm calling on Rockefeller to set up an independent statewide citizens committee to act as ombudsmen for both prisoners and guards in all New York prisons.

Can you conceive of holding a meeting of the Democratic caucus, as we did today, just after a recess during which it became absolutely clear that the upcoming Vietnam elections are rigged, and not once mentioning the issue of the war? Well, that's what happened.

The caucus was strictly given over to reports from the leadership. Everything else was *verboten*.

And what did our great leaders have to say?

Carl Albert: "The purpose of the caucus is to advise members about what's happening, to help formulate Democratic policy, and to help assure the reelection of its members. . . . The caucus is not for confrontation. . . . We don't mean that we're trying to seek conformity. We mean that the caucus is not the place for intra-party bickering or for copy for the press. . . . Anyone who uses the caucus for the press does not attain a public relations credit. . . ."

Yeah, in *his* opinion. Here's more: "Public displays of crying and gnashing of the teeth are counterproductive. . . . I love and respect every Democratic member of the House [I swear these are his words, because I wrote them down] . . . and whether I disagree with you or not, I want each and every one of you to be reelected."

Then we heard Hale Boggs. I was talking to Shirley, so I didn't catch much of his nonsense. Then Wilbur Mills: "We'll be concluding hearings on the full proposals of the President's economic program this week. Then we're going to have some executive sessions next week, and we're going to make some changes in the President's package. You can be sure that we'll be finished in October, because I'm going to be very busy going into lots of Congressional districts."

Shocking! Nothing, no substance, nothing! The man didn't say anything except that he was running for President.

When the time for questions came, Father Drinan, from Massachusetts, got up and said, "The majority of Democrats have indicated in voting for Nedzi-Whalen and the one-year extension of the draft that they want to end the war. Since this represents an expression of the majority of the majority party, I'd like to know what the position of the leadership is on these issues." Nobody answered him. They just ignored him, and went on to another speech.

So I kept standing, trying to get the floor, planning to say, "I'd like to hear Father Drinan's question answered." But they wouldn't recognize me. Finally, I turned to Parren Mitchell and asked him to try and get the floor and ask the question. But he made the mistake of whispering his intention to Tip O'Neill, the Whip, and so he was never recognized either. Parren's going to have to learn.

(237)

Then O'Neill, since he's a leader and he had yet to report, got up and said, "The leadership has been very forthright on its positions on the economy, and never let it be said that the leadership is not also willing to discuss its positions on foreign policy too. Anybody can get any question he has on foreign policy answered simply by walking into Mr. Boggs' or Mr. Albert's office."

So that was that, believe it or not.

And how did my liberal friends feel? They just shrugged. "You gotta change Congress, Bella," is what they tell me. Otherwise, they don't even react at all. They insist, "When you're here as long as we're here, Bella, any little victory is a victory." These tired men are still glowing over the repeal of the detention camp law.

Incidentally, because I'm so often critical of the leadership, I've been denied a few petty payoffs. For instance, various Congressmen are invited to bang the gavel in the House when Carl's not there, but I've never been asked. Also, at the end of a day it's procedure that you can insert articles or statements into the *Record* from the cloakroom. One Congressman is selected by the leadership to get permission for everybody. Of course, I've never been asked to do that either. It's just their petty way of penalizing me, and it doesn't bother me a bit. Anyway, as Sidney Yates from Chicago said to me the other day, "If I were Carl Albert, I'd shudder the moment you walked *up to* the chair, let alone *sat in* the chair."

While I don't care much about sitting in the chair, I must admit that I do have a hallucination—I can't even call it a dream—sometimes, that I'll rise and say, "Mr. Speaker, I ask for a privileged resolution to end the war in Vietnam." And whoever is in the chair will recognize me. And there will be an immediate mass falling over on the House Floor. I already asked Ella Grasso if she'll conspire to do this with me when she gets her turn in the chair. "Are you crazy?" she laughed. But before the session is finished, I think I just might figure out a way to do it.

September 16

The trouble with the Democratic leadership is that half the time they're leading us backward, and the few times when they take a progressive stand on an issue, like today on strengthening the enforcement powers of the Equal Employment Opportunity Commission, they're totally ineffective. Even with their support, we lost—by five votes yet, and there was a total of sixty-nine Democrats who voted *against* us.

The EEOC, which was created under the Civil Rights Act of 1964, has never been given enforcement powers to end job discrimination. It can only investigate and seek redress through informal kinds of conciliation—which is why in more than half of the thirty-six thousand cases it's investigated it hasn't been able to do a thing. The bill we were voting on would have given the EEOC cease and desist powers, among other things, so that women and members of minority groups and others wouldn't have to wait years before they could get back pay or be reinstated to jobs in which they were discriminated against. What we ended up passing was a weak and meaningless Republican substitute bill which keeps the EEOC a watchdog without teeth. But everyone says the Senate will pass a strong bill, and something good will come out of conference. We'll see.

This morning I had the opportunity to testify before the Ways and Means Committee on Nixon's new economic program. I started out by saying "The President's proposals reinforce his position as the superchief of corporate America. Although many Americans have been stunned by the reversal of the

(239)

President's economic policies, from hands-off to sweeping interventionism, there is a consistency that ties these policies together, in that big business remains the favorite and working people and small business are still the victims."

I went into a lot of specific details, but the point I tried to reinforce was that if Nixon really wants to strengthen the economy, then he should end the war immediately, cut back drastically on military spending and turn the money over to such nonlethal projects as providing jobs, repairing our decaying cities, building low and middle income housing, creating and improving mass transit facilities, dealing with drug and pollution problems and assuring 25.5 million poor people a guaranteed annual income. And we'd probably still have money left over—when you consider that we're now wasting $76 billion a year on Pentagon adventures.

September 20

This time we're going to make it awfully hard for Nixon *not* to appoint a woman to fill the Supreme Court vacancy created by the death of Hugo Black. We prepared, through the National Women's Political Caucus, a telegram to the White House, urging the President to appoint a woman, and offering him the names of forty women who are federal judges, state supreme court judges, law professors and members of Congress to pick from. I took my own name off the list. Not that I wouldn't like to be a Supreme Court Justice, but, well, you know, I signed the telegram.

September 22

Frank Annunzio, who's a Daley-machine politician from Chicago, almost got run over by a car at the same intersection where it almost happened to me. The cop told him what I said at the time. So Frank, who's always attacking me for having supported Lindsay for Mayor ("You and that Lindsay of yours," etc.), came up to me on the Floor and said, "What do you mean telling the cop nobody would miss you? I had to tell him, 'She's absolutely wrong. We would all miss her, and her passion and her concern, and her smile, and her carrying on, and her joking, especially when she doesn't win a vote she wants.'"

I thought that was a sweet thing for him to say. And he usually doesn't even vote with me, this guy. And, like he says, when he does, he loses.

September 23

Meeting of the Women's Caucus steering committee. There's still some friction from Betty and a few others. Betty again insinuated that I wouldn't welcome in the Caucus Republicans and middle class people as much as I would young people and minority group women. I mean, it's all such nonsense. All over the country all kinds of women respond to me. I'm a much more total person than most women in the women's movement. Not that the others don't have total personalities—it's just that they have dealt in their careers strictly with the women's question. I am a woman who has proven that I not only care about and am able to relate to women, but care about and am able to relate to all people.

September 25

I was talking politics tonight in Madison, Wisconsin, in a speech to the New Democratic Coalition out here. Mostly presidential politics, because I'm beginning to get a little scared that we could lose this next one, once again, to Nixon. I mean, look who the frontrunner for the nomination is: Muskie. It will be tough to beat Nixon with Muskie. He's a stiff soldier, that guy. We can only beat Nixon with a guy who's willing to go out there and scream and holler about the economy and the war, and Muskie's too damn uptight. You'd never know he was a Catholic, he's so uptight. The guy's off-key on the whole passion thing. He's got none.

Who instead of Muskie? That's what I keep asking myself. Every time I read the papers about Lindsay or McGovern I get sad. I haven't figured out what that means, I haven't analyzed it yet. But I'll tell you, when I get this way there's a reason—and it comes to me sooner or later. McCloskey? Do you know that guy has informed me that he doesn't intend to vote for the Equal Rights Amendment?

"Are you crazy?" I asked him. "You might as well be committing political suicide."

"I can't help it," he said. "I can't bear to see women serve in the draft."

September 27

This you are not going to believe! The New Orleans *States-Item* asked Eddie Hébert if he knew of any women qualified for the Supreme Court. "I'm sure there are many," he said. "Bella Abzug is a love. I admire her. We're great friends. Not many realize she was once editor of the *Columbia Law Review*. . . . She is one of the most brilliant Congresswomen we have."

What's he trying to do? Kick me upstairs?

September 28

In trying to head off the impact of my resolution of inquiry, the State Department arranged a briefing for Congressmen and women on the Vietnam elections, which I agreed to and got a lot of people to attend. But they didn't tell us anything we hadn't already read in the newspapers, which is par for them, and so I'm going to continue to press for passage of the resolution when it's reported out of committee later this week.

Remember Chet Holifield? Ever since the initial meeting of his Government Operations Committee last winter, when I opposed his reorganization plans, he hasn't said a word to me. Until today. "How are you? What've you been up to? How's your family?" Can't figure out what the hell he's up to.

You know what I *think* it is? I think he's one of the many guys around here who are suddenly coming to terms with the potential of the women's vote. A lot of these guys insist that the women's vote is going to be divided, but Holifield's a smarter politician than most. He's an old-timer. I also think he's beginning to catch on to my style.

September 30

A day not to be believed. As Martha Griffiths said to me when it was all over, "You're fast, Bella, but this time they beat you to it, and you had it coming to you, you smart aleck. You should know you have to be here every minute if you have something going!"

All morning I had been trying to get hold of Doc Morgan, the chairman of the Foreign Affairs Committee, because he had told me that he was going to bring my resolution of inquiry to the Floor today, and I wanted to find out at precisely what time. Because I was unable to reach him, I left my office and started for the Floor at around ten minutes to noon. The House convenes at noon, although it doesn't usually get down to business until at least a half hour later, since normal procedure is to listen to the opening prayer and then listen to a series of one-minute speeches by members who have something to say on anything. Figuring I had enough time, I stopped in the bathroom for a minute or so, and arrived on the Floor at three minutes after twelve. By that time Doc Morgan and the leadership had already done me in.

Dispensing with the tradition of first allowing for the one-minute speeches, of which there are often a dozen or more in a day (I'm surprised they didn't do away with the prayer too), the House moved with incredible speed to okay Doc's motion to table my resolution with a voice vote. One, two, three, they killed my resolution—just like that—with only a handful of the members present.

As soon as I arrived and found out what had happened, I started storming around the chamber looking for Morgan. Not that I ever expected to win the vote on the resolution, but legislation is *never* brought up in the first two minutes of the session, and *never* in the absence of the sponsoring legislator. I was mad as hell. I don't like being knifed in the back, no matter how insecure the leadership has become at being challenged. I wanted Morgan to vacate the proceedings under which the resolution had been tabled. But since I couldn't find him—he hit and ran—I decided to do it myself.

"Mr. Speaker," I said, "I ask unanimous consent to vacate the procedure under which House Resolution 595 was laid on the table."

I tried to speak quietly so none of the regular refusers of unanimous consent could hear me, but Carl Albert's too clever for that. He asked me to please step into the well, where there's a microphone, and repeat myself. You see, if nobody objected, he'd be forced to grant my request.

But this time, my amplified voice seemed to reach Hale Boggs, who once more asked me to repeat myself, and then replied he had heard Doc Morgan say "he had been in consultation with the gentlewoman from New York and that he had made some agreement that she would be here."

(244)

Meanwhile, Morgan was still nowhere to be found, so I explained my version of what had happened—that I had been trying to get in touch with him. And then just to prove my good intent about the whole resolution I explained that "in order to make certain that there would be every opportunity to receive the information [about U.S. involvement in the South Vietnamese elections] the resolution seeks," I had arranged a briefing with the State Department, but they had given us nothing we couldn't read in the papers.

Then a guy by the name of Durward Hall from Missouri got up and objected to my request for unanimous consent, and that ended it. The bastards! Whereupon I went over to Boggs and Albert and said, "Okay, fellows, you broke the rules of your own club. If that's how you play, I can play that way too. I'm not going to give unanimous consent to anything anymore—you guys are going to have to vote on everything in this House." And I wasn't kidding. The way I felt at that moment, I would have called for a vote on the opening prayer.

So to placate me somewhat Hale Boggs went into a charade of trying to find Morgan. He didn't, of course, and that was it. I really feel terrible. I've never felt so badly about anything in my whole life. I'm never late for *anything*. All I can say is that these guys have yet to hear the end of it, that much I promise.

An upsetting day on another account too. I got notice from Herman Katz, the City Clerk, that he's rejecting the petitions to put the statehood proposal on the ballot. He claims we didn't have enough valid signatures, and that's largely because he rejected all the signatures of those people who are between eighteen and twenty-one years old, claiming their names did not appear on voter registration lists. They just got the vote, so how could they have been registered for the last election? He claims only persons who registered in the last election were qualified to sign (and witness too). He rejected whole petitions that were witnessed by eighteen- to twenty-one-year-olds.

As far as I'm concerned, he's tampering with some very important constitutional rights, and we're going to challenge his decision in the courts. Nonetheless, and it's very unfortunate, they've accomplished what they intended. They hung us on a technicality, so it's going to be impossible to get the statehood referendum on this year's ballot. All along, to tell you the truth, I had a feeling they'd do something like this. They always try to wear you down until you're too weary to do anything anymore. I feel especially bad about all the hard work put in by the volunteers. They felt deeply committed to this issue, as I still do, and there was real anger at the city's knifing a movement that was designed to *help* the city.

Late this afternoon, as part of a bill extending antipoverty programs for another two years, we passed, 251-115, a child care law. In a way I'm thrilled about it because a good chunk of the Abzug-Chisholm bill was included—provisions like twenty-four-hour child care centers, sponsorship by private groups, retention of existing Head Start programs. But there are also some disappointments. Unlike the Senate's bill, which passed a few weeks ago and authorizes $2 billion to develop child care centers, the House bill sets no money figure. I'm also distressed that the House bill only provides *free* child care services to the very poor—those families with annual incomes of less than $4320. (The Senate set this figure at $6900.) There seems to be an unfortunate tendency on the part of many people down here to think of child care as something that should meet the needs of only the poor. The Abzug-Chisholm bill would have accommodated the poor while moving toward a truly comprehensive system of free child care. Another thing that bothers me about the bill is that it does not call for child care centers to be operated on a nonprofit basis. This means the profiteers will have their day in meeting the basic needs of children for care and education. A chicken franchise business is actually going into the business of setting up child care centers! Of course, all they're interested in is making a buck.

Nonetheless, finally we do have a bill. I've always felt that a nation can be judged by the quality of care it provides for its children—not by its airplanes and its missiles. And since for the longest time we've simply ignored the whole matter of child care, this bill, I guess, can be viewed as a beginning.

October 4

On the first and third Mondays of the month we're supposed to operate on what's called a "suspension calendar," under which the rules are suspended so that noncontroversial bills can be brought to the Floor. I was sitting there when up came this resolution that appeared harmless, but which in fact should not have been on the calendar. It called for the "humane treatment" and repatriation of American prisoners of war.

I got up and pointed out that it doesn't take a great deal of courage to support a resolution like this, but the shame of it was that it was being brought up under the suspension calendar when we didn't have the right to amend it. After all, if we're really concerned about the health and safety of our prisoners, it seems to me we should bring them home. As of three months ago, the North Vietnamese said they're willing to let us do just that. They promised that once we set a date for our withdrawal, the repatriation of prisoners could begin concurrently with the removal of our troops. Instead of mouthing platitudes about the humane treatment of prisoners, it might be a better idea to force Nixon to answer the North Vietnamese proposal, which he has yet to do.

October 5

In view of the fact that the Senate has once again attached the Mansfield Amendment to a military bill, a group of us decided to confront Boggs and Albert and tell them it was time to fish or cut bait. By refusing to support the amendment, they are not only going against the will of the American people, but against the will of the majority of Democrats in the House.

Although he didn't help us, Boggs at least didn't speak against Mansfield the last time. Albert, on the other hand, spoke and voted against it. So we told them, "You're either leaders or you're not leaders." Boggs said he'd think about it, and maybe do something to help us next time; Albert said he couldn't change his position. He believed in consistency, he said. "Just like Mansfield has a consistent position, I have mine." All he agreed to do was not obstruct us by speaking against it the next time.

"You know, Carl," I said, "I can't understand you. We continue to spill blood over there for no reason at all, and you tell us it's not your responsibility to change your point of view."

"I respect your point of view, Bella, you should respect mine," he said.

"You're wrong. You're hurting the Democratic Party."

"Look, Bella, I respect you. Please."

It seemed that he wanted to elicit from me a statement that I respected him too. He didn't get it. I like him personally, but that's not the issue.

Later in the day, on the Floor, the great economic tax package came back from Ways and Means with a rule that it couldn't be amended. We were told, in effect, to take it or leave it. I left it, because it's nothing but a program of giveaways to corporations and a bonanza for big business. The surprising thing was how few Congressmen even bothered to come and say something, one way or the other. As I said, in starting out my remarks, "I must admit that the number of people in the chamber participating in the discussion of the great economic problems of this time is having a chilling effect upon my normal enthusiasm for participating in debate."

Earlier I had bumped into Wilbur Mills, the Ways and Means chairman. "You running for President, Bella?" he said to me through a group of people.

"No," I said, "but Wilbur is, and if I were running, I would have never reported out such an antipeople bill."

October 6

When the House convened at noon I was tied up in a meeting for a few minutes when I got a frantic phone call from Don Edwards, who's chairman of the Judiciary subcommittee that is reporting out the Equal Rights Amendment.

"Get to the Floor immediately," he said. "They've already rammed through the economic tax package with a voice vote, and they're moving right into the Equal Rights debate, and *nobody's* there yet."

Not only that, but they went on, with Don not even being there, to decide by a voice vote the kind of rule under which the amendment was going to be debated. I'm getting very depressed by the rigidity and trickery under which business is done in the House. The leadership seems to be getting into the habit of springing things on us when we're least expecting them, and it's obvious that they're up to no good.

By the time I got there Martha Griffiths was opening the debate. She was followed in the debate by Manny Celler, who was true to form and worse than ever at the same time. He even talked about the fact that as far as he had noticed, "the fallopian tube has not yet become vestigial," and that our sloganeering for equal rights could be compared to a campaign to "Crush Phallic Imperialism." As if it were so frivolous. He worried that if we passed the amendment, family life would be threatened, and marriage as an institution would totter. He pointed out that "women have had the vote for half a century, but used [it] overwhelmingly, not to elect women, but to elect men," and cited some poll to prove that women "were not interested in so-called escaping from the so-called cage." All in all—outrageous. Conceding that there were instances of unfair discrimination against women (other than what he called the discrimination of "nature, the result of germ plasm"), he argued that any remedy should come through the courts and legislation—not by constitutional amendment.

When I got up, I tried to stay away from the silly business of the sex issue and answer his last point: "An amendment seeks national approval for changes in basic problems and basic conditions that exist in our society. Once this amendment is passed by Congress, the people, through the political process called ratification, will be able to participate in this national decision, to have their say concerning the very important principle of equality under the law for women."

I pointed out that we have gotten nowhere with legislation or the courts, especially the courts, which are male strongholds. I then went into a discussion of the real issue at hand—the Wiggins Amendment, which had been added in committee, which would continue to exempt women from the draft or any other law that "reasonably promotes the health and safety of the people." As an example of how preposterous these "protective" labor laws are I cited the night work laws, which prevent women from working overtime or taking jobs, such as elevator operators, at night, when the work is less and the pay is more. These same night work laws do not protect the cleaning women in this country from the back-breaking toil they regularly perform at night while their "protectors" sleep safely in their beds.

That line brought the House down, such House as there was. Maybe forty Representatives were there. Anyhow, it did awaken the gallery.

I just noticed in this evening's Washington *Star* that a columnist by the name of Morris Siegel writes, "White House gossip says President Nixon is seriously considering appointing a woman to one of the two Supreme Court vacancies. . . . Why not get the whole thing over with at one time by appointing Bella Abzug to both seats?"

One will be enough, Morris—to speak from *and* to sit on, thank you.

October 7

No vote on Equal Rights as expected. One of the members died, Congressman James Fulton from Pennsylvania. They always suspend a session when you die. It's like Manny Celler has God, the Bible and death control on his side.

October 8

A couple of months ago Egee got her own apartment, her first, in Brooklyn Heights. It's a fourth-floor walk-up, which is why until today I never saw it. Every time Martin and I drove her home, I'd look at those steps and figure if I climbed them, it'd be the last thing I ever did.

Tonight she invited us over for dinner. I made the climb, huffing and puffing but still in one piece, and it's a lovely little apartment. She has it furnished with items from thrift shops in the neighborhood, and a rug we brought her back from Denmark.

Egee's still in school—she has six months before she gradu-ates. She commutes out to Hofstra every day in a car we bought for her and Liz to share. Liz, of course, is in Boston, and she only uses the car when she's home. They have an inter-esting arrangement for sharing it—I don't know the details, but it seems to work.

It was a great evening. Egee's feeling pretty happy, and she seems to be much more at ease with herself and the world. She doesn't even mind it when people come up to me and fall over me, complimenting me, which is something that used to annoy her.

October 9

Busy day in the community, ending in a rap session with some kids in a rehabilitation drug program in the Clinton area on the West Side, one of the most interesting exchanges I've par-ticipated in all year. For the first time, I guess, I really sensed the depth and vastness of the drug problem. I got the idea that perhaps the only way to go about solving it is to bring all the groups now doing drug rehabilitation work into one giant coalition. Organize it like a political campaign—except as a crusade to educate parents, employers and communities as to what drugs are all about. Next to taking care of the actual physical problem, this might be the best treatment of all for ad-dicts. With all the talk these days about drug-oriented crime, people seem to have lost sight of the fact that addicts are human beings too—very desperate human beings deeply in need of care.

Afterwards, Martin and I had dinner with Liz, who's in for the weekend. Like her sister, she's also a bit more relaxed about "Mama" these days. Having your mother become a major political figure takes getting used to, and I can empa-thize with them both. After all, there are always stupid professors coming up to them saying things like, "I hope you're as challenging as your mother." It puts them on the spot. They both, obviously, want to be on their own. They don't want to have to match up to my standards, and they don't want to have to feel they have to be outstanding just because they have Bella Abzug for a mother.

October 12

We knocked out the Wiggins Amendment (265-87) and went on to pass Equal Rights, 354-23. Now it goes to the Senate, where it was bottled up last year, and where we again expect to have some trouble. In any case, the Senate is not likely to act on it before next year.

The debate today wasn't as exciting as it was last week, but not to be believed were a couple of guys who got up and announced that their wives had "ordered" them to vote against the amendment.

So my first words when I got to the Floor were, "I want to say that I do not come here under instructions from my husband on how to vote."

Anyhow, it was probably our most glorious victory of the year. Incidentally, all the women except Leonor Sullivan voted for it. Why not Leonor? "Old-fashioned girl," as she puts it.

October 13

They hung Eddie Hébert today—his portrait, I mean, in the Armed Services Committee hearing room. I attended the ceremony, which seemed to surprise everybody from the military-industrial complex. "What's this relationship between you and Eddie?" they asked. I tried to explain that before we square off, we're very friendly. "You stick with me, Bella baby," that's how he talks, "you stick with me and I'm going to teach you all the rules."

I met Eddie's wife for the first time—a big Southern woman, very charming. "I'm glad to meet my competition," she said.

October 14

Bad defeat on a bill to create an independent agency to advocate and defend consumer interest. I voted against it when it was reported out of the Government Operations Committee last week, because all the strengthening amendments which would have given enforcement powers to this new consumer agency were voted down. I had fought hard in committee in support of Ben Rosenthal's stronger version, which was prepared by Ralph Nader. We tried to get the amendments in the bill again on the Floor, but they were rejected. Very sad. I ended up voting for the weakened bill, which passed with only forty-four votes against, on the theory that a consumer agency without teeth is better than none at all. But it's very discouraging. If they can't pass a strong consumers' bill, what can they pass?

October 17

More than a hundred people attended an all-day crime conference organized by my office and held in the auditorium of the VA building in New York. It was a very varied group of people from all over the district, including police, representatives from tenant groups and block associations, businessmen, white, black, Puerto Rican and Chinese. It was a good give and take session; everybody was very loose. They seemed to enjoy the opportunity to be able to say what was on their minds without being encumbered by experts. Some pretty good recommendations came out of the session which I'm passing on next week to the Police Commissioner, such as increasing the number of visible uniformed police on the street and setting up a permanent commission to investigate, on a community level, complaints concerning police inaction and corruption.

During the lunch break I ran up to see this home for the elderly which my mother might be going into. They've accepted her, but they're making a big song and dance about how much money they need. She'll go in under Medicaid, so what they're really looking for is supplemental "contributions."

"I'm a *kaptsan*," I said. (*Kaptsan* is Yiddish for somebody who doesn't have any money.)

"Well, you go around campaigning, don't you?"

"Yes."

"Well, you could campaign for contributions."

October 18

Since I had an important meeting to attend in Washington this morning, I wasn't able to testify as scheduled before a City Council committee considering a bill to extend jurisdiction of the city's Human Rights Commission to include discrimination against homosexuals. I was one of the earliest supporters of this cause, and since the organized homosexual groups have come to expect a great deal of help from me, I made it a point to cram in some radio and television appearances specifically to urge support for the bill. Then I sent Dora Friedman to the hearing to read my testimony for me, which in part said, "It has been estimated that there are 20 to 30 million homosexuals in the United States, forced by law, prejudice and ignorance to be so-called closet homosexuals, living in fear of ostracism, reprisals and criminal prosecution. . . .

"But even if homosexuals were only a tiny minority of men and women, the issue would be the same. The issue is the right of the individual to privacy, the right to choose his or her own sexual orientation, the freedom of consenting individuals to engage in private relationships which simply are not the business of anyone else or of society at large. . . .

"It is time to stop treating homosexuals as pariahs and latent criminals. It is ironic that a city so famous for its culture, theater and art should deny protection to the many men and women who have made such great contributions to this reputation. . . . But whether they are famous or unknown, talented or ordinary, homosexuals are individuals, and as such they have a right to expect that this city will provide them with legal redress against unfair discrimination."

The Democratic caucus this month has again been turned into a lecture from the leadership—further postponing all items on the agenda, such as my small proposal to withdraw from Vietnam by the end of December. "What is this?" I said to Olin Teague, the caucus chairman. "You think you're going to turn the caucus into a sewing circle. We have to come here to get lectured at? I happen to have a very important item on the agenda, and I don't have time to fritter away at your lectures." He promised to reschedule my item for next month—providing we're unsuccessful in getting the Mansfield Amendment into a military bill before then. Actually, there's a good chance that we'll be able to get Mansfield back into the military procurement bill. Tomorrow we're scheduled to vote on whether and how to instruct House conferees to seek to reconcile our version of the procurement bill, which doesn't have the Mansfield Amendment, with the Senate's, which does. A number of us have been lobbying heavily for votes to instruct the conferees to accept the Senate version in conference—and we're hoping to have enough votes to win. Some of us went to see Carl Albert and Hale Boggs again. This time Carl said he wouldn't talk against Mansfield and promised us a direct vote on the issue.

October 19

They'll break every rule in the book to beat you if they feel you've got something on them—that's the way the leadership in this House operates. It's brutal and sick. They apparently realized we would win a vote on instructing our conferees to accept the Mansfield Amendment, so they refused to even allow us to have one. I don't know exactly what happened, but obviously the White House got panicky and went to its allies among the Democrats, who unfortunately include our great leaders Albert and Boggs, who, very simply, double-crossed us. I knew something would go wrong. Carl told me before the session that the parliamentary situation might not allow a clear vote.

When the debate opened, Chuck Whalen from Ohio had a motion ready which would have instructed the conferees to accept the Mansfield Amendment in conference. But Carl claimed he was obligated to follow some House tradition that if any motion to instruct conferees were to be made, the Minority (Republican) Leader would have to choose the member to do so. Actually, this was an old tradition (not even a procedure) which they trotted out for the occasion. So Gerry Ford picked Leslie Arends from Illinois, the Republican with the highest seniority on the Armed Services Committee.

Arends, of course, then made a motion instructing the House conferees *not* to accept any Senate amendment not germane under House rules, which in this case meant the Mansfield Amendment. Here's where it gets very complicated. In order to amend the Arends motion we first had to vote on

(257)

what's called a "previous question"—a technical motion to cut off debate and force a vote. In order to amend the Arends motion we had to defeat the "previous question." Since they weren't allowing a clear vote, what it boiled down to is this: Those voting *against* the "previous question" were the supporters of the Mansfield Amendment. And since it got so confusing, we lost. The "previous question" passed 215–192.

Then a few minutes later the Arends motion was defeated by 215 to 193 votes. About twenty-five reactionaries who were against Mansfield switched votes. They wanted the House conferees to be free to accept a Senate amendment lifting the embargo on importing chrome from the racist government of Rhodesia. The effect of all this: to leave the House conferees free to oppose the Mansfield Amendment in conference. Which, of course, they will do, as they already have in the Selective Service bill.

So once again we were double-crossed. They make it so complicated that the public doesn't even know how it's getting screwed. As I said in my remarks, "A majority of this House as well as a majority of the American people want to set a date certain for the withdrawal of all our troops from Vietnam. Yet a minority of this House seeks to thwart [us] . . . from obtaining a clear vote on this question."

In any case, you'll be interested to know that this was the first time all the women in the House voted together against the war (against the previous question; against Arends), and 192 votes are the most we ever had. We only need 218 for a majority, and obviously we're working our way there. The only shame is all the death and killing that'll take place before we can get together those extra twenty-six votes.

Meanwhile, Nixon is escalating the air war over Indochina. Most Americans don't know it but our planes are dropping more bombs there now than even under Johnson.

October 20

Lester Wolff, a Representative from Long Island, introduced not long ago a resolution of inquiry on the South Vietnamese elections, which is almost exactly the same as mine. It came up on the Floor today (he chose not to fight for it, accepting one of those phony State Department briefings instead), and rising to speak in favor of it, I said, "I want to thank the chairman for recognizing me, late though it is."

Everybody says that my one saving grace is that I always have a funny comment to make, but I assure you that was not the case later this afternoon when Eddie Hébert brought the military construction authorization bill back from conference. First I called a quorum, which upset him, and then I called a roll call vote, which upset him even more.

Both times he tried to dissuade me. "Bella baby," he said, "there's no money in it for Vietnam or ABM."

"Eddie," I said, "you're not going to get one penny for the military—and I don't care what it's for—until we end this war. Period."

I was among the 26 who voted against the bill, as opposed to the 370 who voted for it.

October 21

Eddie Hébert's bill today was on pensions for men in the armed services. "I'm not going to fight you, Eddie," I said.

"You're not?" he said, startled. "What's got into you, Bella baby?"

"You can have your pensions, Eddie, but no money for any other military stuff."

"Khrushchev would be happy to hear you say that."

"Listen, Eddie, I knew you were a devil, but I didn't know

you were that much of a devil that you could communicate with the dead."

"Huh?"

"Khrushchev is dead!"

"I mean that other fellow with the 'K' then."

"Who? Kosygin?"

"Yeah—that's it."

October 22

Nixon has done it again. He's appointed two backward *men* to the Supreme Court. It's an awful put-down for us. But I read that even Pat Nixon said if he doesn't appoint a woman he'll have to answer to her. Maybe we'll get her to join the Women's Political Caucus.

After he answers Pat, I say he's going to have to answer to the rest of the women in America in 1972. I knew he was backward, but until today I don't think I was prepared to say he's stupid too. By not appointing a woman to one of those seats, he did a very stupid thing—politically.

He played a typical cat-and-mouse game with the issue. First the White House leaked the story that he was considering appointing a woman. Then he submitted a list to the Bar Association that included a woman judge from California who was so poorly qualified that there was a general outcry. See, he was trying to imply he couldn't find a woman good enough for the Supreme Court. The problem was, he couldn't find one bad enough.

October 26

Lindsay called me today in response to a plea I made to him to open as scheduled a new hospital on the Lower East Side.

(260)

The city's Health and Hospital Corporation budget is running on a deficit, and there have been hints that this is one of the projects they plan on scrapping—even though it's the only medical facility of its kind for people in that neighborhood. He said there was no money, but he'd try to do what he could to see that it opened as planned next year. He was sort of vague, so I said, "Look, this is something which has to be done."

He immediately blew his cool. "Well, if you and your colleagues in Congress weren't so ineffective, maybe we wouldn't have this problem to begin with."

Whereupon I let him have it: "I don't think that's a right thing for you to say to me. After all, I never said how ineffective I thought *you* were when you failed to solve the transit fare problem. I never said how ineffective I thought you were when you gave large increases to labor in this city without regard to the effects on other budgetary problems. I never said how ineffective I thought you were in your failure to mobilize the constituencies of this city and other cities on behalf of urban programs. And I don't think you have any right to talk to me that way." And so on and so forth.

"Are you implying that I'm ineffective?" he said.

"I didn't *imply* any such thing," I said. And hung up.

Since January I've been wanting to swim in the Capitol pool, so today my secretary called to make me an appointment for tomorrow.

"Women can only use the pool early in the morning," she was told.

We're going to have to do something about that!

(261)

My brother-in-law from California was in Washington on business this afternoon. We went out to dinner at what I was led to believe is the fanciest French restaurant in town. The food was a terrific disappointment. After dinner I showed him my little apartment, and he was somewhat appalled at its stark quality. It looks like a hotel room. I hate coming back to it at night, even though most nights I work in the office until eleven or twelve.

October 27

They brought up the military construction appropriations bill today (as opposed to the military construction *authorization* last week) with a new trick, which makes it harder to oppose. They have taken appropriations for certain kinds of military hardware out, and presented the bill to us as primarily a $2 billion appropriation for G.I. housing. On the theory that the money's only going to housing they very correctly assumed that the liberals weren't going to bother to fight it. After reading the bill, however, I got a little suspicious, and asked Robert Sikes, the chairman of the subcommittee on military construction, to yield for a question.

"Are there not funds for five [Safeguard missile] construction sites in this bill?" I asked.

"I intend to discuss that within a very few minutes," he said.

In the meantime, we were scheduled for a New York delegation luncheon, and some of the fellows nudged me into going. A little while after I got there, we were summoned by a quorum call, initiated by Durward Hall, a Republican from Missouri whose vocation and avocation seems to be calling quorums. In calling this one, I later found out, he had said, "I note the Congresswoman who interrupted the distinguished gentleman [Sikes] a while ago is not on the Floor after having made a certain query."

(262)

He was sticking it to me.

So when I got back I decided to stick it to them. I listened to the explanation by Sikes, which he concluded by saying, "There is no construction money for Safeguard facilities in this bill. Does that answer the gentlewoman's question?"

I asked if there was any money for *planning* Safeguard military facilities.

He admitted there was. Fifteen million dollars, in fact, along with another five million to build access roads to the missile sites.

Then I asked if there was any money in the bill for military construction of NATO facilities. Yes, I was told after some fumbling, there was $110 million allocated for that.

I could have gone on and on, but it gets very lonely out there by yourself. Nobody really cares about these things anymore. So I waited awhile, the debate proceeded, and I decided, since everybody seemed full of ennui and ready to pass the bill without any amendments, that it shouldn't be a total loss. I got out a piece of paper and a pencil and scribbled down an amendment to strike out the $20 million that had been allocated for Safeguard planning. I didn't figure I'd get any support, but I thought, what the hell, while there's anything left in me, I've got to keep this up.

I rose and made my amendment to a chorus of yawns. I couldn't even get enough support for a teller vote, so they had a voice vote and my amendment went crashing down with a resounding "No." Then I called a quorum so that I was able to get a roll call vote on the entire bill, which a grand total of me and thirty-one others voted against.

Toward the end of the session I got a little furious sitting there listening to them all attacking China and the United Nations, advocating cutting off funds to the UN and so on. I got up and made a statement in which I tried to explain to these rigid defeatists that China's admission to the UN really opens up a very hopeful phase in the UN's history—that we

(263)

now have a forum in which to communicate with a government that represents one-fourth of the human race.

All in a day's work. One can only try.

October 28

For weeks—months, actually—my Government Operations conservation subcommittee has been holding hearings to determine what to do about phosphate detergents, which pollute the environment, as opposed to nonphosphate detergents, which contain caustic agents that are harmful to health. The government has driven everybody up the wall, first telling us that phosphate detergents were no good, now telling us that nonphosphate detergents are even more harmful. As Betty Furness told some of these guys at one of our sessions, "You fellows have got to get this straightened out, because the laundry's piling up."

It's a very frustrating situation, with government and industry—despite all the money spent on research, technology and development—unable to agree on proper labeling and packaging for the nonphosphates, on allowable percentages of phosphate content, on packaging standards and so on. It's really becoming very boring, because these hearings drag on and on, and we don't seem to get anywhere. I must have listened to the same people from the Environmental Protection Administration, from the Food and Drug Administration, from Lever Brothers and from Colgate a hundred times! Nobody can agree on anything. It's an utter mess!

One of the witnesses was the head of the FDA, Dr. Charles Edwards, who happened to appear shortly after I had finished reading an article that pointed out that there are no women among the top ninety FDA managers and supervisors. Dr. Edwards came into the hearing complaining about how the poor housewife is so confused by what detergent to use, and

(264)

how the FDA isn't quite sure of how to communicate with her.

"Dr. Edwards," I said, "could it be that one of your problems in communicating with the 'poor housewives' is that you don't employ *any women* in the top decision-making processes of your Food and Drug Administration?"

October 29

At a cocktail party in honor of Charles Evers at the home of Carter Burden, I saw John Lindsay for the first time since our telephone conversation the other day. As soon as he spotted me he came over, kissed me and asked if I was still angry.

"No," I said. "Since I'm a great blower of the top, I can't very well be angry at you just because you blew *your* top."

November 2

Election day. I flew back to New York for a few meetings, and to vote. When I got to my polling place, I found that my name was on the "challenge" list as being under investigation as to residence, which is a bit of humor I didn't understand. Obviously some joker at the Board of Elections is up to something, I don't know what.

November 3

I met the Kentucky Fried Chicken King today, a character named Colonel Sanders, who was testifying before my special studies subcommittee on the problems of the aging. This is a man who claims to have started a whole chicken empire at the age of sixty-five (he's now eighty-one) with his first Social Security check.

As we listened to his testimony, it became quite apparent to me that Colonel Sanders had limited concern for the plight of the aging in this country. He made some remark about not approving of people living off handouts, an utterly ridiculous thing to say in light of the fact that there are old, helpless human beings in my district and elsewhere who are forced to live in slums and miserable hotel rooms, eat tea and toast and live in tremendous insecurity about receiving proper medical treatment. And because our society neglects their problems—even though millions of elderly people have nothing to live on but meager Social Security benefits—they are very often the prime victims of crime. All of which I found the Kentucky colonel rather insensitive to when I questioned him. I was getting ready to carve him up a little, but the committee chairman, I think, suspected this and shifted the questioning back to himself.

November 5

This has been a very backward and murderous week in Congress. We were in session until 2:30 in the morning the other night, debating the higher education bill to which they attached no less than three antibusing amendments. On the one hand, they voted $1.5 billion to help communities pay for the cost of integrating their schools. On the other hand, they voted amendments to prohibit the use of federal money to pay for the cost of buses or drivers; to prohibit federal education officials from requiring or even encouraging local communities to use busing; and to prohibit federal court orders from going into effect until all appeals have been exhausted. All of which amounts, very plainly, to preserving segregation as it exists. Each of these amendments passed by a two-to-one margin, with the help of Northern liberals, no less.

All of these provisions were in a bill that for the first time allocated federal general purpose grants to every college in the country. What were antibusing amendments doing in a higher education bill? We were more or less told that the only way we were going to be able to get any money for higher education was if we voted money for desegregation in primary and secondary schools. So what they did, in effect, was vote the money to desegregate schools and then prohibit anybody from spending it in any sensible way to accomplish that purpose.

And that's not even the worst of what they did. Title X of the Higher Education Act, as reported out of committee, provided that federal funds could be withheld from universities that discriminate against women in admission practices, or in other aspects of university life. Then John Erlenborn from Illinois raised an amendment that exempted undergraduate schools' admission policies, leaving this aspect of Title X, in effect, to apply only to graduate schools. He and his supporters said they were concerned about establishing a precedent of federal meddling in the operation of colleges and universities —a view shared by a number of college presidents, which is outrageously hypocritical. They don't mind taking federal money, do they? Actually, what they're really afraid of is that once they start admitting women to their elite male-dominated colleges, they're going to have to admit them to the professorships and they'll also be opening the door for women to other aspects of the power structure—political, social and economic. Title X only applies to universities that accept federal money in the first place. It seems to me that if a university accepts tax dollars from women, then it's got to accept the women with them. Is that asking too much?

Apparently for the House of Representatives it is. The Erlenborn Amendment passed, 194-189. Since half the guys who voted for it had just a few weeks ago voted for the Equal Rights Amendment, it proves that they were only giving us lip service to begin with—because this was the first real test of the intent of the Equal Rights Amendment.

Later on, through the efforts of Edith Green, Patsy Mink and myself, we were able to convince some more men to sup-

(267)

port Title X when it came up for a second vote. But by this time it was nearly two o'clock in the morning and a number of men had already flown the coop. Notably, Mr. Ed Koch, who had gone to New York to demonstrate an anticrime whistle at a neighborhood meeting. He not only missed that vote but nine other key votes, including those on the antibusing amendment. He was teaching people how to blow a whistle while on the Floor of the House they were once again blowing the whistle on our fundamental rights. We lost Erlenborn again, by five votes. It's utterly shameful.

November 6

I had a wild experience at a big peace rally in Central Park. I had to climb up on an unsteady platform in order to speak, and no sooner did I get started than a large group from the Progressive Labor Party, who were standing right underneath me, began shouting, "Bullshit! Bullshit! Bullshit!" This is the first time this has ever happened to me—and I wasn't prepared for it, especially with the TV cameras grinding away. I was told that even though I could hear the hecklers (hear them? I couldn't even hear myself talk), they couldn't be heard on TV. So I tried to ignore them, but truthfully, it was a disaster. I couldn't wait to get off that platform. But as somebody said afterwards, "Sarah Bernhardt couldn't have a perfect performance."

And those hecklers even got wilder after I got down. They started throwing rocks at Senator Vance Hartke. Martin said he was afraid they were going to do the same to me. "If they had, I would have thrown them back," I told him.

People are so fed up, this is what happens. It's all part of the disorientation of our times. On top of it all, I wasn't feeling very well the whole time. I've got some kind of a bacterial infection, and my bladder is very much in trouble.

(268)

November 11

A New York delegation luncheon was scheduled for noon, but when I heard that Ben Rosenthal, with the approval of Ed Koch, who's the delegation's unofficial secretary, was bringing a guest speaker, I decided not to go. The usual practice is to ask the permission of the entire delegation in advance. This time we weren't even informed. The speaker was Matt Troy, a New York City Councilman and the Democratic boss of Queens County. Ben's been feuding with him, and I guess now he wants to make up. Which is okay with me, except I didn't feel like sitting through it. I don't meet with county leaders in New York, let alone Washington. And a county leader from Queens? What's Queens got to do with me? Even Manny Celler, the head of the delegation, refused to go. Only about nine guys showed up.

Later in the afternoon I had a meeting with Senator Kennedy in his office, and we talked about the fact that none of the prospective and announced presidential candidates has struck the country with any great lightning. I got the feeling that he's going to take a wait and see attitude, that if none of the other candidates caught on and he showed some strength, he would come into the picture. He's taken some good positions lately, I told him, and when the time comes to pick a candidate I'd like to have the broadest possible range of choice.

Flew to Chapel Hill tonight for a speech to the students at the University of North Carolina. As I have been doing for the last month or so—I've been in Philadelphia and St. Louis for other speeches like this—I mixed a little about women, economics and the war into a potpourri of passion and concern. They gave me a dinner and a reception afterward. Tomorrow morning I'm due to lecture at the School of Public Health. These are really concerned, interested people. My trips to the South have been very enlightening—for all of us.

(269)

November 12

When I got back to New York my staff showed me an article in the *New York Post* which made it sound like I organized a boycott of yesterday's delegation luncheon. They also said that Koch was on the Barry Gray radio show last night where he called me a purist, and insinuated that I wouldn't sit down and talk to people. Obviously, either he or Ben or both leaked the story to the *Post*, which is really shameful. The real story is that Ben was trying to mend his fences with Troy—and he was using the delegation luncheon for that purpose. I didn't care one way or the other about it, except that the luncheons are usually working sessions on legislative matters, and since nobody consulted me about making an exception for this one, I didn't care to go. It's that simple. I didn't plan any boycott. That's stupid. In fact, I didn't even hear that Troy was going to be the speaker until yesterday morning, and I went over to Manny Celler and asked, "Why?"

"Why?" Manny laughed. "I suppose Ben Rosenthal wants to be a judge."

Later I called Troy and told him that my not being at the luncheon had nothing to do with him personally. "In fact," I said, "these guys made you the patsy."

"I agree," he said.

November 16

I made a special trip back to New York tonight for a fund-raising dinner in honor of Bill Ryan on the occasion of his tenth anniversary in Congress. Seventy-five bucks a plate. Ryan, Don Edwards, John Dow and I almost didn't make it because we were debating the Defense Department appropriations bill and we couldn't leave until we were sure there wasn't going to be a vote before tomorrow.

(270)

It wasn't exactly my night once I got to the dinner. I was seated at a table over on the side with Pete Seeger and some of Bill's staff, who were a little overly self-conscious about our potentially running against each other next year. Teddy Kennedy was the main speaker and in his opening remarks he referred to Dow and Edwards, the only other two Congressmen there, but not to me. When he saw me afterwards, he said, "My God! Bella! I didn't know you were here. Here, I'll show you my green slip. Your name isn't on it."

"Don't worry about it, Teddy."

Somebody obviously wasn't very happy about my being there, but I had figured it would be very uncomradely not to go. After ten years Bill's certainly entitled to be recognized by those of us who agree with his positions and recognize his devotion.

As soon as people discovered that I was there, hidden at Bill's staff table, they insisted that I say a few words. I got up and made, in a few seconds, what was called by others a most gracious and laudatory speech about Bill. Everybody thanked me profusely and thought I was very big-hearted. That's funny, because they should know by now that I always say what I really mean.

One guy came up to me and said, "I guess that speech was your declaration of intention to run against Koch."

"I wouldn't count on it if I were you," I said. "One has nothing to do with the other." The sad thing is that the three of us should be in competition.

November 17

A Democratic caucus was scheduled for this morning with my Vietnam item on the agenda, but I agreed to pass it up because we were scheduled to vote this afternoon on Ed Boland's amendment to the Defense Department appropriations, which would cut off funds for the war by June 1. Since I had put in a lot of time organizing for this moment, I wanted to save all my steam for the Floor debate, and a good debate there was. The best we've had since I've been here. So many people had so much to say that they were only allowing us each three-quarters of a minute to say it. I went through my three-quarter-minute breathlessly ("In the time that I've been in this Congress, I have grown to have great sympathy with the members of this House who were forced to support this war under false assumptions . . ."), and then when my time was up Herman Badillo yielded me his three-quarter-minute, and then Shirley Chisholm gave me hers—amounting to a grand total of two and one-quarter minutes. What I tried to explain, in the course of this, is that while we had done well in stating our policy to the President that we wish him to withdraw from Vietnam, he has chosen to ignore us, and so now it's time we forced him to do so by cutting off funds. I also said that it would not be a bad reflection on anybody's loyalty to do so, that in fact it was our obligation as an independent branch of government to carry out the people's wishes, since the President won't. The amendment lost 238 to 163, but this was the first time we had a vote on actually cutting off funds for the war.

November 18

I led a delegation of representatives from national Jewish organizations in my district to an hour-long meeting with Joseph Sisco, the Assistant Secretary of State for Near Eastern and South Asian Affairs. I always felt that an activist has to do more than just sign statements—and that's why I arranged this meeting and why I also introduced my own bill, once the Senate defeated the foreign aid program, to continue to provide support to Israel.

(272)

Sisco told us that no decision had yet been made on whether to discontinue the sale of Phantom Jets to Israel. Then he went into a song and dance about how he was afraid that our disengagement from Vietnam would lead to a feeling of neo-isolationism among the American people, and make it harder to get support for Israel. I told him he was wrong on all points. First, I said, we're not disengaging from Vietnam; and second, the American people—unlike the State Department—have never had any difficulty in distinguishing between the immorality of our government's support for a repressive one-man regime in South Vietnam and the morality of our support for the democratic government of Israel, which is simply trying to survive and has never asked us for soldiers.

November 19

Word came from the Lindsay Administration that they're going ahead, as planned, with the opening of the Governeur Hospital on the Lower East Side. Maybe I should encourage the Mayor to blow his cool more often.

Tonight I was the guest speaker at my own synagogue, the Town and Village Synagogue. When I arrived, I discovered I had forgotten my glasses, so the first thing I had to do was go around the synagogue to find somebody of about my age with my degree of farsightedness so I could read my notes.

Once I found a similar prescription to mine, I gave my speech, which was a report of my meeting with Sisco. Afterwards, Martin and I went downstairs for what they call the *Oneg Shabbat*, where they serve cake, coffee and wine. As usual, one guy cornered me and started badgering me about my views on Israel.

"I just told you about my meeting with Sisco," I said. "I told you about my bill for aid to Israel."

That wasn't enough, he said. So I ran down everything I've ever said or done about Israel, which apparently still wasn't enough, because in a formal question period which followed, he asked me the same questions. So I said to the guy, "It's obvious all you want to do is make a speech, so I will repeat to you in public what I just told you in private."

Later on they told me he was an old Farbstein supporter who's never gotten over my being elected. It figures.

November 21

In Dallas with Martin I gave a really hard-hitting speech to a group called the Bill of Rights Foundation, a mixture of liberals (Southern-style) and conservatives. Figure that out.

I'm still fuming about Nixon's statement of a few days ago in which he said he was signing the defense bill but would simply ignore the provision instructing him to set a date for total withdrawal from Indochina. This was a compromise version of the Mansfield Amendment. Congress didn't say *when* we should get out, but it did say we *should*. "Nixon, who calls himself a law and order man, is actually a lawbreaker," I said in my speech. "He's guilty of contempt of Congress."

Texas will never be the same again.

November 22

Martin and I planned on going to Corpus Christi with Bob Eckhardt, the Congressman from Houston, who was at the dinner last night. We visited his house, sat around the fire and had some wine and good conversation. But the weather's rotten, and so instead of going to Corpus Christi we decided to fly to Las Vegas, where we hear it's clear and sixty degrees. We've never been there.

November 23

It's atrocious.

November 25

By now I've been introduced at every major nightclub in this city—by Harry Belafonte, by Sammy Davis, Jr., and by Alan King—as the greatest woman of the twentieth century. I've had it, frankly. I mean, I love all these people, but I don't like being on display and I don't like being in Las Vegas. We're getting out of here tomorrow.

November 26

We couldn't reach Tony Marzani, who works on my New York staff and drives me around, so we arranged for Egee to bring out her new car and meet us at the airport. Although on the one hand she felt very self-sacrificing, on the other I think she enjoyed the fact that we asked her to do it. We don't see too much of her since she got her own apartment. Liz is another story. She's in touch constantly—for money. When her father says no, she calls me.

At the airport an older black woman came up and introduced herself to me and said, "You're Bella Abzug, aren't you?"

"Yes."

"You're hailed as the liberator, aren't you?"

"Some people say that."

"Well, I want you to know, Mrs. Abzug, that I don't want to be liberated. I like it just the way it is."

"You do, huh? Do you work?"

"Yes."

"How much do you make?"

"Seventy-five bucks a week."

"Did a man ever have your job?"

"Yes."

"Do you happen to know how much he made?"

"Yes, come to think of it, I heard he made $10,000 a year."

"Well, you see, that has something to do with liberation. We think women should get equal pay for equal work. Do you have any kids?"

"Grandchildren—but I take care of them."

"Are they pre-school age?"

"Yes."

"Do you leave them at a free child care center when you go to work?"

"Are you kidding? I have to pay somebody to watch them."

"That's another thing women's liberation is all about."

"Mrs. Abzug," she said. "Can I have your telephone number?"

December 3

A couple of fiery meetings this morning in my New York office. The subject: the economic development of the Lower East Side. We succeeded last month, after a great deal of effort, in persuading the Economic Development Administration in Washington to approve the OEDP—the overall economic development plan drawn up by the groups participating in the Coalition (the Lower East Side Economic Planning and Development Coalition) and City Economic Development officials. The plan outlines several approaches and projects for

(276)

revitalizing the neighborhood, developing new kinds of industries and most importantly creating jobs for some of the 190,000 blacks, Puerto Ricans, Italians, Eastern Europeans, Jews, elderly, poor and middle class people who live there. The unemployment rate in the area is over 11 percent and lowering that is one of the major goals I have set for myself.

Now, however, as understandably happens when you're dealing with all sorts of people who've been screwed for so long they want to be sure they aren't getting screwed again, there's a lot of controversy about the actual development plan. A few groups claim they weren't properly consulted. My meetings were to try and iron out their complaints, so that we can get on with the important task of building the broadest possible coalition of every element in the community and all work together to create the kind of economic activities that will bring jobs into the area. The next step is to apply for a technical assistance grant to hire a staff, which, once the bickering stops, we'll be able to do.

As I said, these things happen. It's sad, though, that *poor* people, whether white, black, Puerto Rican or Jewish, can't understand that they're all on the same side. It's such a waste for them to dissipate themselves by fighting each other.

December 5

I'm in Chicago for the formation of a National Youth Caucus, a gathering of three thousand young people from all fifty states. Since I'm practically an honorary member of the Black Caucus, and since I was present five months ago for the birth of the Women's Caucus, my presence here, as I told the group, makes me sort of a political midwife. In 1968, I said, their generation was on the outside getting clubbed and teargassed while inside Convention Hall in this city their hopes for a peaceful democratic America were being trampled. I told them I was happy to see that they had not given up, and that this time they were going to be inside "ripping off" a piece of the power structure for themselves. They were so excited they interrupted my speech twelve times for applause, and then gave me a ten-minute standing ovation at the end. I've never seen anything like it.

The kids are not only enthusiastic. They're being very hard-headed and planning a state-by-state campaign to get young people selected as delegates to the conventions. Best of all, they're going to work closely with the Women's Caucus, and the Black Caucus. I love them!

December 6

Back to Washington for a policy council meeting of the Women's Caucus. Virginia Allen and I were named co-chair-women for the next three months. Virginia, a very able woman, was head of the President's Commission on the Status of Women which produced the definitive report on women, "A Matter of Simple Justice." All of the report's recommendations have been ignored by Nixon. What else? He governs by commission and omission.

I've been putting in a lot of time for the Caucus directing a political task force that's concerned with getting equal representation of women among delegates to the Democratic Convention next summer. Elly Peterson, who's also on our council, is heading up a task force that's directed at the Republican Convention.

We're really beginning to move. A couple of weeks ago I arranged a meeting for us with Larry O'Brien, Democratic Party Chairman, and Patricia Harris, who's temporary head of the convention credentials committee. She's a lawyer, and very sharp. (In fact, she was one of our nominees for the Supreme Court.) O'Brien had Don Fraser of Minnesota and some staff people there and we talked for almost three hours. Our side also had Shirley Chisholm and Patsy Mink, Fanny Lou Hamer, Carleen Waller of Tennessee, Milly Jeffery of the UAW, Phyllis Siegel, a young law student who's been doing a lot of research for us, and Anne Wexler of Common Cause.

I made the opening presentation, and the others pitched in. The upshot was that Pat Harris agreed that failure of any state delegation to include 50 percent women would constitute a *prima facie* showing of noncompliance with the convention guidelines worked out by Don Fraser's committee. And O'Brien had to agree.

Don wrapped it up for us later in a letter to O'Brien, and now O'Brien has sent out orders to all state parties to submit their affirmation action plans for compliance with the guidelines to the National Committee by January 15.

Now we'll have a basis for making credential challenges, if we have to. But I'd rather we didn't have to. I'd rather we get the delegates.

December 7

Well, we did it. The House and Senate have both finally passed a child care law as part of an overall antipoverty bill. The vote was 210-186. The next step is the White House. Since it's the single most important piece of social legislation to come out of this Congress, Nixon has already made it clear that he's not happy with it, and that he's considering a veto. It would be a perfect opportunity for him, after all, to express his disdain for women, minorities and youth—all of whom are benefited by this bill—in one swoop. This time our people-be-damned President is even toying with some new victims: children.

December 9

Incredible! He vetoed the child care law. "Fiscal irresponsibility," he said. This, mind you, is from the same man who spends billions for death in Vietnam. He also made another remark about the law's "communal approach" and "family weakening implications" that's so ignorant and hypocritical it makes me sick. He doesn't care that millions of women *have* to work and leave their kids home alone or with off-and-on babysitters.

This veto proves to me positively that Nixon has no intention of allowing *any* money to get to anybody other than the vested interests he figures will help him get reelected. He's so callous. This bill had the support of one of the broadest coalitions ever put together and it was enormously popular among all kinds of women—middle class and working women as well as groups like NOW (National Organization for Women). It's becoming obvious to these women, among others, that if we don't defeat Nixon, he's going to defeat us, and good.

December 10

Yesterday that miserable veto, and today a great victory, a really great victory. In twenty-four hectic hours I conceived, lobbied for and presented an amendment, which passed late this afternoon and may very well wind up saving New Yorkers a good deal of money on their rent bills.

Here's how it happened: On November 22, even before a Rent Advisory Board had been appointed, the Price Commission announced that "rent increases on rent-controlled units authorized by state and local rent control agencies will be allowed to go into effect." For New York City, where there are between 1.4 and 1.7 million rent-controlled and rent-stabilized apartments, this meant scheduled rent increases of

light of controls on wages and prices. How much the land-lords will be able to raise the rent still hasn't been determined, and won't be until the Price Commission issues the federal guidelines, which will probably be sometime next week.

December 14

Wilbur Mills, the chairman of the House Ways and Means Committee, came up to me on the Floor. "Bella," he said, with great concern in his voice, "I must ask you a question."

"Go ahead, Wilbur." I figured he wanted to know my opinion on the devaluation of the dollar.

"What," he asked, "is 'Bella Abzug is one' in the crossword puzzle? You know, sixty-six across? I can't figure it out!"

December 15

I'm an absolute physical wreck. These past several days, during the most tense and important days of the session as we move toward adjournment, my Public Works Committee has been meeting from ten in the morning until six at night marking up the water pollution bill. I've had to run back and forth between the committee room and the Floor, a good ten minutes each way. The committee adjourns every time there's a roll call vote, but the system makes it impossible for you to function. You can't be in two places at the same time and keep your finger on everything. It's a horrendous way of doing things, totally unfair, and it should be changed. Committees should meet on certain days, and the House on others.

During the hearings on the water pollution bill—which the Senate has already passed unanimously—we've heard testimony from numerous officials from the Administration who are trying as hard as they can to scuttle the bill in its present form, since it bites their big business pals. One provision they've been particularly concerned about sets a goal to end discharges of industrial pollutants into the water by 1985. In other words, to make all waters in this country once again safe for fish and humans. This is in the Senate bill. Paul McCracken, the President's chief economic adviser, and others from the Nixon camp have testified that this is impossible, and want the provision removed. There's also, as usual, the problem of money. Our bill provides for $20 billion over the next four years, but McCracken claims that the real costs would be in the neighborhood of $60 billion to meet our goals, which he contends is too much money in light of current budget difficulties. I pointed out to him that isn't it strange that on the one hand he's crying poverty, while on the other Nixon is giving away upwards of $10 billion annually to the corporations with his new tax program. The real issue is one of priorities, damn it. Are we going to continue to spend $76 billion a year on military programs, or are we going to start to commit the funds to cleaning up the water, building housing and improving education, health and child care?

Then we also heard from Mr. Governor Rockefeller, who also sang the Administration's tune, except even more shrilly. He put the cost of meeting our goal at $2 to $3 *trillion*.

I asked what the basis of his figures was, in light of what McCracken told us.

He said the estimate had been prepared by his technicians by multiplying what they thought would be the cost of cleaning up the waters in New York State by ten.

Hardly a scientific way of preparing an estimate, I told him. Then I asked him if the American people might not be convinced that their tax money would be better spent for a program to clean up pollution than a military program.

"*You* might convince them," he said, and everybody laughed.

After I put him through a tough cross-examination, and got him to concede on almost every point, he said, "The distinguished Representative from New York has questioned my figures. My concern is that in challenging my figures, she has none to substitute except a very beautiful figure of her own."

"That's one demerit, Governor," was all I could say to that sexist remark.

The testimony of McCracken and Rockefeller and others, as well as incredible pressure from industry, proved damaging to our cause. The committee effectively knocked out the 1985 goal, and required a study by the National Science Academy to determine what the real attainable goals will be. Once the study is completed, in about two years, Congress can then act again if it chooses to.

I argued: Let's keep the 1985 goal. It's only a *goal*. Let industry realize it's got to start shaping up to achieve it. If we find out for legitimate reasons that it's technologically impossible, we can always change it, but if you take away the goal you are preventing the development of the necessary research and technology. And the longer we wait, the more expensive it's going to be.

I did not succeed. Bob Jones, who's filling in as chairman for John Blatnik (he had a heart attack), says we were lucky to have held the line as much as we did, in view of the Administration's opposition. When I had to leave this afternoon, he asked me if he could have my proxy vote in reporting it out favorably. "Yes," I said, "but only because I'm in favor of *a* water pollution bill. But I'm putting you on notice that I'm going to file separate views."

Now, most people would not believe that a freshman would handle a committee that way. All week I badgered the hell out of them, then, since I had to leave early, I also asked them for a special request to skip ahead of themselves (they go through the bill page by page) and put in my sex amendment, which prohibits discrimination on the administration of the program by reason of sex. A lot of people thought it was rather nervy on my part. The ranking Republican member, William Harsha from Ohio, who sits on the tier above me in this committee, turned around and said, "I want to ask you a question about this sex amendment."

I turned to him, peered over my glasses and drawled, "Yes?"

He burst out laughing and said, "Never mind."

I got unanimous consent for the sex amendment.

December 16

I've been shuffling back and forth every day this week between Washington and New York, because the Senate, very rightfully, is tying us up and keeping us from adjourning the session until the House acts on the Mansfield Amendment, which establishes as national policy the total withdrawal of American forces from Indochina in six months, contingent upon the release of American prisoners. Monday night I spoke at the B'nai Jeshurun, one of the oldest synagogues in New York, then I flew back at 7 A.M. for the session Tuesday. Wednesday night I flew back to New York again, this time for a fund-raiser at Carol Haussaman's gorgeous apartment on Central Park South. (We're gradually knocking down that deficit, but it just doesn't go away. Claire Scheinbart, a devoted political co-worker and friend from way back, and Bina Racine have been working like dogs to raise funds for me, even though they hate doing it.) This morning I'm back in Washington, and Martin's with me, because tonight he's flying to Miami with me where I'm to speak at another synagogue. I have tremendous requests to speak at synagogues all over the country, because, after all, I'm the only Jewish woman in Congress.

Finally, this afternoon the impasse on the Mansfield Amendment, which had been attached to the foreign aid authorization bill, was broken. The bill had been hung up in conference because the House conferees had refused to accept the Mansfield Amendment, which was in the Senate's version, and in retaliation Mansfield would not allow the Senate to vote on the foreign aid appropriations bill, which the House had already passed. (The authorization sets a ceiling on spending; the appropriation provides money for specific programs.)

Ever since the Senate defeated the original foreign aid bill—because it's much more advanced in its views than the House, which is essentially the rubber stamp chamber—the whole question of foreign aid has been a tremendous problem. The intent of the Senate's action was to cause a reevaluation of the foreign aid program, which has been tied all these years to cold war policies and used to prop up antidemocratic regimes like Franco's in Spain. The Senate revived the bill only after splitting it into two parts—economic and military aid—as it should be. In addition to the Mansfield Amendment, which they attached for the third time this year to a major bill, they put on various other policy restrictions, which include limiting spending in Cambodia and measures to keep the President from using foreign aid funds to carry out some of his backward foreign policy objectives, as well as requiring him to release some impounded funds for domestic programs before he spends our lives away on foreign policy.

It's all very complicated, but what it comes down to is this: We, at the moment, have neither a foreign aid authorization bill nor a foreign aid appropriations bill, nor a continuing resolution, which would allow the Administration to spend money on the same level as before until Congress takes final action next year. A couple of days ago, the rubber stamp House leadership pushed through a stopgap continuing resolution. The Senate, fortunately, refused to act unless the House conferees agreed to let the Mansfield Amendment come through

(287)

conference on the foreign aid authorization legislation. In effect, they said, "No continuing resolution comes out of the Senate until the House takes up the Mansfield Amendment."

This morning the conferees were still haggling, and on the Floor some of the members were pressing Hale Boggs about when the deadlock was going to be broken so we could adjourn. He said the Speaker was conferring with some of the important people involved in the legislation, but that he had not yet received word as to what would happen. So while we were sitting around twiddling our thumbs he came up to me, first off the record, then on the record, and said, "Bella, why don't you get up and make a speech. They're all badgering me. Everybody's asking me questions, and I don't have the answers, and I need some time."

I took up his invitation—not to waste time, as he would have liked—but to lay out the real reasons we were deadlocked. Simply, that the House conferees were not agreeing to the Mansfield Amendment, which reflects the will of the majority of the American people. I suggested that there should be a motion to direct our conferees to accept the Senate's position on the Mansfield Amendment.

Then we recessed for lunch, and when we came back, Bill Ryan made such a motion. Doc Morgan moved to table it, and, I'm sorry to say, he won his motion by a vote of 130-101. We certainly could have used some of the 193 members who supported Mansfield on an earlier vote, but they had already left town.

Even though we still hadn't had a direct vote on the Mansfield Amendment, Mike Mansfield said that in view of the vote we did have he would allow the Senate to act on a continuing resolution for foreign aid appropriations, which it will do tomorrow. I think he was trying to get off the hook. So the logjam was broken. But the fact remains that we have not yet had a direct vote on the Mansfield Amendment—and that

(288)

becomes the single most important item of business, as far as I'm concerned, once we reconvene in January.

Another case study of how government runs over the little people may be nearing its conclusion—this time, hopefully, with the people winning out in the end. The whole thing started back in 1962 when the Post Office acquired a block of property in the Chelsea section of my district for what it said would be an annex to the Morgan Post Office in the area. Once it got hold of the land, it evicted some three hundred low-income tenants who were living in apartments there, and proceeded to demolish the buildings, as well as a public gymnasium and an indoor swimming pool, one of the few such facilities on the entire West Side.

You guessed it: The Post Office never built its annex, having since decided to move its bulk-mail operation to New Jersey. Instead, it abandoned the construction plans and callously turned the block into a parking lot for trucks. For years now they've been parking their trucks there, while people in this city, suffering through one of the most severe low-income housing crises in history, are without homes!

Logically enough, the community wants the land back for housing. During the primary election last year, Farbstein said he got the Post Office to commit itself to declare the land in excess of its needs. There was a big celebration, and it was heralded as a big victory for Farbstein. Fine and good.

Then when I came to Congress, I found out what Farbstein had neglected to mention: the Post Office said it would not give the land back until the New Jersey facility is open early in 1973—when they will no longer need the annex lot for their trucks. So way back last winter, I started raising hell. At one point I brought my subcommittee on public buildings and grounds to New York to hold hearings, and then we held more hearings in Washington. We documented the desperate need

(289)

for housing in New York City, but otherwise we got nowhere. We still couldn't get the Post Office to release the property *right away,* even though the plans for housing and financing arrangements were already completed. This summer when the Post Office became the U.S. Postal Service, once again it promised that the land would be declared in excess of its needs, but not until *early* 1973. So we were right back where we started, except for all the time that had been lost in between.

Then I discovered that I wasn't the only one with Post Office troubles. Seven other members of my Public Works Committee had postal facilities in their districts that were needed by the communities for other projects and that were of no great importance to the Post Office. So we all attached amendments to the Public Works Act. Mine required the U.S. Postal Service to transfer the property to the city for "housing and related purposes." No sooner had we all attached our amendments than the Postal Service turned around *again* and claimed they would still have to park their trucks there even after the mail operation was moved to New Jersey. Can you imagine? After all those times they said they wouldn't need it, now they say they need it again. Except this time they say we can build housing on top of their parking lot. Well, needless to say, my amendment does not include their parking lot!

Today the entire matter came up before my full Public Works Committee which is marking up the bill. All the guys were kidding me. "Why don't you accept their plan? We'll put your name up in lights. We'll call it 'Bella Abzug Apartments.'" Jokes aside, I convinced the committee to accept the amendment as is.

So now it's in the House version of the bill, and the people of Chelsea are very happy. In the next session we'll have to get it passed on the Floor and through the Senate. Our only problem will be to convince the legislators that housing is more essential than parking, which I'm afraid, considering the makeup of Congress, and the terrific pressure from the Postal Service, is not as easy as it sounds. But it is possible, maybe even likely. One thing that helps: Senator Javits and the city agencies involved are with me on this one.

December 17

Martin has heard me complain all year about how my schedule leaves no time to take care of personal needs, and these past few days he's finally had a chance to see exactly what I mean. He flew to Washington yesterday, saw the mad rush there, and then we barely made it to the airport on time to get to Florida, where I was scheduled to speak at a lecture series in a synagogue at 8:30. We landed at eight o'clock, and without even having a chance to wash up, I was rushed off to my lecture, and then in the reception afterwards barely had a chance to say hello to a whole slew of relatives who were there from his family and mine. Then we had to rush to stay at a hotel near the airport in order to get up at seven o'clock to make the plane back to Washington by the time the sesssion convened. We voted on the continuing resolution, the session adjourned and then we flew back to New York—where I had to go right away to speak at another synagogue. Martin was so bushed and tuckered by this time he simply went home and went to sleep.

December 18

A very moving experience at the United Nations this morning. Shirley Margolin and Jane Weissman of Women Strike for Peace arranged a farewell tribute to U Thant, who's leaving after ten years as Secretary General. They asked me to be their spokeswoman and present him with a scroll and a dove tie clip.

It so happens that U Thant became Secretary General at the very same time that WSP got its start. I still remember that first big demonstration we had outside the UN to protest resumption of nuclear testing. We carried balloons and signs and some of us were holding babies in our arms. We were scared as hell about strontium 90 from nuclear fallout poisoning our kids' milk. From out of nowhere, it seemed, thousands of women turned up at the UN that day. Most of us didn't know each other. We didn't even have a name for our group yet.

Now here we were, several hundred women this morning, older and wiser, inside one of those big, fancy General Assembly conference rooms honoring U Thant. He was honoring us too as one of the really significant peace groups. His staff had wanted him to cancel his appearance because of some emergency meeting, but he said, No, he couldn't disappoint "the women and Bella."

He's a small, graceful man with the kind of face that looks as if it's been purified by suffering. We sat next to each other on the dais and he looked intently at me all the time I was talking. It was a tough speech to make. It had been a bad few weeks for the UN because of the Indian-Pakistani war and we were all feeling pretty disheartened. So I couldn't pretend that the UN was an outstanding success, but I also had to convey that we weren't down on the UN, we just want it to be stronger and more effective.

"As the UN has had its triumphs and its failures," I told him, "we have felt, with you, the frustrations that often follow our most earnest efforts and the sense of relief when wars that might have been did not take place and when wars that should *not* have been finally ended."

I talked about how WSP had helped get the limited nuclear test ban treaty in 1963 and how I had just introduced a resolution in Congress after the perilous Amchitka nuclear bomb test asking our government to declare a moratorium on underground tests until a comprehensive ban could be negotiated. I talked too about how we in WSP had learned to reach out to other women in Vietnam and foreign lands and how we have joined in an international sisterhood of peace.

"We must begin to think in terms of 'What's good for the world is good for my country,' instead of the other way around," I told him, mentioning that earlier in the week he had said the concept, "My country—right or wrong," is the most dangerous threat to world peace.

His speech was very simple, really very spiritual without being religious in the formal sense. "I have seen war," he said, "and it is even more terrible than you can imagine." He praised WSP for its work and made it sound as if he was practically a member. Over the years he has been one of the most eloquent voices against the arms race and for the kind of UN that won't be just a debating society but will really help nations work together to prevent wars and save our planet and its people. After listening to him, I felt that I had heard a great man. One of the women taped his speech, and I'm going to put a transcript into the *Record*. Just to counterpose some of those wild speeches the know-nothings were making after China was admitted to the UN.

After I pinned the tie clip on him (it took both of us to do that), we embraced and he left. Then the women wanted me to make *another* speech to them. "You've got to pep them up," Shirley said. Can you imagine?

December 21

At five o'clock last night we got word that the Price Commission announced that it was going to ignore our rent amendment—even before the President signed the law to which it was attached, and even before it issued its own federal rent guidelines. The announcement said that New York could go ahead with its rent control raises subject to a review by the commission to determine whether these local increases met federal objectives. Utterly illegal! They caved in to the real estate lobby in outrageous haste, and they've broken the law!

I called a press conference for this morning in which Frank Brasco and I and some other local legislators announced our support for a coalition of tenant groups that is going to court to seek an injunction against the Price Commission, which has shown a wanton disregard for the right of citizens. The tenants are also planning to get a restraining order against the city to stop the rent increases of 7.5 to 13 percent from going into effect.

The whole thing is preposterous! It's not even enough anymore to pass a law, because if it annoys the vested interests they simply use the power of the state to ignore it. To put the increases into effect first and then say you'll review them later is to deny people their due process—as if there were no Constitution.

December 28

A group of young Vietnam war veterans has seized the Statue of Liberty. They're going to stay there, they say, to remind the American people that the war is still going on. And just to underscore the point Nixon has ordered massive bombing of North Vietnam, the heaviest since 1968. This is how he's winding down the war! Some American pilots have been downed, and so now there are *more* American prisoners of war, not less. The guy's timing is great. Just when Congress is in recess, and most people don't want to think about anything but their families and parties. If he'd done this when we were still in session, the Mansfield Amendment story might have had a different ending. We're just going to have to try again, even harder, when we reconvene next month.

In the meantime, I've announced that I'm going to introduce a resolution to censure the President for flouting the will of Congress. Some people want me to introduce an impeachment resolution, but I tell them that the voters will do it their own way.

I live in hope.

Epilogue

What's the epilogue, anyway? Where am I going? We're facing a presidential election about which I'm very concerned.
None of the candidates has yet shown the brand of activism
and leadership that the people in this country are desperate
for. I'm facing a major redistricting in New York, which, once
the new district lines are drawn, is going to throw me into a
very tough fight to keep my seat in Congress.

However, the response I've gotten from people in my district and all over the country requires that I run again. My
job isn't finished. I've just begun, really. I say this, not knowing how the redistricting will come out. I have a feeling,
though, that the Republican legislature, which I have probably
attacked more vigorously than any other member of Congress,
and the Republican Governor, whom I have also attacked
more vigorously than anyone else in Congress, will obviously
not be seeking to make my reelection a simple matter.

No matter. Wherever the new district lines are drawn, I
will find my district and I will run. I know only one thing:
My approach to politics, what I have done and what I have
yet to do, is very different from almost any other member of
Congress. No other Congressman has the commitment to
activism that I have. None is as prepared as I am to really
delve and pierce and pressure the process and shake it inside

out, as I am. So it doesn't matter who runs against me. I am fundamentally different from any of my potential opponents.

It's also important for me to run again so that other women will be encouraged to do the same. One thing that crystallized for me like nothing else this year is that Congress is a very *unrepresentative* institution. Not only from an economic class point of view, but from *every* point of view—sex, race, age, vocation. Some people say this is because the political system tends to homogenize everything, that a Congressman by virtue of the fact that he or she represents a half million people has to appeal to all sorts of disparate groups. I don't buy that at all. These men in Congress don't represent a homogeneous point of view. They represent their *own* point of view—by reason of their sex, background and class.

Take my friend George Andrews, who was a Congressman from Alabama. (He died at the end of the session.) He was a typical Southern politician in every respect. A few days after the Pentagon Papers were published, I bumped into him, we started talking and he said, "I don't like the way we were deceived and lied to about Vietnam."

"So why don't you do something about it?" I asked. "Why don't you start voting with me?"

"Well, Miss Bella," he said, "I'll tell you: It's like one strawberry said to the other strawberry, 'If we hadn't gone to bed together, we wouldn't be in this jam.' "

As if to say: We went along. We did what they wanted us to do. We now find out they lied. So what do we do?

You'd think, in coming to that kind of realization, that these guys would start voting a little differently, especially with their constituents clamoring for peace. Well, a few have, but the great majority are determined, at all costs, not to rock the boat. Now—who are they representing? Themselves or their constituents?

I've been all over this country this year, and I've talked to all kinds of people—businessmen, blacks, women, students, senior citizens, workers, Chicanos, a good healthy cross section —and they *always* respond overwhelmingly to what I have to tell them. And believe me, I give it to them hard about the war, the military, the racial, economic and sexist discrimination, about the perverted national priorities and so on. Who represents these people in Washington?

Their own Congressmen only pretend to, while they go on voting against money for housing, health, education and child care on the one hand, and go on giving Nixon a blank check for making war on the other. Take this whole fight we had this year on strengthening the enforcement powers of the Equal Employment Opportunities Commission. There isn't a single Congressman who doesn't have a district full of women and/or minorities who are daily suffering discrimination in employment. Then how do you explain so many Congressmen fighting like hell to make sure the EEOC does not become an effective enforcement agency? You explain it by understanding that the men in Congress represent essentially their own class interests and are opposed to any kind of real change that might benefit people at large. This holds true, I'm sorry to say, not only for individual Congressmen, but for the Democratic leadership as well. How, in this day in history, can the Democratic Party elect a Speaker of the House who talks about bipartisan foreign policy as if we were still fighting Hitler? Foreign policy aside even, on important domestic legislation—like the EEOC, for instance—you don't even get the feeling that the leadership is visibly working to get the legislation passed, even when the party is behind it. We simply don't have a strong leadership, because they seem to be so often at odds with the real sentiment in the party and the country, and because they're always busy building those ridiculous coalitions with reactionary Republicans.

And then there are the liberals. They've not only been a terrible disappointment to me, but further proof that the nature of Congress must be changed. Unfortunately, the liberals have failed to take notice of the massive and fundamental movement for social change in this country, so they're still too busy patching things up when what we need is a whole new set of works. I'm sympathetic with them; I think they did very well in such things as defeating the SST and getting the detention camp bill reversed; and I know they've been trying hard to get us out of Vietnam; but I'm also very annoyed that they aren't out there fighting for and organizing people, encouraging the young to register and the underfranchised to run for office. We need activists for leaders—and they aren't filling the bill.

Some suggest that the reason is that you have to go along to get along. Well, now that I've been around a year, I certainly don't buy that. I don't *go along* and I've seen that those who do don't get anything more out of the leadership than I do. I get as many favors from the Speaker and my committee chairmen as anybody; I get the Floor more often than most people; I get response to the needs of my district—just witness in the closing days the rent amendment and the Morgan Post Office amendment. And when I call up a government agency, I almost always get immediate results. (I've been told it's because they're concerned that if they don't respond to me, I'll bring down a thousand people and sit on their doorstep.) I've probably helped more G.I.s with their hardship cases with the United States Army than any dozen Congressmen put together. I call up the generals and I almost always get immediate action! I call Joe Sisco and I get an immediate appointment. Now, let's face it: If they all thought I was somebody they could ignore, they would.

In fact, not going along to get along has made all the difference in being able to create some feelings on the part of people, both in and out of Congress, that things *can* and *must* be done, and that there are different kinds of people, like myself, who can come to Congress to do them. I think I've accomplished a lot—maybe more than any other newcomer.

(300)

I can't prove it, but I'm sure it's so from the way people talk to me. Hale Boggs said to me just the other day (and Carl Albert has said it too), "I don't think there's ever been a freshman who's learned as much about this place and put it into practice as you." No other freshman, as far as I know, has ever gotten amendments into bills which were then passed into law—as I have with the rent provision and the sex discrimination amendments. And these aren't even my major accomplishments.

I opened up a long-forgotten and very important procedure —the resolution of inquiry. I've made people see that it's not heresy to question the procedures on the Floor, to ask questions of the Chair or committee chairmen, to challenge the operation of the Democratic caucus, to take a leading role in committees and not be just another junior member waiting his turn to occasionally ask a quiet question. But perhaps the biggest thing of all that I've done is to establish myself as a representative of women, of young people, of minorities, and as an outspoken and uncompromising advocate of turning the nation's priorities around to benefit the poor and lower-income people. I symbolize these new priorities because of my actions inside and outside of Congress.

People begin to understand that you stand for something, that you have principles. They know what *I* stand for. In the midst of the controversy about building a lower-income housing project in middle-income Forest Hills in Queens, I met a group of people who spotted me in the airport and said, "Hiya, Bella. Will you help us get rid of that project?"

"What?" I said.

"Oh," they said, "that's right. You would be *for* it. We understand."

That's exactly the same reaction that most of my colleagues in Congress have to me. They understand that I'm not unreasonable. I'm tough about what I think is right, but I'm not an obstreperous human being. I fight hard, and I try to win.

If I don't win, I keep fighting. Anybody who's ever had anything to do with me—inside Congress or out—knows that if I feel strongly about something there's no point in stepping on my toes to change my mind. To the contrary, they stay off my toes as much as they can because they're afraid I might take them on.

The major drawback to my being in Congress has been its effect on my personal and family life. It hasn't, for one thing, been easy on my kids. They are constantly in a struggle where their own identities are being eclipsed, and they don't like it. People are always approaching them as the daughters of Bella Abzug, when they, like everybody else, only want to be known as individuals in their own right. And they are individuals—strong and lovely ones. Slowly, they've learned to feel pride in the situation, and they're not quite as upset by all the clamor as they once were. They realize that if they don't overreact to people overreacting to them, in time it all dissipates and they're accepted as themselves.

Both Egee and Liz, incidentally, are political beings, having been brought up in an integrated neighborhood in Mt. Vernon. They're both very involved in the peace movement and humanist causes, though of course they're not engaged in the kind of mass activism I am. Through Egee, in particular, since she's older, but also through Liz, I've received a lot of insight into some of the differences between young people today and people my own age. And the fact that I've been associated with young people in various movements for ten years now also helps me to relate to them.

Egee is especially important to me in helping me to understand where I can and where I cannot move young people. On the one hand, she shares their disdain for the establishment, but on the other, she's very good at conceptualizing and seeing things in historical perspective. While she's part of her generation in terms of consciousness, she does not use the same routes for expression—such as pot or escapism or overinternalization. She tends to relate to my larger-world outlook, and has much more of a grasp on the way society operates than most kids her age.

Martin? He loves every bit of what I'm doing. He's always been extremely supportive, and now he enjoys how I'm being recognized. You see, he felt that I'd never be appreciated, and so he's glad to see that he's wrong.

The tough part of it, of course, is the diminishing amount of time we have to spend together. We don't even have weekends anymore, unless—as he's been doing recently—Martin accompanies me where I go. During the week it's a lonely life for him—and for me. But he loves the movies and the theater, and friends are always inviting him to dinner. In Washington, I don't even have time for those kinds of things. And the few hours I do get to be alone down there at night, I don't like. It's very unpleasant, and it makes me very unhappy.

Traveling around the country is not pleasant either. The few times I've been able to convince Martin to come along, it's been a little better—but it's still always such a strain. He wishes I'd cut down. He thinks what I'm doing is injurious to my health, and that I won't be able to last for long if I keep it up. He's not wrong.

He said he only really understood what kind of life I'm living when he saw me at work in my office the last few days of the session. As he sat there waiting for me, he realized all the upsets and disappointments and failures and achievements and chaos. He saw that it wasn't simply a matter of having a committee meeting at ten and being on the Floor at twelve, but that *in between* every minute is *action*. There isn't a second I waver, not knowing what to do with myself. If it's not a committee matter I have to discuss, it's a letter to the Price Commission. If it's not a telegram to the Mayor, it's a response to a group seeking help in New York. If it's not a "Dear Colleague" letter asking me to co-sponsor a bill, it's my own bill I'm preparing on the elderly, or water pollution, or health care or whatever. And everything is going on at the same time. Five hours of work to be done in every hour.

Martin says he doesn't know how anybody can stand all the pressure. And he's only seen me those two days! He hasn't even seen all the calls and the letters, the meetings with my staff to prepare for upcoming committee sessions, the five bills that are coming up on the Floor at the same time with me trying to figure out what to do about them and say about them, all the activities and organizing connected with the Women's Caucus, the Youth Caucus, working to get women elected as delegates to the national conventions, pressuring the presidential candidates to start speaking to people's real needs, getting prepared for the Democratic caucus, lobbying for the Mansfield Amendment, seeing that the Lower East Side coalesces behind an economic development program, seeing that all community groups get together when needed to put pressure where it needs to be felt—there isn't a minute, one single minute that's free. There are always groups visiting, always groups that want to hear from me about housing and health and welfare and crime and jobs and food and peace and schools. Every block has a block party, and they want me there. Every group has a Christmas or Hanukkah party, and they want me there. Every constituent with a problem wants an appointment. Every public official who needs your help always gets in touch with you when it's too late, so that everything has to be done frantically. Every group that makes an application for funds from the federal government wants you to be in there pitching for them—whether for language programs, training programs or dental care programs—and there are scores of these programs that I've worked on. People write us every day about problems with the Army, problems with landlords, problems with jobs, problems with the government, problems with facilities and discrimination; we are forever trying to help addicts in need of rehabilitation programs, people who have no place to live, people who have no food, no winter clothing. It never, never ends. Every second requires that I do, move, push. People are desperate for help, for leadership. There's no place else to go but to me, they say, and the sad thing is that very often they are right. That's what I want to help change.

Looking back over the year, is there anything I would have done differently? No. If anything, I should have done more of it.

Index

U.S. State Department, 227, 229, 242, 245, 259, 273
U.S. Supreme Court, 86, 121, 240, 242, 251, 260, 278
University of Michigan, 117
University Settlement, 149
Urban Priorities Division, 180

Van Horn, Edith, 177
Vanderbilt University, 116, 119
Vanik, Charlie, 149
Veterans Administration, 254
Veterans' Affairs Committee, 27
. Vietnam, 31, 53, 55, 60, 62, 65, 87, 101, 108, 128–129, 132, 157, 164, 183, 189, 194, 207, 210, 234, 236, 238, 243, 245, 247, 256, 258, 259, 271–273, 280, 292, 294, 298, 300
Vietnam Disengagement Act, 53, 62, 92–93, 120, 127
Vietnam Veterans Against the War, 118
Village Independent Democratic Club, 68, 127
Village Voice, The, 24, 28–29, 89, 155

Waldie, Jerry, 99
Waller, Carleen, 279
Washington, D.C., 123, 169, 199
Washington, Walter, 139
Washington Post, 75, 90, 151
Washington Star, 251
Ways and Means Committee, 26, 130, 239, 248–249, 283

Weissman, Jane, 291
Weizmann Institute, 12
Westchester County, 171
Wexler, Anne, 279
Whalen, Chuck, 94, 257
Wichita State University, 205
Widnall, William, 281
Wiggins Amendment, 205–206, 250, 251, 253
Williams, Alice, 40
Willowbrook State School, 213
Wilson, Jerry, 73, 145
Wolcott, Jean, 89
Wolf, Judy, 137
Wolff, Lester, 259
Wolman, Gil, 178
Women Strike for Peace, 13, 26, 82, 86–87, 105, 135, 157, 177, 178, 197, 201, 291–294
Women's National Press Club, 17–18, 21
Women's Political Caucus, 101, 177, 219, 232, 235, 260, 277–279, 304
Women's Political Conference, 124
Woodcock, Leonard, 50
World War II, 69
Wu, Peter, 74–75

Yarrow, Peter, 181
Yates, Sidney, 238
Young Americans for Freedom, 157
Young Lords, 181
Youth Caucus, 304